Aloha

[illegible]

March-2000

THE PLEASURE PRESCRIPTION

"Aloha" versus "Haole"

Haole — The mental and physical exhaustion of the millions of overstressed and overworked individuals in today's society leads to what Polynesians call a "*haole* life" (*ha* = breath, *ole* = without). *Haole* living is an urgent, breathless existence in pursuit of an elusive "better" that leaves one disconnected and fatigued.

Aloha — The Oceanic people taught that a joyful and healthy life is based on following our "seventh sense" or *aloha,* the instinctive drive to do what is pleasurable and healthful. *Alo* means to share and *ha* means breath, so *aloha* literally means to give and share the breath of life.

The Pleasure Prescription is about rediscovering your sense of aloha—literally and metaphorically "catching your breath." (To find out how much *aloha* is in your life right now, turn to page 40 and take "The Aloha Test.") Once you've caught it yourself, you will learn that true relaxation, happiness, health, and longevity come from giving and sharing this breath of life.

Dedication

For my *ku'uipo wahine* (loving wife), Celest Kalalani, who saved my life, fills it with pleasure, and teaches everyone who knows her the true meaning of *aloha,* and for my sons Roger and Scott, who are the source of our pride and joy.

Other Books and Audiotapes by Paul Pearsall, Ph.D.

Superimmunity: Master Your Emotions and Improve Your Health

Super Marital Sex: Loving for Life

Super Joy: Learning to Celebrate Everyday Life

The Power of the Family: Strength, Comfort, and Healing

Making Miracles

The Ten Laws of Lasting Love

The Pleasure Principle: Discovering a New Way to Health (Audiotape Series)

A Healing Intimacy: The Power of Loving Connections

The PLEASURE PRESCRIPTION

To Love, to Work, to Play — Life in the Balance

Paul Pearsall, Ph.D.

For further information contact:
Hunter House Inc., Publishers
P.O. Box 2914
Alameda, CA 94501-0914

Library of Congress Cataloging-in-Publication Data
Pearsall, Paul.
The pleasure prescription : to love, to work, to play—life in the balance / Paul Kaikena Pearsall. — 1st ed.
p. cm.
Includes bibliographical references and index.
ISBN 0-89793-208-0 (cloth). — ISBN 0-89793-207-2 (pbk.)
1. Pleasure. 2. Stress management. 3. Conduct of life. 4. Polynesia—Social life and customs. I. Title.
BF515.P32 1996
158—dc20 96–28108
CIP

Cover Design: MIG/Design Works Book design: *Qalagraphia*
Project Editor: Lisa E. Lee Production: Paul J. Frindt
Editorial Assistance: Jenny Moore, Tami Wisniewski
Sales & Marketing: Corrine M. Sahli Publicity Assistant: Enver M. Casimir
Customer Service: Edgar M. Estavilla, Jr., Christine Arciniega
Fulfillment: A & A Quality Shipping
Publisher: Kiran S. Rana

Printed and bound by Publishers Press, Salt Lake City UT
Manufactured in the United States of America

9 8 7 6 First edition

Contents

Contents (cont'd) . . .

Part Three: Living Aloha

The numbers in superscript in the text refer to endnotes organized by chapter and starting on page 233

Acknowledgments

Any wisdom on these pages comes from the graceful genius and profound *aloha* of the *kanaka maoli* (full-blooded Hawaiian people). I give my fondest *mahalo* to all of my Hawaiian teachers, including *kumu* Frank Kawaikapuokalani Hewett, *kupuna* Aunty Betty Kawoniokalani Jenkins, her husband Jack, and her mother Elizabeth (Tutu Mamma) Nalani Ellis, Fred Cachola of Kamehameha Schools, and Clay Park, all of the Island of O'ahu. *Mahalo* also to Charles and Nina Maxwell and Keali'i Reichel of my home island of Maui, and to Hawaiian studies teacher Pua Case Lapulapu, Kia Frond (taro farmer of Waipio Valley), and the Pai *'ohana* of Honokohauiki, all of the Big Island of Hawai'i, and to Sabra Kauka and Kai'opua Fyfe of the Island of Kaua'i. Any mistakes, distortions, or misrepresentations I may have made in my attempt to make the very deep and sacred Oceanic lessons of Polynesia accessible to the modern continental mind are all mine. *Mahalo* also to my mother Carol, my brother Dennis, and the memory of my father Frank, all of whom taught me the loving power of *'ohana.* All of these people have helped me to write my prescription for pleasure—finding enchantment in every moment of living.

My warmest *aloha* also to the entire *'ohana* at Hunter House Publishers, including my most caring and careful editor, Lisa Lee, patient publisher, Kiran Rana, and my energetic publicist, Corrine Sahli. *Mahalo nui loa* to all of you for having faith in my work. I hope our efforts have resulted in a book that will help a lot of people find more healthy pleasure in their lives and that we can, as we say in Hawai'i, *hana hou!* (do it again).

Important Note for the Reader

The material in this book is intended to provide an overview of the health and healing implications of the traditions and practices of Polynesian cultures, and related scientific and medical research, especially in the field of psychoneuroimmunology. The research is extensively referenced for readers wishing to pursue further inquiries. Every effort has been made to provide accurate and dependable information. However, the reader should be aware that professionals may have differing opinions about the implications of research, and change is always taking place. Any suggestions for techniques, treatments, or lifestyle change described in the book should be used under the guidance of a licensed therapist or health-care practitioner. The author, editors, and publisher cannot be held responsible for any outcomes of trying the ideas and suggestions in this book in a program of self-care or under the care of a licensed professional. The ideas, suggestions, and techniques in this book should not be used in place of other medical therapies.

Introduction

Consider these glimpses of the lives of just a few of today's "successful" people:

- The young coach of the University of Nevada at Las Vegas Runnin' Rebels basketball team is rushed to the hospital.[1] Days later, he quits the job he had sought all of his young life, citing total fatigue and the stress of winning as his reasons. He says he can't take the pressure and is finding "no joy in life anymore."
- After working most of his life to assume the prestigious position of president of Harvard University, Neil Rudenstine begins to fall asleep during major meetings. At the peak of his career, he goes on sabbatical to "find some pleasure in life by reading Lewis Thomas, listening to Ravel, and walking with my wife on a Caribbean beach."
- Los Angeles District Attorney William Hodgman grabs at his chest as millions watch during his opening statement in the O. J. Simpson trial. He is later rushed to the hospital suffering from what his wife Janet calls "meltdown from overwork with no time for himself."
- Accountant Marge Smith quits her job just days after a promotion to full partner in her firm, a position she had sought since college. She says she is overwhelmed with "trying to have it all and ending up feeling like all I have is trying." She sells the new Mercedes Benz purchased with the advance on her new salary, puts her home on the market, and gathers her children up to board a plane for the Caribbean. She says to the ticket clerk, "We're out of here. I'm maxed out and the kids are maxed out. We're never even together to complain about it. I'm going to sell fishing tackle in Jamaica and play on the beach with my kids before it's too late."

These people are experiencing what increasing numbers of people throughout the world struggle with every day: "toxic" success, a lack of delight in daily living, and the illnesses that go hand-and-hand with too much work and too little play. And all of them are being unconsciously prodded by their "seventh sense," an awareness that lies beyond the physical and psychic senses. This seventh sense attracts us to what is basic and necessary for a truly healthy, blissful life and leads us away from things that rob us of our natural ability for pleasure.

Throughout the world, there are different approaches to dealing with the problem of "burn out," or exhaustion from stress. The Western world has devised several stress management techniques, but fails to confront the *sources* of stress. As a result, stress reduction becomes just another stressful life obligation. Eastern culture considers this condition a failure in self-enlightenment and says introspection can alleviate it. As a result of more time spent turning inward, however, intimate personal relationships become neglected and loneliness results for the contemplator and his or her family. The Japanese call burn-out *karoshi,* which means working oneself to death, and it is now Japan's leading cause of death. Many Japanese try to deal with their overwork by taking hurried and intense one-week vacations they call "the golden week."

This book identifies the underlying cause of our variously named stress reactions and shows how to change them by following an entirely different path: the pleasure prescription.

Books, TV gurus, magazine headlines, and self-styled therapists today all hope to sell us on how exercise, diets, stress reduction approaches, and strategies for a constantly positive attitude will make us happier, healthier, better people. Their strategies seek to scare us or train us into health. This book presents an entirely new way to wellness based on "enlightened hedonism" rather than "fearful healthism." It is not a book about eliminating, giving up, or keeping under control. It's not about how to be happier . . . always. Instead, *The Pleasure Prescription* is a prescription for listening to the messages of your body and mind to find health and happiness. It is about how to balance unhappiness and happiness in daily life to fulfill our basic desire for meaning and connection. If wholeness is healing, then we need the lessons from our unhappy moments as much as we need to be open to our joyful times. We need independence from the relentless pursuit of happiness or avoidance of pain and a graceful acceptance of life's natural chaos.[2] Author David Shaw points out that life is a sexually transmitted condition with a mortality rate of 100 percent—none of us gets out of it alive. So, we might as well get as much learning, loving, and pleasure as we can, while we can.

The Inspiration for This Book

The pleasure prescription I offer comes from Polynesia and is based on the idea that we are made for shared joy, that what brings joy brings life, and that joy is not just elation but a kind of balanced spiritual toughness that allows us to derive pleasure from every aspect of daily living. It is a grit that allows us to learn from all emotional states so that we have the grace to deal more harmoniously with and offer help to our turbulent world. Philosopher Ding Ling writes, "Happiness is to take up the struggle in the midst of the raging storm and not to pluck the lute in the moonlight and recite poetry among the blossoms."[3]

Throughout this book, I refer to the aesthetic of Western science and its powerful medical and psychological research findings alongside the introspective insights of the Eastern spiritual orientation. These are the two philosophies that have the strongest influence on the way we live our lives today. I draw on them to give context to the secret of the pleasure prescription: five principles of life based on traditions of the Oceanic cultures. I also refer to recent medical and scientific findings, to show you exactly how and why the pleasure prescription works.

Polynesia is not just a set of tiny island paradises scattered in the Pacific. What some call "Meganesia" to more accurately reflect its size is defined by modern maps as extending from the archipelago of Hawai'i Nei (the Hawaiian islands) north of the equator to the north, to Rapa Nui (Easter Island) to the southeast, and to Aotearoa, a pair of huge continental fragments and small offshore islands that form New Zealand to the southwest.[4] Because the islands span the oceans, I refer to their cultures as Oceanic. They are not the opposites of Eastern and Western continental traditions; they are a different, third perspective.

Both Western and Eastern traditions glorify the individual, either in the pursuit of self-fulfillment or self-enlightenment. The Oceanic or

Polynesian tradition glorifies the Whole. Most books on health are written from the cultural orientation of the West, East, or a mixture of both. Though we accept and grapple with both traditions, many of us feel a need that has not been met, a hunger for deeper spiritual connection. With this book, I hope, you will find the way to fill that yearning.

First and foremost, I hope that, despite many of the warnings given about how we live, you will find this book *enjoyable.* If what you read doesn't bring you joy, I've defeated my whole purpose. I hope that you will see how Polynesia, like pleasure itself, is not simply a nice place to visit but offers a radical way to think and live based on a two-millennia-old wisdom that anticipated our most recent scientific breakthroughs. This book presents five of the oldest lessons in the world about a joyful, healthy, long life and supports them with the newest and most important discoveries about our complex and very sensuous and responsive immune system.

The book is divided into three parts, followed by endnotes, a glossary of the Polynesian terms used throughout the book, and a bibliography. The first part, The Pleasure Paradigm, introduces the concept of "enlightened hedonism" as the key path to health and well-being. It discusses our current approach to life in the context of our evolutionary, biological, and spiritual needs. It also presents the new fields of psychoneuroimmunology (PNI) and psychoneurocardiology (PNC), the modern sciences that are revealing the power of the pleasure prescription. The last chapter in Part One is about quieting the "selfish" brain and reclaiming the natural pleasure paths and our seventh sense which have been hijacked by our brain's acquired taste for urgency neurohormones.

The second part, Learning Aloha, presents the five principles of *aloha* in detail. Each of the five chapters in this section presents current scientific discoveries that validate the Polynesian concepts that build *aloha,* and each ends with a specific lesson for practicing the *aloha* components in your daily life. The third part, Living Aloha, shows you how to apply the pleasure prescription to the various challenges of daily living.

If you are experiencing a delight deficiency in your life right now because of illness, work problems, or family strife, you many want to begin reading the chapter in Part Three that relates to your immediate concerns. If you are the type of reader who enjoys skipping and sampling through a book, you might first want to check your "pleasure pulse" by taking the Aloha Test in Chapter 3. If possible, take the test with someone who knows you well, discuss the results, and then read the specific chapters that relate to your needs or interests. If you are a health-care professional, you many want to begin here with Part One, which deals with the theoretical and medical bases for the pleasure paradigm. If you like to read books from beginning to end, by all means go ahead!

At the back of the book is a glossary, which begins with an explanation of Polynesian pronunciation and has short definitions for the Polynesian terms used in this book.

Throughout the book, I have included several tests and used simple formulas and catchphrases that summarize complex ideas. I have also included the actual words from interviews of 100 Polynesian *kupuna* (elders) and *kahuna* (healers). These words are touchstones and, I think, will guide you through some difficult lessons in learning to follow the pleasure prescription. Please know that there are many complex aspects to the Polynesian culture that cannot be addressed in this book. Hawai'i is my home, but I have traveled throughout Polynesia. While many differences exist within the islands, the one common theme is the five elements of the way of life called *aloha*: patience, unity, pleasantness, humbleness, and tenderness toward others.

A word on reading this book: the pleasure prescription is about connection—understanding how your body, mind, and spirit work together, and how your health and your happiness are not only connected, but connected to the world around you. Because the ideas behind the pleasure prescription and the research that supports them are connected in a network of ways rather than a linear progression, I talk about them in a similarly interconnected, holistic fashion. The pleasure prescription is not something to be "taken" like a pill; it is something to understand and internalize. By reviewing these ideas in many different contexts, I hope you can become familiar with them, recognize your experiences of them, and get to know them from the inside out.

As another objective of this book, I hope health-care workers of all specialties—teachers, clergy, and anyone in a position to offer professional guidance and comfort to others—will add the teachings from the Oceanic paradigm to their own theories of caring. I hope they will nurture their own awareness of and responsibility to the seventh sense and consider prescribing these *aloha* principles in their work.

The Pleasure Prescription is not a self-help, feel-good book. It is a course in a new way to well-being, a "healthy hula," if you will: learning to dance with others to the joyful, harmonious rhythm of daily living.[5]

Mahalo nui loa (thank you very much) for being willing to consider a new way to wellness.

THE PLEASURE PARADIGM

In this section, you will learn...

To diagnose the "Delight Deficiency Syndrome"

To discover your own "seventh sense" for the healthy pleasure that leads to a longer, healthier, happier life

That a long and happy life depends much less on diet, exercise, stress reduction, and the achievement of success than on a daily life of enlightened, moderate, shared hedonism

The pleasure prescription, which is a large portion of optimism to provide hope and learn from times of suffering, a dash of pessimism to prevent complacency during the times of great joy, enough realism to distinguish those things we can control from those we cannot, all blended into a shared delight in being alive

A third way to well-being based on the five components of Polynesian *aloha,* the key ingredients of the pleasure prescription

How the new fields of psychoneuroimmunology (PNI) and psychoneurocardiology (PNC) are confirming the healing and immune-enhancing principles of *aloha*

The neurology of glee and how addiction is natural and necessary for total health

Chapter One

CATCHING YOUR BREATH — AND SAVING YOUR LIFE

"Fear not that life shall come to an end but rather that it shall never have a beginning."

— John Henry Cardinal Newman

A new plague has struck the world. It is the cause of more than one of every four health complaints in the United States, the leading cause of death in Japan, among the top five reasons people call their doctors, and directly or indirectly contributes to early death more than any other factor.[1] It is a silent killer that not only destroys its victim but spreads to the victim's family, friends, and the community. This modern epidemic is even more threatening because it kills slowly, allowing itself to be spread by its host for years without knowing until too late that she is slowly killing those she loves.

This lethal killer is not a virus or bacteria, although it severely weakens the body's defenses against these invaders. It is not the result of poor diet, lack of exercise, or failure to reduce stress. It is a lack of joy, the lack of sufficient daily bliss to bring about psychological and physical health, and I call it "Delight Deficiency Syndrome."

Checking for Delight Deficiency Syndrome

Before we talk about the "Third Way" of living that can bring us daily delight, why don't you check to see if you have a touch of Delight Deficiency Syndrome yourself? How many of the symptoms below, each of which begins with the letter C, do you have?

1. *Chronic fatigue,* usually accompanied by difficulty sleeping or sleep onset insomnia (falling asleep immediately, waking in a few hours, and then not being able to get back to sleep).
2. *Constriction,* usually experienced as a stiffness in the "tense muscle triad" of the forehead, neck, and upper shoulders.
3. *"Chronophobia,"* a fear of having too much to do in too little time.
4. *Consumerism,* a constant need to get more, better, newer stuff.
5. *Feeling conflicted,* torn between the need to be with your spouse, family, and friends and still fulfill work obligations.
6. *Feeling cornered,* trapped between daily obligations and dreams of a life not pursued.
7. *Being controlling,* feeling that you must stay on top of things or they will get ahead of you, or that others are trying to take advantage or control of you.
8. *Feeling challenged,* feeling that you must prove yourself constantly or someone else might "get your piece of the pie."
9. *Becoming careless,* making mistakes in even the simplest and most common activities.
10. *Being cynical,* expressed in sarcasm, being unwilling to trust people, and having difficulty enjoying what would seem to be enjoyable activities because they seem frivolous or distracting.

The more you find yourself suffering from these symptoms, the more likely you are suffering from Delight Deficiency Syndrome. Fortunately, there is a cure for this: daily doses of pleasure!

What is the nature of this magical medicine? It is not a drug, potion, cure-all exercise, or talisman. It is a basic way of life, much more a way of "being" than another thing to do. So, before you learn to take the pleasure prescription, it is necessary to understand why your current approach to life may not be bringing you the joyful well-being you hope for. In this chapter and the next, we will explore the conflict between your current lifestyle and your body's instinctive needs and desires. From there, you can see how an alternative approach to daily living can give you the keys to physical, mental, and spiritual health.

Taking the Pleasure Prescription

Are you taking full advantage of the fact that you live in paradise? Is your life a real pleasure for you and those around you? Do you feel "at home" with yourself and do others feel at home with you? More than the results of any medical test, your answers to these questions predict how long, happily, healthily, and heartily you and those around you will live.

Research shows that what you think about your health and how long you expect to live may be more important than any assessment made by a doctor. Those who relish life and expect to enjoy it for a long time are three times less likely to die young than those who expect an early death. This is supported by research that showed that people who physicians considered in poor health but who believed that they were in good health survived at a higher rate than those who accepted their doctors' view.[2]

Most of us will live much longer than our great-grandparents, but are we living better? Are we living more joyfully than they did? With its technical wizardry, Western science has made miraculous contributions to our physical welfare, but it has made far fewer contributions to our spiritual and emotional well-being. As technology evolves more rapidly, we increasingly separate our physical health from our mental and spiritual self. As a result, we suffer a variety of physical and emotional ailments and a disenchantment with daily living.

With *The Pleasure Prescription,* I will show you how you can glow with health—what Polynesians call *lamalama ka'ili*—and enjoy every moment of your journey to this wonderful state even when you are not very happy or when you feel sick. The approaches described in this book offer the one thing that can save and lengthen your life: helping yourself and others to life's simple pleasures rather than avoiding them, and immersing yourself in the wonder of the world as it is.

The Oceanic people taught that a joyful and healthy life was based on following our seventh sense, an instinctive drive to what is healthful and pleasurable, manifested in what they called *aloha. Alo* means to share and *ha* means breath, so *aloha* literally means to give and share the breath of life. The pleasure prescription is about "catching your breath," and once you've caught it, finding that relaxation, happiness, and long life come from giving and sharing this breath.

Catching Your Breath

Before you embark on the pleasure prescription, I have one more suggestion. If you are very busy and distracted and don't have much time for pleasure right now, you may be addicted to the stress hormones that numb your sense of pleasure. Before going any further, I suggest you catch your breath.

Sit down in a quiet place, close your eyes, and take in a few breaths. Breathe in very deeply through your nose until your abdomen goes out. Say the word *alo* to yourself or softly aloud. Remember, *alo* means to share. Then breathe out, softly saying the word *ha,* which means breath.

Imagine that you are on a Polynesian beach just after you have awakened in the morning. Feel the warm, new-day breeze coming in off the ocean and listen for the waves lapping at the white, sandy shore. Smell the fresh tropical air, which always feels as if a gentle rain has just ended, and notice the subtle changing scents of all the fresh flowers misting around you. Feel your heart beat and let it represent the deep drums of the Pacific gently thumping their healthy rhythm within you. See the rainbows that smile over the mountains on a fresh new Polynesian day.

Once you feel a little less *haole,* or breathless, stand up and stretch. Call someone you care about and tell him or her you are going to start bringing a little more healthy pleasure into your life and hopefully into his or her life, and into the world in general. Remember, just catching your own breath is not enough to experience the full bliss of *aloha.* The true sense of *aloha* requires the catalyst of continually sharing the breath of life.

Dancing in the Moment

In his book *Full Catastrophe Living,* psychologist Jon Kabat-Zinn focuses on the importance of paying attention to all that life has to offer and quotes 85-year-old Nadine Stairi, who told him, "Oh, I've had my moments, and if I had to do it over again, I'd have more of them. In fact, I'd try to have nothing else. Just moments, one after another, instead of living so many years ahead of each day."[3]

In many ways that thought is the essence of the pleasure prescription. However, this is not just another book about taking life "one day at a time"—life is not so simple as that. When I was struggling with cancer, dozens of health-care workers and well-meaning visitors said, "Just try to take it a day at a time." Those of us who have come back from dying know that life is made of moments, not days. Think of your best memories and you will know them as moments, not specific days; as experiences, not events with beginning and ending points.

I first noticed the power of the pleasure prescription and its moment-to-moment joy through the ups and downs of life when I watched a young Hawaiian hula dancer. I saw that she was crying. She smiled and swayed gracefully to the gentle chanting and music, but teardrops slid down her cheek and moistened the floral lei around her neck. After her dance, I said, "You did such a beautiful dance today. You moved so wonderfully even though you seem sad." She smiled, wiped a tear from the corner of her eye, and said, "I am very sad. I have just learned that I have a tumor in my breast. This is the best time to dance. Dancing is easy when you are happy, but it is healing and necessary when you are hurt. Life is a hula, and you must learn to love and share the hula no matter what life has given you. Hula helps me keep the harmony in my life even when the music nature plays for me is not pretty. When you hula, you always move both right and left. Right is no more important than left. Your hula is a way of being in *pono* (balance) and staying in *pololei* (connection)."[4]

Are you dancing through your life, or just going through the motions? Are you a well-adjusted robot or a learning, struggling soul? Do you move in harmony, with balance and connection, or are you rushing to the next step? What is it that keeps you from dancing in the moment? Are you as healthy as you could be?

Escaping From Health Terrorism

The Cassandra complex In the classic legend, Cassandra, the prophetess of ancient Troy, was doomed never to be believed. She had many revelations and made prediction after prediction. In part due to the sheer number of her prophecies, people stopped listening to her. Our health-care system has become a modern-day Cassandra, crying out health warning after health warning, many of which appear contradictory. Unable to separate speculation from reality and numbed by the barrage of bad news, we no longer trust these prophecies and warnings. We either live in fear, constantly trying to avoid the dire consequences predicted by modern medicine, or we decide to recklessly ignore them, denying what may in fact be important to our well-being.

If we feel alienated from modern medicine, we may turn with despair to so-called "alternative" medical approaches. Too often, however, these approaches fail us as well, because we fail them. We do not learn, respect, and practice the philosophical and cultural perspectives from which these systems originated. We seek a magic pill, and when taking it doesn't work, we move on to the next one. We wonder why so many people who ignore the health warnings seem healthy while others who listen seem to die too soon. Why are there sick health saints and flourishing health reprobates?[5] In part it is because health is the result of a complex, dynamic process, one which draws on our body, mind, emotions, spirituality, and relationship to others and the world around us.

Even the most conservative physicians concede that most of what causes illness or results in healing is still largely unknown, and that what makes for health is not a simple "magic pill." Physician James McCormick, writing in the respected medical journal, *Lancet,* warns against the "health puritanism" that takes away much of the fun of fitness. He says, "Physicians would do better to encourage people to lives of modified hedonism so that they may be able to enjoy, to the full, the only life that they are likely to have."[6]

Physician Arthur Caplan, Director of the Center of Bioethics at the University of Pennsylvania, is concerned about the new Cassandraism of Western medicine. He suggests that roles once played by abstract ideas of hell, limbo, and eternal damnation have found secular expression in the somewhat abstract ideas of high blood pressure, bad cholesterol, and ideal weight. In subscribing religiously to the prophecies of scientific research we have elevated medicine beyond the physical and created a belief system that governs the way we experience our lives. Ironically, for all its good intentions and scientific "proof," this approach to life only makes our numbers look better—it does not actually make us *feel* better.

Someone once pointed out that medical statistics are like a bikini. What they reveal is interesting, but what they conceal is vital. Hidden behind the impressive statistical power of modern science are the remarkable, neglected lessons from our spirits and a seventh sense that can guide us to what nourishes and protects us. And what nourishes and protects us is *pleasure.*

In carefully designed, on-going research, psychoneuroimmunologist Arthur Stone at the State University of New York has discovered that positive events have a stronger positive impact on immune function than upsetting events have a negative one.[7] Simple enjoyable activities, such as having a few friends over for dinner or sharing a sunset with a loved one, can have immediate results such as strengthening the immune system and temporarily reducing blood pressure.

The worried well We read about risks to our health every day, but we seldom read about the "robust factors," those aspects of living that are great fun and lead to good health. We seldom read that, despite the nagging, transitional, and, as you will read later in this book, necessary illnesses we all experience, most people are generally healthy for much of their lives, whether or not they eat a perfect diet or exercise appropriately. So what has happened to us? We have become the worried well, focused on fear and checking for symptoms, popping vitamins and spending hours in doctors' waiting rooms, often to be sent home at best with the encouragement, "it will get better," or at worst with unnecessary medications that are beginning to lose their effectiveness through overuse.

Much of our health worry is related to a joyless, paranoid lifestyle. Many of us feel increasingly unable to control our destinies. In our failed attempts to find a sense of safety in life and control in our world, we feel increasingly vulnerable. We feel in constant danger from contaminated water or food, a new bacteria that has outsmarted our most powerful medicines, a drunk driver, an addict who might kill us to support a drug habit, or the random gunshot from a disgruntled worker. To continue to live in an increasingly threatening world (that we ourselves help to create), we withdraw from it. We also turn inward to monitor and protect the one thing we think we can control—

our own body. But we are blind to the fact that there is no such thing as "self-healing." Health and healing are dynamic—and interactive. They come from both inside us and outside us. Only an approach that is connective, based on respect, love, and caring for ourselves, others, and the world around us, can save us.

Instead of becoming "harmonious healers of the world," we have become individual worried warriors, fighting to stay alive as long as possible in an increasingly uncivilized society. We try to keep up our strength for the war by checking our pulse, taking our blood pressure, counting our calories, watching our weight, and exercising to stay in shape so we can be the fittest who survives the daily and nightly conflict between the haves and have-nots. We don't realize that our physical ills and social ills are related.

Can't buy us health or happiness How are we addressing our health and happiness? How do we tackle the problems around us? Researchers have shown that money does not buy happiness.[8] Money has also failed to buy us health or satisfaction with our health-care system. We spend more than 2 billion dollars a day and 900 billion dollars a year on one of the most advanced health-care systems in the world. We spend 7 billion dollars a year on heart bypass surgery alone. Unfortunately, as the Harvard School of Public Health Report shows, most of our financial investment to buy health has failed to get us what we paid for—a longer, happier, healthier life.[9]

Not surprisingly, the majority of us feel robbed. Dr. Michael Allukian, President of the American Public Health Association, says that we have ended up with a health-care system that doesn't promote health, doesn't seem to care, and isn't much of a system. At the current rate, our medical system will constitute almost half of our gross national product by early in the next millennium, but 89 percent of Americans say they are dissatisfied with health care.[10] Of the 10 most advanced countries in the world, we rank ninth in satisfaction with our health-care system. Like people rearranging deck chairs on a sinking *Titanic,* we are urgently trying to make our short cruise through life look better, but the real problem at hand is whether we're on the right boat.

An alarming global twist has occurred in our quality of life as well. We have so neglected living in cooperation with our planet Earth that we are now almost beyond being able to pay to repair the ecological damage we have done. For example, the median life-year saved by cancer prevention programs costs about $750,000. However, to stop factories from releasing the chemicals such as benzene and formaldehyde that cause cancer in the first place would, at today's prices, cost more than $2.5 million for that same life-year.

It is clear that we cannot buy our way out of the problem we have created. It does little good to spend more than $21 billion a year on drastic, life-saving measures when we are creating a planet with a toxic environment, on which life shortly will not be worth living. Something must be done to bring us back in balance. So what have you been doing?

Risk roulette Overwhelmed by all the spending and worrying, many of us have become health gamblers. We occasionally escape from our hectic lifestyle by "stealing a few moments," distancing ourselves from the environment we ourselves have made so demanding and threatening. Or we sequester ourselves in the safety of home offices, missing the social contact of the workplace, communicating by Internet rather than interaction, and rendering homes places of business rather than bliss.

Many of us have not learned that real joy comes only with shared pleasure. We also play a "risk roulette" where there is only one possible good outcome—good health, as promised by medicine—and hundreds of bad ones, which we focus on as we spin the wheel of life. Physician Larry Dossey writes, "It is as if all our potential thoughts are a roulette wheel of possibilities, with only a single, positive slot amid thousands of black negative ones."[11]

If we land on black and become ill, we seek repair. We think that we can be fixed by medicine, but, as medical writer René Dubois writes, "To ward off disease or recover health, man as a rule finds it easier to depend on healers than to attempt the more difficult task of living wisely." Living wisely is our task at hand, and where better to look for advice on living wisely than from those who have lived long and successful lives before us.

A Hawaiian *kahuna* (healer) described the Oceanic way of "living wisely" when he said, "Health is harmony. To live in harmony with our *'aina* (earth), we must learn that we are like parts of its body. The earth is alive and we are its organs. We guarantee ourselves great unhappiness when we live like cancer cells multiplying selfishly without regard to the whole organ system called earth."[12]

Secrets to a Long Life

As the first "installment" of the pleasure prescription, here are 20 research findings that challenge the "health terrorism" and medicalism of today. I hope they offer relief from the "risks" you've wasted your pleasure time trying to avoid. Let these pieces of good news take the threat of early death out of your daily living and replace it with the reward of being totally alive now. Each one is based on studies done by respected researchers who are challenging the Cassandra complex of modern medicine.

Twenty Happy Findings About Health Risks

1. *Don't worry about the most commonly used medical test results.* Low blood pressure and cholesterol levels are not the best predictors of health and longevity.[13]

2. *Don't worry about your salt intake as related to your blood pressure.* More than 90 percent of us are not "salt sensitive" and do not react to salt with increased blood pressure.[14]

3. *Don't worry about cancer.* There are now more researchers, health-care workers, therapists, administrators, and insurance people involved in the battle against cancer than there are people with cancer. Most people diagnosed with cancer get better. I did! In fact, I survived stage IV lymphoma that had spread through my body, three courses of chemotherapy, full body radiation, and a bone marrow transplant. Those whose cancer does not remit often become happier and more alive than they were before cancer, and more so than people who have never had cancer.[15] We fight a war against cancer, but we have not yet learned to enjoy the daily peace of blissful living that might significantly reduce it and help us heal if we have it.

4. *Don't worry about the impact of negative events in your life.* Pleasurable experiences have much more powerful health effects than negative experiences and can negate most of the effects of negative experiences.[16] In addition, you *need* the challenges of life to be able to appreciate the gifts of being alive.

5. *Don't worry about the stress in your life.* You need stress to live. Stress is not as bad for you as you've been told; it is actually essential to health and longevity. Those who experience the most stress often develop a "stress hardiness" that helps them when serious illness strikes.[17] While too much "hot" stress reaction is not good for you, too much stress-free "cool" reaction can impair the development of an adaptive, balanced physiology. Life without stress would be no life at all. In fact, we are often so pressured to avoid stress that we miss out on the pleasure that comes with positive, challenging stress, which psychologists call *eustress.*

6. *Don't worry so much about your diet.* Dieting isn't good for you, no diet works for long, and what tastes good usually *is* good for you, otherwise your body would not have been made to think it is good. Some fat, sugar, and cholesterol are essential for life. Gaining a little weight as you age is natural and good for you also. Eating an occasional high-fat meal won't hurt you; a little meat once in a while can actually help lower your cholesterol with its "good fat" content. A high-fiber diet isn't always necessary. Indulging in a high-butterfat milkshake every other day does little to raise cholesterol. Even the dreaded dietary risk-factor, ice cream, can lower your cholesterol.[18] As much or more so than *what* you eat, joyful eating with people you care about produces healthy nutritional benefits. Or, as this little poem puts it,

   Those who eat beer and franks,
   With cheer and thanks,
   Will be healthier than those who eat
   Sprouts and bread, with doubts and dread.[19]

7. *Watch, but don't worry about, symptoms.* Most illnesses go away in a few days, some illness is essential for your immune system to develop, and what causes your symptoms are processes that may actually be essential for you to heal. Most symptoms should not be relieved too quickly—the immune system is strengthened and develops new defenses by encountering and defeating illnesses such as measles and chicken pox.[20] A

runny nose, slight fever, and hearty cough all serve important and essential healing functions. Almost all common illnesses are self-regulating, yet doctors' often bland, crowded, boring, poorly lit offices are full of the worried well, who are missing out on the sunshine outdoors that might make them feel better. Don't forget: one of the best ways to keep your mind off of your own body is to get interested in someone else's!

8. *Don't worry about being a little depressed.* Unhappiness is not an illness. While chronic deep depression requires immediate professional help, some depression can be very healthy. It can serve as an emotional coolant for an otherwise hot lifestyle. It injects a dose of needed reality that can help make our dreams come true and promotes balance in our thoughts and physiology. As you read in the introduction to this book, the pleasure prescription is not based on a positive attitude but a blended balance of optimism, pessimism, and realism. A depressed state is often accompanied by insightful contemplation and followed by elation, and depressed people are usually very perceptive and more in touch with reality than those who delude themselves by pseudo-happiness.[21]

9. *Don't worry about always trying to be up-beat.* Irrational cheerfulness can shorten your life. People who are almost always cheerful also tend to be dangerously impulsive and to disregard commonsense health habits. People who experience depression have the skill of seeing reality, not denying it.[22] Trying to be up all the time can really bring you down. If we get too high, we crash.

10. *Don't worry about your body image.* A big behind can be a sign of good health, and how you are shaped is mostly beyond your control.[23] Tuning into and enjoying your body is more healthy than worrying about its shape. The obligations we place on ourselves about trying to stay young, firm, and shapely only add more burdens to an already pressured life. When we let go of our focus on the ideal of young, slim, and beautiful, we free ourselves to enjoy the sensuous pleasures of the only body we will ever have.

11. *Don't worry about getting old.* Studies show the older we get, the happier we get.[24] So stop trying to satisfy your "inner child" and start developing your inner elder. On the day of his one hundredth birthday, comedian George Burns offered his secret of long life. He said, "Don't worry about getting old, just get up. Have something that makes you want to get out of bed."

12. *Don't worry about getting enough exercise.* Don't kill yourself to save your life. Intense exercise isn't necessary for good health or a long life.[25] The "no pain, no gain" approach is counterproductive to fitness. A half hour of walking, swimming, or other enjoyable exercise with another person several times a week is enough to reap the benefits of regular movement. Pleasurable exercise is vital to keep the mind and body energized. If you exercise because you "must," you miss the pleasure boost that makes exercise even more healthy. Mark Twain was on the right track when he said, "Whenever I feel I *ought* to be exercising, I just sit down and enjoy doing nothing until the urge passes."

13. *Don't worry about feeling rushed.* There is a difference in the health impact of a "glee rush" and a "goal rush." When you feel a glee rush, the thrill of all the potential life has to offer, your body reacts with the bliss response. On the other hand, if you are constantly too busy to enjoy the simple pleasures of daily living, you end up with a "busy body": a body too distracted to experience delight and too busy to defend itself against disease. Much has been written about the "Type A" personality. Being a persnickety or ornery Type A may have negative effects on your cardiovascular system, but being a pleasant and pleasured Type A is *not* a major risk to your heart.[26] A full, even hectic life can be good fun and mean good health if you balance it with shared moments of bliss.

14. *Don't worry about your heart.* Your heart is the strongest muscle in your body and, unless denied a daily dose of delight, it does not weaken with age. Constant concern about "heart risk factors" can turn us into cardiac neurotics. Yes, it is un-

wise to press your luck and abuse your body with reckless eating, smoking, drinking, or drug use, but most people who have some of the major heart attack risk factors will never have a heart attack. And 50 percent of those who do have a heart attack have none of the risk factors we are taught to fear.[27] Rather than bypassing our hearts, we would be better off connecting them with other hearts to more fully enjoy living and loving. The more you open your heart, the less likely it is that you will need open-heart surgery.[28]

15. *Don't worry about causing your own illness.* There is no conclusive evidence that personality predisposes you to any disease. If you want a role model for long life, don't look at joggers, health-food fanatics, or new-age gurus. Look at those who have actually lived long lives. You will find that they subscribed to a life of constantly seeking and giving daily pleasure.[29] The great philosopher/comedian Redd Foxx once pointed out that all those exercise fanatics and health food nuts are going to feel mighty silly when they're lying in the hospital, dying of nothing.

16. *Women shouldn't worry about job stress making them as susceptible as men to high blood pressure.* Professional working women actually have lower blood pressure than women who stay at home. It is clearly how you are, more than where you are or what gender you are, that counts when it comes to hypertension.[30]

17. *Don't worry about not being relaxed enough before a medical procedure or surgery.* While relaxation training before surgery helps people feel less tense, researchers have found that the greatest postsurgical increases in the stress hormones that impair healing and immunity are found among patients given relaxation training. Those who did not learn to relax and worried had fewer stress hormones after surgery. The key seems to be "Don't relax, worry!"[31]

18. *Don't worry if you haven't yet joined the "total fitness" movement.* A study of nearly 13,000 men by researchers at 22 medical centers in the United States showed that, despite a successful reduction of health risk factors for heart disease (smoking, fatty

diet, lack of exercise, and such), the death rate was higher for these 13,000 men than for a control group of men who did not reduce their risk factors.[32]

19. *Don't worry if you missed your annual physical exam.* The periodic health exam was introduced over 80 years ago, but there is as yet no strong data to document the physical exam's efficacy for adults.[33] While some regular tests, such as pap smears, mammograms, and prostate and rectal exams, can offer early detection of problems, a total physical exam every year may not be the cost-effective magic bullet we thought it was.

20. *Don't worry about "the Big Two": high cholesterol and little exercise.* Studies now show that elderly men with low cholesterol levels suffer from problems such as depression and suicide and have a higher degree of general hostility and unhappiness than men with high cholesterol levels.[34] While exercise can be shown to have good effects on the heart and circulatory system, as pointed out earlier, there is no clinical evidence that conclusively demonstrates that increasing physical activity for sedentary people significantly and consistently reduces their rate of disease.[35]

These 20 bits of good news about the bad news we often get from the medical establishment should not, of course, lull us into a false sense of security. It is careless and potentially lethal to ignore the gifts that modern biological science offers, but it is silly and life-limiting to govern our lives by the as-yet unproven myths about healthy living. The pleasure prescription calls for balance. As author Jeremiah Abrams pointed out, "The one-sided get blind-sided."

These health findings and the many more that will be discussed throughout the book show that, in general, we are working too hard to be healthy, suffering too much undeserved guilt about what we eat, weigh, do, and look like, and taking the *fun* out of life just to make our life "longer." But you don't need to rely only on me and these Western science research findings to understand the pleasure prescription. Your body and your seventh sense for healthy pleasure will tell you that you are most hardy when you are the most happy—you don't have to kill yourself working harder to live longer.

Chapter Two

PLEASURE—THE SEVENTH SENSE

"Polynesia . . . a place where one can enter into truth, become one with nature and, after the disease of civilization, life is a return to health."

— Paul Gauguin

Paul Gauguin found little pleasure in life. Despite acclaim as a great artist, he experienced long, deep bouts of depression and poor health. Although he had achieved much he dreamed of, Gauguin agonized over his failure to achieve his own version of perfection. Unable to find peace in his everyday life in Paris, he fled to Tahiti to rest and recuperate. There he was introduced to an entirely different way of life. Like many other writers, scientists, musicians, and artists, Gauguin fell in love with the people of Polynesia and their daily practice of five principles of pleasure that brought them health, happiness, and long life.

Gauguin found ultimate fulfillment in a way of life called *aloha,* a 2000-year-old prescription for living based on embracing life by sharing its sacredness with others. He was soothed by the sensuality of an island paradise where daily life was characterized by a powerful combination of patience instead of urgency, connection with nature instead of attempts to control it, collaboration in place of competition, humbleness instead of self-glorification, and gentle kindness instead of hostility. Gauguin was amazed at the harmony in which the people lived with and protected nature, and was rejuvenated by a lifestyle that nurtured stamina, strength, and endurance. He said they seemed to communicate with a sense beyond the basic human senses, one that allowed them to connect with the world around them as easily as they connected person-to-person. Gauguin rediscovered his health and happiness in Polynesia and remained there, agreeing with Mark Twain, another visitor, that this magical place was "heaven on earth."

Gauguin's discovery of paradise was less the discovery of a place than a way of living. The displeasure and despair that sent him to Tahiti are not strangers to us today. Luckily, the secrets of *aloha,* shared for the first time in *The Pleasure Prescription,* can bring us all a longer, healthier life in our modern world. If you want a healthy harmony in your own love, work, play, and family life, then read on. And you don't have to travel to Tahiti, for here it is, in your own backyard!

Disconnection from Ourselves

Hawaiian scholar Michael Kioni Dudley asks, "Who is really happy in the world? Is it the high-powered, fast-paced individualist who spends every resource of time, energy, and thought building and maintaining a financial empire? Is it those who have embraced the consumer mentality, believing that more possessions bring more happiness?"[1] This book shows that the mental and physical exhaustion of the toxically successful people mentioned in the Introduction and the millions of others following in their footsteps is traceable to leading what Polynesians call a *haole* life, (*ha* = breath, *ole* = without). *Haole* living is a breathless, urgent daily existence spent in pursuit of "better." It is a never-ending journey that leaves us discontented and fatigued. A major cause of *haole* life is our disconnection from ourselves, the earth, and those around us. It so pathologizes unhappiness that it keeps us from learning from the natural chaos of living. Our energy is directed at avoiding any unhappiness rather than benefiting from the insights of a well-rounded, meaningful life that includes all emotional states from despair to great joy.

Neurologist Antonio R. Damasio refers to the disconnection we feel as "Descartes' Error," because it springs from the assumption that our brain is separate from our body. An extension of this error is our separation from our environment. Because we affect our environment and it affects us, it is a part of us. We have come to see nature as insentient, mechanical matter to be used in competition with others who also seek control of the world.[2] Many of us have welcomed mind-over-body medicine as an attempt to address the separation of our physical body from our whole selves. Although it is often called "holistic medicine," it is still an extension of the "self-over-the-world" approach to life. It is another version of separation: one mind trying to take charge of one body. We have yet to learn the Oceanic history of healing the earth and others as a requisite step to healing ourselves. No matter how much stuff and success we may achieve, the *aloha* lesson is that if other people, and the earth and its creatures, are unhappy, ultimately so are we.

Brain and Mind

Pleasure is the mechanism that connects all aspects of ourselves, our senses and our body, our mind and our brain. Right now, consider what is on your mind most of the time. Ralph Waldo Emerson pointed out that "Life consists of what a man is thinking of all day." Is your mind crowded with obligations, pressures, needs, wants, aspirations, planning for the future, trying to do more, and have more? When you jog, do you think about the wonderful scenery or your latest work challenge? When you go to the gym to lift weights, are you thinking about the beauty in your world or about how to firm your buttocks? When you eat, do you discuss family problems or the taste and texture of your food? When you take a vacation to "get away from it all," what is the "all" you are getting away from? Does the "all" stay on your mind? Why do you want to get away from it? Are vacations an escape from your own way of living—brief pleasure probations from a life sentence of obligations? As John Lennon warned, *is your life what is happening while you are making other plans?*

If so, your mind has been "Westernized" and your indigenous, "pleasure mind" is being neglected. The Aloha Test in Chapter 3 will help you measure the degree to which you have lost touch with your indigenous mind. Chapter 6, Cranial "G-Spots," will give you a more detailed picture of the neurology of pleasure and how it works.

What's On Your Brain?

We often don't stop to distinguish between the brain and the mind, but the difference is profound. Right now your brain is processing the light that conveys the pattern of print that makes up what the brain sees as words. Your mind gives the words meaning now and as compared with the past and future. Your mind is where pleasure is born or aborted, and it is the source of your seventh sense.

Your brain is capable of talking louder than your mind, droning out the messages of your seventh sense. To see who's getting the most airtime in your life right now, try the following exercise.

At the end of the day before dinner, sit down in a quiet place with a pad and pencil. Without any effort at censorship, write down what your brain is saying to you. Don't edit, just write. Is your brain urging you to eat, to work or worry about work, to avoid something you should be doing, or telling you that you need sex? What brain commands are traveling over your system? Write down at least ten thoughts from your brain, what my patients call "brain bulletins." Put this brain command list away until late evening. Later, put on some music you find relaxing, sit down again, and re-read your list. How many of those thoughts do you want on that list? How many represent the way you want to lead your life?

If you are like most people, you will find that the brain's messages were recycling the four Fs of survival: feeding, fighting, fleeing, and fornicating. The brain may try to fool you by hiding its basic four-F orientation, but if you look carefully you will see these scripts repeating themselves as basic life motives. Look at the list with your mind, not your brain. Your brain will see the list as reminders of obligations and assignments, but your mind can assess the value of the messages in terms of your own chosen way of living. You may even see your mind make breakthroughs on the list, items that seem strangely out of place. These might be thoughts such as "I want to take a slow walk with my sweetheart," countered by your brain saying, "You don't have time to walk. Have a quick jog so you can keep my body in good shape." Your mind might say, "I'd like to eat a nice, fat cheeseburger and savor every bite." Your brain might respond, "Get some food fast. I don't care what, so long as it stops my hunger."

The mind is your "high self" and is the process of your dreaming, hoping, praying, and attempting to be one with everything and with all other minds. It directs you outward to join, not to turn inward or against. Where the brain seeks the stimulation of the new, the mind appreciates and is soothed by the old. The mind enjoys quiet peace, but the brain is hyperactive and keeps sending signals to eat, fight, flee, or make love instead of just sitting there connecting with the world.

Neurologist Richard Restak writes, "Mind can affect brain; brain can affect mind. But can either be separated from the other? Not any more than the other side of this paper can be separated from the side that you are now reading."[3] The illusion that the brain is in charge of our life is an obstacle to finding the healthy balance and connection necessary for pleasure in living. The brain has its job to do, but it is a part of and not director of our destiny.

Controlling the Selfish Brain's Agenda

Our brain has lost its mind. Although it thinks otherwise, our brain is not "us."[4] It is an important part of the most wonderfully integrated biosystem in the world, but it is not who we are. Its primary function is to regulate health maintenance, but it is often blinded by its total commitment to keeping us alive in the short run. As a result, we must teach our brain to be a team player and work with our mind, our seventh sense, and our body to help us practice the *aloha* that leads to health and well-being. This lifestyle encourages a mindfulness that brings us the most pleasure. What kind of brain do you have?

The impatient brain Does your brain keep telling you that there is plenty of time or that there is never enough time? Unless we tell it to be, the brain is not patient. It is interested in gratification—now, and it will use every body resource to keep itself alive at the moment, disregarding later health consequences.

The brain has no built-in sense of or for others. It is absorbed by the four Fs that make up its internal directive. It thinks that if something cannot be eaten, fought, escaped, or made love to, it is not worth too much attention. As a result, the brain is prone to a constant state of urgency, and any bliss is at best a distracting rest period used to re-energize for a return to the daily battle of survival.

The disconnected brain The brain is cerebral-centric and not much concerned with unity. It only thinks about its own welfare. Our brains have to be taught to cooperate, care, and nurture the world. Without the higher connective consciousness that leads to pleasure, the brain follows the rule of survival of the fittest. It uses the basic six senses more as weapons than ways to healthy pleasure.

When someone behaves obnoxiously, does your brain say that this person is in need of your help and understanding because her behavior shows that she feels frightened and disconnected? Or does your brain react selfishly, telling you she is a jerk and figuring out ways to let her know it? Connected brains think in the first, more forgiving way.

The angry brain Because it is impatient and disconnected, the brain is not naturally amicable or agreeable. It easily goes into fight mode. It does not discriminate between the symbolic threat of a verbal insult and the real threat of physical harm. It is usually in the "fight or flight" urgency response state, ready to ward off anything it sees as trespassing in its narrow territory. Like a hungry animal, it is easily irritated.

What is your first thought when someone cuts you off in traffic? Do you think, "That poor person is so rushed that he didn't even see me?" or do you think, "Who does he think he is? I'll cut him off, too." The first thought brings pleasure and health, the second thought is the angry brain protecting its turf and using up the body's resources in the process.

The arrogant brain The brain is very powerful and controlling, thinks it is brilliant, and does not easily accept humbleness. It thinks its way is "the" way. Unless we teach it differently, it has little regard for any other brain unless its owner is a source of food, someone to fight or flee, or someone to have sex with.

Does your brain tell you that most people are not as smart and clever as you are or that everyone has their unique brand of intelligence that it can learn from?

The anesthetized brain While every sensation passes through some level of the brain, the brain itself cannot feel. It is simply a processing place, and unless we take control of our brain, it cares little about less urgent pleasures. Unless we tutor our brain in tenderness, it does not take a gentle, kind approach to life.

Does your brain tell you to get what you can when you can, or does it tell you to touch, hold, give, care, help, and embrace? The second way is a way of thinking about life that tells the brain that the body needs tender, loving kindness or it will eventually stop sending the nurturing the brain needs to stay alive.

The Seventh Sense

We live primarily by five basic senses: sight, smell, taste, touch, and hearing. Sometimes we experience a sixth, "psychic" sense, which conveys and reads an energy we cannot always describe or measure. Our six senses evolved to make sure that we seek what we need to survive and that we avoid things that threaten our survival. Beyond these physical and psychic senses, though, is a seventh sense, one that modern society often fails to nurture. It is an intuitiveness composed of all the basic senses. It directs and employs the other senses to detect what is true healthy pleasure. Consider it an evolutionary sense for bliss and an enchantment with living.

The seventh sense mediates all of the basic senses and gives them purpose. The seventh sense is the gestalt of all of our basic six senses and more than the sum of them. It is the "something tells me there is something missing, something more" sense. The seventh sense is subtle; it gets our attention by entering our consciousness and inspiring us to think about a meaningful, joyful, enjoyable life.

The seventh sense regulates the brain, mind, and body and ensures that we "feed" ourselves the basic things necessary for happiness and health. Like food for the body, the seventh sense seeks food for the soul. The seventh sense is a moderator; if we follow it, it will direct us away from what hurts us and lead us directly to what brings us and others the greatest joy and health. My study of the links between current medical research and Oceanic tradition has convinced me that the way of feeling, thinking, and behaving in the world that Polynesians called *aloha* is the key to the discovery and development of your own seventh sense.

Pleasure Paradoxes

During more than thirty years of clinical practice, I have noted many paradoxes about pleasure. One of the most significant is that those who seem to have been given the best of life's fortunes appear to find less joy in their lives than those who have been dealt a less fortunate hand. The latter seem to know, as Robert Louis Stevenson pointed out, that life is not a matter of always getting a good hand but of playing any hand well; that experience is not what happens to you but what you make of what happens to you. They almost always are able to find joy in simple things while their more "fortunate" counterparts struggle to find a little joy and peace in their more complex lives.

If you want to see this pleasure paradox in action—and meet some very healthy people practicing the pleasure prescription—visit a cancer ward. These people know that well-being is much more than not being ill. I lived as a patient for months in a bone marrow transplant ward where each of us was near death, and I have never seen so many happy people in one place.

One of the patients, Alice, noticed this difference and explained, "Cancer patients have a survivor's pleasure. The 'silver platter' people were given a gift they could not receive. Our pleasure is earned through the school of hard knocks and we're more than ready to receive the smallest gift of pleasure." Alice went on to explain that the "silver platter" group had become numbed in their ability to develop a sense of pleasure—the seventh sense—while cancer patients are forced to learn to use it because many of their more basic senses have been impaired by chemotherapy or radiation. She added, "Cancer cures selfishness real quick. You so badly need to stay connected with life that you drink in every bit of joy that makes you feel alive. Cancer patients are often less afraid of dying than of not being able to die when we must. Maybe that's why we find so much more in life. Dying isn't controlling our life anymore, enjoying being alive is. We know there are two parts to death: letting go of life and dying. When you think about the idea of letting go of life, it is like letting go of your child as he gets older and must leave. You don't want him to go, you know he must, so you really try to enjoy the time you have with him." Another patient said to her visitor, "I think I see more from my hospital window than you do when you're out there. You seem more institutionalized than me."

People who faced death Like many therapists, I have also noticed in my practice that personal crises are not so much catalysts for drastic life changes as incentives to look at life differently. Chapter 15, "Loving and Learning Through the Hard Times," addresses this in depth. What I have learned differs from some of the popular ideas about surviving crises.

Contrary to popular fiction, people who face death are less concerned with making a new life for themselves or trying to milk all they can out of life than simply pausing to take in the beauty around them. Most return to their prior life but live it more mindful of every moment. They are more likely to go fishing than sky-diving, to sit with their family than to contemplate alone. They become less self-interested and more altruistic. The light that transforms them when they face death is less the glow of a beckoning afterlife than the radiance of being blissfully alive in the moment. They have much less fear of death than those who have not known it first-hand, and are less motivated to try to avoid death at all costs. I consider them "people of the seventh sense," because of the depth to which they are in tune with life and with what brings them pleasure, and the degree to which they use their mind, not just their brain.

The people of the seventh sense cannot be characterized as any "type" of person, and I've known fighters, acceptors, martyrs, liars, and exaggerators among them. But they share a common thread: they *changed what was on their minds,* and in doing so, changed their approach to life. They began dealing with life on a holistic level, making an emotional and spiritual decision to be more a part of everything. As a result, their seventh sense blossomed. Their pleasure sense took over their eyes, and they could see thunder. It took over their ears, and they could hear lightning. It took over their nose, and they could smell the rain. It took over their sense of touch, and they could feel the flowers. They no longer took vacations, but instead took regular *vocatios*—the Latin word for brief pauses to enjoy beauty.[5] Instead of setting out on a world cruise, they were much more likely to stop the car to take a long, slow look at the sunset.

Beauty neurosis People of the seventh sense have overcome what author James Hillman calls "beauty neurosis," a hyperactive lifestyle that confuses intense activity for the ability to engage with the world.[6] According to Renaissance writings, the three graces of life are beauty, restraint, and pleasure—all three of which the beauty neurotic lacks. Our pleasure-mind craves beauty, and in its absence suffers from the beauty neurotic's robot-like life, devoid of meaning. They become prone to unhealthy addictions, replacements that mask their chronic delight deficiency.

Beauty neurotics' five basic senses remain under the control of the selfish brain, which abuses them and wastes their pleasure potential in its joyless search for survival. They show little restraint, and often become workaholics. They are often unknowingly skin-starved for the gentle touch of someone who loves them, but seek sex more than share sensuality. People of the seventh sense, on the other hand, seek less to be "up" or "on" than "among." They don't live to work, they work to live. They not only feed the sense of touch, but their other sensual abilities as well.

Because people of the seventh sense often have had intense spiritual experiences, they may take a different view of the soul. They are less concerned with saving their private, inner soul than having their soul join lovingly with all other souls here on earth. Psychologist Carl Jung viewed the soul much as Polynesians and other people of the seventh sense do. He wrote, "The soul is for the most part outside the body."[7] Many of our religions focus on individual salvation, fostering the same risk mentality as modern medicine. We are told to prepare for judgment day, when our soul will graduate from "earth school" and present its credentials for entrance into something higher. People of the seventh sense are free of such fear because they see themselves as part of a collective soul—something Polynesians call the *aumakua.* For them, we are all in this together and *we are already living in paradise.* One cancer patient said, "To get to heaven, we have to spend less time worrying about saving our own soul and more time loving all souls."

Above all else, "seventh sensors" seem to be blissful and persistently patient enough to take the time to feel life rather than be led by it. I'll say much more about this in Chapter 7, "The Pleasure of Patience—Success Aloha Style." Seventh sense folks seem to personify the statement by Rabindranath Tagore, "The butterfly counts not months but moments, and has time enough."

When I was in the cancer unit receiving intense and painful chemotherapy and radiotherapy, I also noticed another paradox of the pleasure principle: *the patients being visited by friends and family give emotional support as much and often more than they receive it.* I saw fellow patients who had to give up life because of the severity of their illness finally die for their families. Knowing their own life was at an end and wishing to free their loved ones of personal and financial burdens, these patients would pass on in the night after settling family affairs and saying their good-byes. Other patients often comforted the medical staff and cheered up the visitors as much or more than the staff and visitors were comforting them. Transcending the fear that they too could become ill, the visitors left energized by the *mana* (spiritual energy) of those in crisis and touched by the power of their seventh sense.

Kumu: Teachers of the Third Way

There is only one nonclinical group I have known whose members have developed their seventh sense to extraordinary levels, and they are the teachers and healers of Polynesia. They first introduced me to the pleasure prescription and the power of *aloha,* and I am humbled by the degree to which they have developed their seventh sense. I have spoken with and learned from hundreds of Polynesian *kumu* (teachers) at home in Maui, Hawai'i, and during several trips throughout the South Pacific. While many people know and have experienced first-hand the beauty of the islands, few know of the remarkable 2000-year-old wisdom of this Oceanic people.

The Third Way of Polynesia and the five key elements of *aloha* are only a small part of the lessons from Polynesia. Polynesians do not teach by the written word, so my attempt to introduce their powerful psychology, spirituality, and medicine in book form is an interpretation of the range of their ideas. The quotes I include throughout this book are taken directly from my interviews with the island people. I have been trained by Western minds, so my presentation of Polynesian thought is by its very nature an approximation. I hope to bring their wisdom to you, but I cannot speak for them. I hope, however, to at least pique your interest to consider the lessons from paradise as loving principles for you and your family to live by, sharing ever more pleasure and bliss.

The wisdom of the islands is grounded in experience. The essence of the pleasure principles and how they affect our lives biologically, psychologically, and spiritually is dynamic—it is not linear. It is known more by *feeling* than by *thinking.* I hope to encourage you to learn the Polynesian style by using your indigenous mind, not just your Western brain. As one Polynesian put it, "I think it's okay if you have a brainless mind, because we all end up that way someday. I don't think it's okay to if you have a mindless brain, because then you cannot find healthy pleasure in life."

Chapter Three

THE ALOHA TEST

"It is not the threat of death, illness, hardship, or poverty that crushes the human spirit; it is the fear of being alone and unloved in the universe."

— Anthony Welsh

Mark Twain once said that the ancients had stolen all our best ideas. Two millennia ago, the wise people of Polynesia anticipated the miraculous discoveries we are just now making in modern physics, psychology, and medicine. They knew the sacred secrets of a blissfully connected life and practiced them everyday. They were the ultimate scientists, understanding the stars and planets, reading the ocean, building fish farms, sailing small but powerful canoes thousands of miles without navigational instruments. They could decipher clues from the waves, stars, and the ocean's creatures, looking at them as if searching a lover's eyes for signs of passion. Hundreds of years before the Vikings went to sea to conquer and plunder, the Polynesians had already sailed the vast Pacific by learning from it and joyfully accepting its mysteries.

United by a common culture and similar languages, the Polynesians spread out over 2,000 miles of ocean in their invisible triangle of islands that spreads over almost one-third of the Earth's surface. The first Atlantic sailors who stumbled upon these people could not comprehend the possibility that an entire nation of people had sailed the largest ocean on earth centuries before they themselves learned how to sail. They could not understand how these patient, simple, harmonious, pleasant, humble, gentle "savages" could be such powerful explorers and run such well-organized and efficient communities. The European sailors had come from a "civilized" world that equated success and happiness with being competitive, combative, and aggressive, with seizing power and controlling rather than giving to others. The Polynesians were reverse images of the Europeans, and there was something about these island people that strangely moved and even saddened the explorers, who perhaps saw in them their own missed potential for a more blissful life.

To the Polynesian, life is not linear. What we call the Polynesian Triangle is really an infinite pyramid extending into the sea and up to the heavens. It is a way of life and not a geographic location. It cannot be accurately represented on our Western maps because it has no boundaries, no territory to protect or conquer, no borders to patrol. Like the ancient Egyptian pyramids, Polynesia is an idea represented by its triangular shape, a three-dimensional oceanic depiction of the sacred trinity of humanness, divinity, and all of nature.

The Polynesians are not Peter Pans of the Pacific who spend their days swimming and relaxing, as stereotypes depict. It is degrading and wrong to see them as "noble savages." They also were not and are not perfect people. They have, however, developed a "health care" system for living together, solving their problems, and finding pleasure in living that is far in advance of our own.

Because the ancient Polynesians lived primarily by their seventh sense, the sense of pleasure that was so distorted and abused by European explorers, those sailors made the same error many others did. They saw these loving people as noble but naïve savages blessed by a wonderful climate and bountiful land. Even today, the islands remain a fantasy land for many continental people, a place for vacation, not education, a nice place to escape to rather than a center of wisdom and healing. One Hawaiian *kupuna* (elder) told me, "They used to call my people savages. Now that we see how these Western people live, we wonder who are the real savages. We wonder what civilization means. We wonder who is really happier and healthier and who treats the *'aina* (earth) with more *aloha.* We wonder who will survive, those they call savages or what they call civilization."

Person, Place, or Thing?

Much of Western culture is grounded in "things" to be used by the individual, while Eastern culture is based more in "person," learning more about the self. The Polynesian way is based mostly on "place." The Polynesians are people of the land and their idea of *aloha 'aina,* or love of the land, is central to the pleasure prescription. A Polynesian man told me, "We are at home. So many people who come here seem lost and emotionally or spiritually homeless. They keep moving, but they never really live anywhere. We love being in our place in the sea. We will never leave because we *are* this place."

Our land-locked minds have trouble comprehending the physical "place" of the island nations of Polynesia. If what we call the Polynesian Triangle were superimposed over the Eurasian continental mass, it would encompass an area stretching from London across Northern Europe to Siberia, down to China and Tibet, over to southwestern Asia, and back up to Southern Europe and England—an "Eurasian triangle" that includes the better part of two continents.[1] It is the people in this Eurasian triangle who, though they think they have conquered and dominated the world with their strong personalities and abundant things, have really failed to claim their natural birthright of bliss through a profound sense of place.

To explain his concept of place, one Polynesian *kahuna* told me, "The world thinks that we are islands far off in the sea, but we do not see that. Continental people live in cities and countries separated by boundaries on the land. We are part of one big family all connected in the sea. We travel on water roads. We are small islands far from the larger islands Westerners call continents. Their continents are just larger islands in the sea, but they don't seem connected by anything. They are moving farther and farther away from each other. Perhaps their islands are just too big and they can't see beyond them to know that they are all connected. They think in terms of lines and borders, so maybe that's why they thought for so long that the Earth was flat. We have known for thousands of years that Earth itself is an island in the cosmic sea. We are all navigators, not owners. We are all on a canoe in the sky."

The New Science with Polynesian Roots

Many of the new findings about health, happiness, and longevity come from the new field of psychoneuroimmunology (PNI). This still-emerging field is the study of the relationship between human behavior, psychosocial factors, the brain, the body, and resistance to or immunity against disease, viruses, and infections. Like the holistic Polynesian sense of "place," PNI is a view of the body/mind without boundaries.

Over the last three decades, PNI has documented remarkable new ways in which we can fight off disease and heal when we are sick. In just three decades it has amassed dramatic—albeit incomplete—evidence of what the Polynesians already knew: that psychological factors influence the body's ability to control symptoms and recover from catastrophic illness.[2] At least two Third-Way assumptions about a joyfully healthy life—*pololei* (connection) and *pono* (balance)—are beginning to float ashore again, like old wine in new casks, heralded by enlightened, open-minded, and open-hearted scientists. We must look beyond the containers, however, for the real lessons of life that are emerging from PNI and other medical fields.

Western medicine still applies a mechanical model to understanding and implementing the findings from PNI. Its mind/body focus stops short of the all-minds-in-one-body approach of the Oceanic peoples. It focuses on techniques, such as relaxation, stress reduction, imagery, and group therapy, as immune boosting and healing strategies. The Eastern models of healing have interpreted the findings from PNI to mean that meditation, contemplation, and seeking inner truth are the ways to access and communicate within this newly understood immune "internet." The Oceanic path to wellness has always known that nothing in this world is separate from anything else and that a balanced, pleasurable life is crucial to health and healing. For the Polynesian, it is not just clearing the mind by relaxation or meditation that brings well-being. It is what we put into our mind and what we help put into other minds that counts. It is learning to think in a connected, unified way that matters most—what might be called *E*PNI or *eco*-psychoneuroimmunology.

Although PNI is a most complex and complicated area still in need of much more study, my own examination of the valid preliminary findings shows that you can maximize the power of your own and others' miraculous immune system and even boost the Earth's immunity by practicing the five principles introduced below.

Taking the Aloha Test

Hawaiian Pilahi Paki describes *aloha* as the fundamental principle of life in Polynesia.[3] There are several variations of the Hawaiian word *aloha* throughout Polynesia, and they all sound and convey the same emotions. Like most Polynesian words, *aloha* has numerous meanings, including love, giving of the sacred breath, hello, and good-bye. *Aloha* is the perfect word to remind those of us who are so busy that we don't know if we are coming or going that we must slow down and find more pleasure in our life.

In the next section, I will encourage you to take a test of your own *aloha*. In the rest of Part One, I will discuss the five components of *aloha* as they relate to some of the newest findings from psychoneuroimmunology and psychoneurocardiology—the ideas that the ancients "stole" from the modern PNI and PNC researchers.

I designed the Aloha Test in 1991 after conducting interviews with *kahuna* (healers) and *kupuna* (elders). Most of these interviews were conducted in Hawai'i, but several were done in other islands of Polynesia. While the Polynesians told me they were glad to help design the Aloha Test, it was only their own gentle patience and tolerance of my Western mind that allowed them to do so. I needed to put the test in "Western" form, so the Polynesians often laughed when I came up with items intended to "measure what can't be measured." One Hawaiian joked, "You really don't need paper and pencil to learn about the mind, but I guess, when it comes to tests, West-est is best-est!"

"If you're looking for true wisdom, just watch how they treat their family," said one *kupuna*. "Watch to see if their family comes first and if they pray with their family and have good fun with their family and enjoy every day in their life. If they are sharing great pleasure in life, they have *aloha*. You really can't test *aloha,* you have to feel it." Despite these reservations, the elders and healers sat with me for hours and talked about the elements that could "estimate in a Western way" some aspects of each of the five components of *aloha* that make up the pleasure prescription.

After collecting my interviews, I tried to match various aspects of the five components of *aloha* with findings from Western and Eastern medicine that substantiated these ancient principles. The result is the 50-item test at the end of this chapter.

Unlike most Western tests, the Aloha Test is not designed for a high score. The lower your score, the less your indigenous mind has been silenced by modern living and the brain's urgency response.

Since 1991, I have given the Aloha Test throughout the world to a total of 10,952 non-Polynesians and, as a "control group," to 100 Polynesians, for a total of 11,052 tests. Because this exam was given at formal business meetings, to large audiences attending my lectures, on cruise ships touring the Pacific, after my appearances on TV talk-shows, in classrooms, and sometimes on the beach, it cannot be processed through the statistical system used by the West. I share it only as a starting point for interpreting your own score on the Aloha Test and understanding the strength of your own seventh sense for healthy pleasure and the role of the five *aloha* factors in your life.

Another reason why any statistical processing of my test results is not possible is that most of the persons taking the test were a biased sample of those who had come to hear me speak. While they cannot be statistically considered a "random sample," there is quite a range of backgrounds. I encourage you to draw your own conclusions about the meaning of the scores you will see from this group as compared to those who would never take such a test or come to a lecture by a psychoneuroimmunologist from Hawai'i.

Aloha Test

Scoring
2 = That's me
1 = Sometimes that's me
0 = That's never me

Ahonui—Patience, Expressed with Perseverance

1. Do you drive aggressively, use your horn out of frustration, just pause at stop signs, curse at other drivers, or speed up to beat a red light?
2. Do you push buttons on elevators that are already lit?
3. Do you hate lines and crowds?
4. Do you like to do several things at once?

5. Do you think "time is money," reluctantly taking tests like this one which seem to be a waste of your valuable time?

6. Is your mind always racing or do you mentally or verbally talk to yourself in an attempt to stay organized?

7. Do you feel guilty when you sit and do nothing?

8. Would others say that you seem rushed and in a hurry?

9. Is your work area messy, with many piles you have not had time to file?

10. Do people who move, think, and talk slowly seem to be "in your way" or make you angry?

    Total Ahonui Score _________

Lokahi—Unity, Expressed Harmoniously

1. Do you try to be all that you can be, better tomorrow than you are today, and to be a success?

2. Do you seek the thrill of victory, love a challenge, and make even little things into a contest with others or yourself?

3. Do you judge others or yourself by accomplishments, achievements, acquisitions, power, or status?

4. Do you think you must first love yourself before you can love someone else?

5. Do you think you get things done more quickly and efficiently by working alone?

6. Do you think you can accomplish anything you really put your mind to, that unsuccessful people lack commitment or motivation, have the wrong attitude, or just aren't willing to try hard enough?

7. Do you think that there is only so much to go around in this world and you have to work harder and think quicker to get your piece of the pie?

8. Do you assert yourself easily and like to use subtle put-downs and clever cynical comments?
9. Are you without many close friends with whom you can confide, tell anything, and show the real you?
10. Do you feel uncomfortable holding hands, hugging, kissing, singing, or dancing in public and think that "touchy-feely" behaviors are silly?

▼ Total Lokahi Score _________

'Olu'olu—Agreeableness, Expressed with Pleasantness

1. Do you frown, pulling up one corner of your mouth, rolling your eyes, and sighing to express your disgust?
2. Do you "stonewall" by turning off, tuning out, and ignoring people who criticize you or express their emotional frustrations to you?
3. Would it be difficult being married to you?
4. Do you like to argue?
5. Do you have all your emotional eggs in one basket, with your happiness centered primarily on your work, your effectiveness as a son, daughter, or your role as a parent?
6. Are you critical of others, either publicly or privately?
7. Do you try to "get even" for transgressions and what you view as trespasses against you?
8. Do you think your way is usually the best way?
9. Do you talk more than you listen?
10. Do you "vent" your anger and think it is best to get your hostility out even if you sometimes have to swear?

▼ Total 'Olu'olu Score _________

Ha'aha'a—Humility, Expressed with Modesty

1. Would others say you tend to brag and boast?
2. Do you like to impress others by owning and showing off expensive things?
3. Do you want others to know about your accomplishments?
4. Do you like to challenge others and put them on the spot?
5. Would others say you are outspoken, more than willing to share your opinions, and tend to lecture people?
6. Would others say you are sure of yourself to the point of being cocky and arrogant?
7. Are you often involved in disagreements, arguments, and conflicts at work, in public, or at home?
8. Do you usually know what people are going to say before they say it, interrupt, cut them off, or finish their sentences for them?
9. Do you say negative things about people who are not present?
10. Have you sued anyone, been sued, or often think about or threaten law suits?

▼ Total Ha'aha'a Score ________

Akahai—Kindness, Expressed with Tenderness

1. Would you sooner send a check to a charity than give several hours of your time personally helping complete strangers?
2. Do you expect a pay-back for your good deeds?
3. Are you uncomfortable around animals?
4. Do you think talking to plants, rocks, and trees is silly?
5. Do you litter?
6. Do you eat quickly and talk while you are eating?

7. Do you think praying might be a nice thing to do but not as powerful as good medicine?
8. Are you privately jealous and envious of others' good fortune?
9. Are you intolerant and impatient with people based on physical characteristics such as men with pony tails or women with tattoos or with certain nationalities, teenagers, or the very old?
10. Would your most intimate partner say you lack romance and prefer sex over sensuality?

▾ Total Akahai Score ________

Interpreting Your Aloha Score

Total your *aloha* score by adding your score on all five of the ingredients.

Ahonui (patience) score	________
Lokahi (unity) score	________
'Olu'olu (agreeability) score	________
Ha'aha'a (humbleness) score	________
Akahai (kindness) score	________
Total A-L-O-H-A score	________

Before you analyze your Aloha Test score and what it indicates about your present lifestyle, consider other peoples' scores. I leave it to you to interpret the differences in the scores and their meaning for each group—and for yourself.

Groups I have tested include:

- Some of the most successful business executives in the world, including CEOs and high-ranking military officers. (N = 1,465, where N is the number tested, mean Aloha score 82)
- Physicians from almost every major specialty. (N = 212, mean Aloha score 87)

- Nurses from every professional background, most with Bachelors, Masters, or Doctoral degrees. (N = 953, mean Aloha score 62)
- Health-care workers of all backgrounds, including physiotherapists, massage therapists, hypnotists, social workers, and psychologists. (N = 2,113, mean Aloha score 73)
- Law enforcement personnel, including police officers, judges, administrators, and polygraph operators. (N =210, mean Aloha score 81)
- Cancer, heart, and transplant patients (heart, kidney, liver, bone marrow). (N = 2,113, mean Aloha score 41)
- Public school, college, and university teachers and professors. (N = 766, mean Aloha score 70)
- Passengers on board cruise ships, including retirees, business men and women, and English-speaking men and women from all walks of life from all over the world. (N = 1,264, mean Aloha score 57)
- Seniors (age 65 and over) in senior centers. (N = 209, mean Aloha score 52)
- National television talk-show producers I met while appearing on these shows, including two nationally known TV talk-show hosts. (N = 14, mean Aloha score 89)
- Students from my college classes, aged from 17 to 76. (N = 1,733, mean Aloha score 83)
- A "control group" of Polynesians, mostly Hawaiian, aged 29 to 92. (N = 100, mean Aloha score 8)

Total N = 11,152
Mean Score for Total N = 74
(excluding Polynesian control group whose mean score = 8)

There was a significant difference in the scores of men and women. Again, not including the Polynesian scores, the mean score for the 7,576 men tested was 76. For the 3,576 women tested, the mean Aloha score was 67. Research shows that women typically, but not always, have higher emotional intelligence than men.[4] This factor may explain in part the nine-point difference between the genders on the Aloha Test.

Now that you have an idea of the test and the results of those who have taken it so far, what does your own score say about you? What does it say about your temperament? your work or professional life? your personal philosophy?

Based on others' prior scores, here is the meaning of your score compared with the average total score of 8 of the Polynesian control group and allowing for several additional points above that score to compensate for powerful, external Western influences that detract from *aloha.*

(*Note:* If you were intentionally trying hard to get a low score, add a 20-point pressure penalty!)

Over 30 Points = Severe Aloha Deficit
You have a Euro-American mindset

20–29 = Moderate Aloha Deficit
You have an almost completely Euro-American mindset

10–19 = Mild Aloha Deficit
You have a strong Euro-American bias

9 and below = Aloha Abundance
You have recovered your indigenous mind, think like a Polynesian, and will have an easy time learning and practicing the pleasure prescription

If your *aloha* score is high, take a look at which of the five elements accounted most for your high score. As you read Part Two of this book, your highest *aloha* component score is the one you will need to focus on first.

Thinking and living *aloha* requires a new way of thinking about daily living. Before you explore Part Two, read the last chapters of this section, which deal with the neurology of pleasure, so that you may be better able to use your indigenous mind.

Chapter Four

YOUR INVITATION TO PARADISE

"How I wish that somewhere there existed an island for those who are wise and of good will."
— Albert Einstein

Imagine a pill more powerful than any known medication, able to significantly reduce your chances of developing heart disease, cancer, and almost all other diseases, and guaranteeing a longer life. Imagine that the only side effect of this magic elixir is a euphoria hundreds of times more satisfying than that induced by any opiate yet free of the letdowns and risks of drugs. Imagine that this pill could replace intense exercise, radical diet programs, and stress reduction techniques while healing you when you are sick, enhancing your immunity, and reducing the negative effects of aging. Finally, imagine that this natural narcotic is completely free and that, when you take it daily, its effects automatically extend to those around you. In the chapters that follow, you will read about the existence of just such a medicine—the regular daily dose of pleasure.

Modern research has begun to verify the validity and health importance of the five elements of *aloha* that compose the pleasure prescription.[1] Western researchers call these factors the five elements of a healthy psychological character or the "Big Five" dimensions of the hardy and healthy personality, one that has strong immunity and healing powers and is relatively free of depression and despair.[2] So alongside explaining the five ingredients of *aloha*, I will mention the scientific and psychological research that makes them so important today.

Ahonui: Patience, Expressed with Perseverance

The word *ahonui* literally means "the great breath." It is central to practicing *aloha* because the breath of life sustains everything and everyone. One who is without patience is without the breath of life. Not only his health but the health of everyone and everything around him is placed in jeopardy by his breathless living. *Ahonui* means being patient at times of trouble and also at times of great joy. It does not mean leading a quiet, passive life. It means not being carried away and being calm enough to be fully part of whatever happens. It means being forbearing and patient enough to stay fully connected with all of life, to breathe in the sacred breath of existence in all its forms.

Modern researchers in PNI are now learning more about the role of *ahonui* in health and healing. When PNI was in its infancy, two cardiologists, Meyer Friedman and Ray Roseman, noticed that patients with heart disease left a telltale sign in their waiting room. Their impatience at being delayed in this room—named the "waiting room," after one of their greatest frustrations—had resulted in worn edges on all of the seats. These men and women were literally living "on the edge," constantly pressured by time.[3]

Subsequent research has shown that many other crucial factors related to a sense of urgency more directly influence the risk of heart disease. It is likely that a hostile approach to everything—including time—is the major heart risk that Meyer and Roseman were seeing, and that being pressured and impatient are really manifestations of other factors, such as egocentric hostility.[4] Nonetheless, the chronic state of urgency that comes with impatience disrupts biological oscillation (healthy balance), described in Chapter 2, and weakens health.

In their effort to beat the clock, "Type T," or time-consumed, people end up beating themselves. Suffering from the nagging fear that there never is or will be enough time, they lack the patience to do one thing at a time, instead taking pride at being able to do and think many things at once. It is not just a busy life but a "clock complex" that creates health risk.

Unfortunately, Type T people do not understand what quantum physicists are now discovering and ancient Polynesians taught years ago about the nature of time: there *is* only "the now."[5] The Type T person is, as Ralph Waldo Emerson warned, "always getting to live but never living." As you will learn in Chapter 5, *ahonui* means living in the eternal now with no boundary between past and future, and being available for what mythologist Joseph Campbell called epiphany, or instant enlightenment.

Author James Ogilvy writes, "Pleasure can be counted but not calculated."[6] The bliss response is not elicited by urgently trying to save time. Recent PNI findings suggest that goal-driven, time-focused people put their immunity in peril. They have not learned the enjoyment of what psychologist Mihaly Csikszentmihalyi calls *flow,* acting with selfless, effortless involvement right now, right here, with almost no sense of time passing."[7] Even when they "have some time," Type Ts feel frustrated and don't know what to do with themselves. They seek immortality but seem unsure of what to do with it or how to "spend" any "extra" time they already may have.

New data shows that prudent, dutiful, ethical people who show patience, not only with others but with themselves, tend to live longer and happier lives.[8] In concrete terms there seems to be a biological reward for "doing the right thing," such as taking the time to return a grocery cart to the store, pick up someone else's litter, leave places better than you find them, and drive courteously.[9]

A *kupuna* (elder) on the island of Maui warned against rushing though life: "If you are wondering if you are as happy as you should be, you aren't as happy as you should be. You can't fool yourself for too long. Your lack of joy in life will catch up to you. Something will get your attention—an illness, loss, or other personal problem, but something always tells you that you're squandering your greatest treasure—the gift of now. That's why they call it 'the present.'"

Lokahi: Unity, Expressed Harmoniously

Lokahi refers to behaving in a constant state of accord with the world, both natural and spiritual. It means living with a sense of enchantment, in harmonic unison not only within oneself but with others now and from the past. It means not moving a rock or picking a flower without being aware that you have changed the Wholeness of the universe.

Most modern psychology has focused on "self-health." Therapists deal with creative parenting, assertiveness training, sexual enhancement, healing the inner child, defeating codependence, and finding more intimacy within relationships. Meanwhile, the air gets fouler and the ecosystem is breaking down. Thousands of species have disappeared from the earth and each hour five square miles of the earth's rain forests, which enable the planet to breathe, are destroyed. The newly emerging field of ecopsychology suggests that we are focused on petty, personal-relationship issues at the expense of promoting a healthy relationship with the Whole that would probably heal these more trivial hassles and certainly put them in the meaningful context required for a healthy and happy life. It teaches that our ego is too narrowly defined and needs to expand—to the size of the earth. It suggests, like the concept of *lokahi*, that no health or healing can take place without simultaneously healing the planet.

The new ecopsychologists are asking old Oceanic questions. Instead of "Are you getting all you can out of life," they ask "What is the responsibility of a therapist in a dying world?" Instead of asking about the nature of our unhealthy intimate personal relationships, they ask "What is the nature of your relationship with the planet?" Instead of focusing on family strife, they extend their concern to asking "Who will help stop the abuse of the earth?" Less concerned with saving our "inner child," they ask "Who will help heal the 'entire planet'?" When a patient moans about her lack of orgasms or his failure to get all he can out of life, the ecopsychologist, practicing modern-day *lokahi*, may interrupt, "By the way, are you aware that the earth is dying?"[10]

Practicing *lokahi* does not mean disregarding individual welfare. It means that the pain of personal suffering is inseparable from planetary pain. Wellness cannot be accomplished by the pursuit of self-enhancement without regard for the Whole. Research now shows that cathexis, or the ability to form and maintain healthy human bonds, is crucial to health and happiness and that disruption, neglect, or abuse of relationships can be lethal.[11] If you want to bring pleasure into your life, first be a person who brings great pleasure into life—and into someone else's life.

A Polynesian *kahuna* said, "All bonds are forever. Divorce never annuls a relationship, and if you want to find joy, stay closely related to others and the world. The brain may think it has voided a commitment, but the heart does not think that way. Like a loving child, once it has loved, the heart loves forever, no matter what. You can never truly separate, even if you live a world away. It is a law of physics and a law of Polynesia. Once things join, they are transformed by their joining and are One forever."

'Olu'olu: Agreement, Expressed with Pleasantness

The word *'olu'olu* comes from a word meaning flexible, pliant, and at ease. It is the exact opposite of one of the leading modern killers—hostility. Polynesians consider going along and being congenial as not only a nice thing to do but essential to well-being. This pleasantness is not limited to people; it should be extended to all of nature as well. Ancient Polynesian fishhooks carved out of bone were worked on for hours to make them not only effective but attractive, so a fish would have a "beautiful last moment."

At least one in five of us has levels of anger and hostility high enough to constitute a serious risk to our health.[12] As you will learn in Chapter 9, most anger comes from feelings of being trespassed against. Modern life is often a constant contest for territory and time, and anyone who takes either away from us is seen as an enemy.

Anger and hostility result in a chronic urgency response, which is discussed further in the next chapter. The heart is put on alert, blood pressure sky-rockets, and the immune system shuts down. Cardiologist Robert Eliot refers to a person in a chronically reactive state of anger as having the "hypertension habit," because we gradually acclimate and even become addicted to the "rush" of anger in our daily life.[13] Habitual hostility may be the single greatest thief of our pleasure and our health. The Polynesians were well aware of the dangers of a hot style of living. The word *'olu* also means "cool," the exact opposite of the hot reaction of the egocentrically impulsive and quick-to-anger person.

Research shows clearly that anger kills.[14] One key component of finding pleasure in living is forgiveness, and modern research shows that leading a life of gentle mercy is the most joyful and healthy way to live long.[15] Cardiologist Redford Williams and his wife show the joyful way of an absolving amiability with what they call the ABCs of forgiveness, which are exactly the same three elements of *'olu'olu* or agreeableness taught by the Polynesians. These are (a) start with small matters, (b) make the forgiveness policy decision to forego anger and remember its pleasure- and health-robbing characteristics, and (c) evolve your forgiveness skills to deal with ever more complex and difficult grievances.[16]

A Hawaiian *kupuna* said, "You have to forgive three times. You must forgive yourself, for you will never be perfect. You have to forgive your enemies, for the fire of your anger will only consume you and your family. And perhaps most difficult of all, if you want to find pleasure in your living, you have to forgive your friends, for because they are friends they are close enough to you to hurt you by accident. Forgiving is the meaning of and making of friendship."

Ha'aha'a: Humility, Expressed with Modesty

Ha'aha'a means unassuming and unpretentious. It means having what Western researchers are now calling the "emotional intelligence" to be aware of our own weaknesses, to calm ourselves down, and to be tolerant of others and not thinking we are more important than anyone else. It means understating one's accomplishments and not trying to be better than others. In Polynesia, bragging is seen as the highest form of rudeness and disrespect and a health-damaging way of distancing oneself from others and nature. Said one *kupuna,* "Bragging is like coughing without covering your mouth. It sends the virus of separateness and arrogance everywhere and makes everyone weaker."

Egocentric impulsivity, hot temper, and selfishness lower immunity, increase risk of early death, and rob life of joy.[17] Polynesians consider arrogance an insult to ancestors and the gods because it misuses and falsely claims ownership, credit, or exclusive responsibility for the natural sacred breath of life given to everyone. It is a public announcement that we are choosing to be separated.

More than a century ago, author Edward Bellamy wrote, "Competition, which is the instinct of selfishness, is another word for dissipation of energy, while cooperation is the secret of efficient production."[18] Modern sociologists have learned that the theory that competition is natural and inevitable is incorrect.[19] Altruism and allocentrism, not egocentrism, are the ways to the general health of the community and thus the individual. Most competition wastes the energy that could be used much more constructively.

A *kupuna* spoke to me in Hawaiian about her favorite quote about temper. She had read it in *Sayings of the Fathers* and translated it for me. She said she thought it summarized the Polynesian approach to the type of humble, underreactive, benevolent life that brings what she called "daily gladness."

> "There are four kinds of tempers:
> He whom it is easy to provoke and easy to pacify, his loss disappears in his gain,
> He whom it is hard to provoke and hard to pacify, his gain disappears in his loss,
> He whom it is hard to provoke and easy to pacify is a saint,
> He whom it is easy to provoke and hard to pacify is a wicked man."[20]

Akahai: Kindness, Expressed with Tenderness

One of the most valued behaviors in Polynesia is giving. Polynesians believe strongly in the idea of reciprocal rebound, or "what goes around comes around." If kind, considerate behaviors are sent out, the same will come back. When a flower is picked for a lei, thanks are given and something is left in return. Voice quality and manner are to be soft and gentle because loudness and roughness chase away the friendly gods and spread negative *mana* or energy. One *kupuna* said, "Think of your every word and deed as a boomerang and remember that it will come back to you."

Modern research shows that one of the most pleasurable of all human acts is also one of the healthiest things you can do for yourself and for others. Gentle, caring selflessness results in significant health benefits.[21] Putting in time caring for strangers has the same positive effect on health as putting in that same amount of time exercising. It translates to immense immune and healing benefits.[22] Polynesians call this behavior *kokua,* meaning to render assistance and relief to others, and they have known for centuries that the best way to help yourself is to silence your self and give of it.

A *kahuna* told me, "Giving to your family is automatic. You must, even though it is often very tiring and difficult. Giving to strangers takes effort. The reward of good cheer is very strong and comes from making strangers a part of your life. It becomes easier the more you do it because you become a way the created joins with the Creator."

Mature Pleasure

The five principles of *aloha*, when practiced together, awaken our awareness of our human potential and the sacredness of our life. We taste the profound and lasting joy this awareness can bring, and we begin to actively seek the things and lifestyle that bring us this type of joy. We forsake empty, momentary thrills for whatever brings deeper, lasting, meaningful pleasure.

To fully appreciate the Third Way of thinking that underlies the pleasure prescription, you must understand the concept of Oceanic maturity. Healthy pleasure is an experience beyond brief intense, uninhibited, and childlike stimulation. To live by the pleasure prescription is to develop a maturity that transcends socioeconomic security, social approval, or private success. Healthy pleasure requires much more than the economic ascendancy emphasized by Western psychology or the spiritual transcendence stressed by Eastern psychology. It requires the type of emotional maturity understood and practiced by the Oceanic cultures.

In Western culture, adulthood is defined by independence, and cleverness in acquiring, keeping, and protecting assets. In the Eastern paradigm, maturity is based more on individual spiritual criteria. Introspection is emphasized and acquiring individual wisdom and knowledge is a major focus. The Polynesian definition of maturity—being in a growing relationship with others and the world—is seldom a criterion for status in the East or job advancement in the West.

The Third Way, living by the principles of *aloha*, emphasizes tolerance and forgiving interdependence. People are *of* the world, not in it, and so a person is judged adult by behaving responsibly and caringly for the world and by being able to take great pleasure from small things. The enchanted view of the world held by children is seen as the way to adult maturity, not a distraction from it.

Maturity is a pleasurable life based on daily balanced, respectful interaction with the earth and a freedom from needing some thing or some insight to flash us into happiness. Unhappiness is not to be avoided but learned from; happiness is to be appreciated but never taken for granted. And pleasure is a natural gift for caring, not an entitlement. Pleasure is the experience of living life to our full potential without diminishing—but enhancing—others' potential for a joyful life.

If we view pleasure as a reward for doing and having, we will forever seek it but never truly possess it. This is because it is based on "things," fulfilling internal desires with outside rewards. All desire states are by their very nature temporary, and desire causes desire. Thus, when we have everything we want, we always seem to want more. Progress, development, and change can be highly valued, but only serve to stimulate the drive to more "getting."

If we take the view that pleasure is to be found in self-knowledge and individual insight, too much contentment becomes suspect as indicating worldly rather than spiritual involvement. Like the happiness derived from consumerism, joy from personal discovery is also transitory. The brain never says "that's enough" because, as Chapter 2 explains, the brain is wired to pursue never-ending self-preservation.

Both these approaches stress the importance of not being happy with what you have or how you are. The Third Way of the Oceanic cultures teaches the exact opposite. Instead of always going somewhere, Polynesian culture understands being here. Pleasure comes from joining and helping more than from competitive winning or comparative individual wisdom. It is enough to fish today, to talk to the ocean and its inhabitants, and to share the catch of the day with your neighbors even if you give all your fish away before you get home. They are involved in the joy of sharing all aspects of their existence. What is acquired along the way of the Polynesian path is a true feeling of belonging.

Buddha taught that "the cause of suffering is desire, and the antidote to suffering is the cessation of desire." As you will read throughout this book, we are often directed more by our desire for intensity and things than by the soul's need for beauty and shared delight. We think that having what we want will bring us joy, but the pleasure principle teaches that true happiness comes with wanting what we have.

We spend about 15 percent of our waking life eating and taking care of personal bodily hygiene.[23] The health terrorism I described earlier has taken much of the fun out of even these activities, almost ruining what I call our vegetative joy. We are told that taste is secondary to or even a distraction from our health and that we must eat only low fat, high fiber, low cholesterol diets. We have little time to linger in the shower or enjoy a leisurely toothbrushing without attending to ridding ourselves of deadly germs and dental plaque. We seldom even have time for a slow, restful, contemplative bowel movement because we are thinking about our next obligation or attending to the texture and consistency of our waste as another possible health alarm. We are given more and more medical self-test kits so we can detect the earliest possible warning signs. Like people with overly sensitive home security alarms, we end up prisoners of our own fears. As if the purpose of life itself were to be healthy, we lead our lives not knowing that the purpose of health is to find the higher purpose in life—mature, shared pleasure.

Three Questions of Maturity

Here are three questions to ask of yourself and, perhaps more important, to ask of someone who knows you very well. These are basic questions many philosophers and teachers have asked in different ways throughout the world over the centuries.

Are you living fully?

Are you loving totally?

Are you letting go completely?[24]

To live fully in Oceanic terms means to connect completely with the world, not use it or pass though it in search of personal wisdom. It means to recognize yourself as a part of the earth and to be responsible, respectful, and appreciative of all its species, plant and animal, rainbow and hurricane. It does not mean just enjoying nature but being of nature. To the Polynesians, living fully is learning, marveling at, and celebrating your closeness to nature's power—even as Pele the volcano goddess' streams of fiery hair slowly embrace, and then destroy, your home as she creates new land.

To love totally in Oceanic terms goes beyond the romantic love of the West and the spiritual love of the East. Love is not devotion to just one person but to all persons and things. It is adoration in action, more behavior than private feeling, and more intercourse with everything than one partner. The *aloha* principles do not use sex to do the work of love or love to do the work of sex. Love is timeless commitment, caring and passion in equal balance, and it is measured not by self-fulfillment but by how much better the world is because you have lived and loved.

To let go completely in Oceanic terms is to silence the self, not just to express it or enhance it. It means to dance, to hold, to sing, to chant, to laugh, to cry, and to pray openly and completely. It means freedom from the pursuit of riches at others' expense. It means appreciating the role of unhappiness in life and having the patience to learn its lessons. It means seeing pleasure as a way of life and not a temporary reward. It means accepting and even relishing the natural chaos of the world and marveling at both the destruction of a tidal wave and the small swell created by a dancing dolphin.

You may be saying to yourself now, "This sounds very simple . . . What's the catch?" There are three psychospiritual dynamics that make these principles difficult for us to fully accept and live by. They arise from our human nature and are socially reinforced by our society's consumer orientation. They are strengthened by our focus on individuality and individual consciousness. Once we come to terms with them, we can be freed from them.

The Three Bliss Blockers

These three mental errors contribute to our Delight Deficiency Syndrome and get in the way of healthy, mature pleasure; I call them "bliss blockers." They are: bliss bulimia, the desacralizing defense, and misappropriated divinity.

Bliss bulimia Try the following test. Give up the walk to the refrigerator and watch an entire commercial break during one of your favorite television programs. With a pad and pencil, count how many times during the break the image on the television screen changes. Every time a new face or scene appears, make a mark on your pad. After the break, count up the scene changes you witnessed. Before you count, make a guess as to how many changes there were.

Although it may seem longer, most commercial breaks last about three minutes. Because our selfish brains are so addicted to and driven by the urgency response, advertisers insert about 150 changes of image during a commercial break.[25] For a comparison, watch three minutes of an old movie. The average scene change during a three-minute period in the movie *Casablanca* was eight. The difference in stimulation rate between what it used to take to keep our brains' attention and what it now requires reflects today's exhilaration orientation.

We are so dependent on the urgency response and so used to letting it dictate our lives that we have become "bliss bulimics." Our society deals with pleasure much like a bulimic deals with food. We binge and purge on pleasure, depriving ourselves of joy for days in our pressured search for survival and then indulging madly for a short time, only to purge ourselves of pleasure again. Learning the pleasure prescription requires learning balance, *pono.* As the Aloha Test showed, Polynesians are relatively free of the urgency response. They understand its intended use—to save a life or to avoid harming another.

Our tendency to get high automatically predisposes us to get too low. It also robs us of the blissfulness of taking joy in the ordinary, of appreciating sameness as much as change, enjoying the old as well as the new. Seeking self-insight while losing sight of others also leaves us without the sharing that validates and makes our experiences of the little things in the world richer. Jack Kornfield, philosopher and author, points out that even the most exalted states are unimportant if we cannot be happy in the most basic and ordinary ways, if we cannot touch one another and the life we have been given with our hearts.[26]

The desacralizing defense The second bliss blocker is something within us that seems terribly afraid of what can happen once we *do* open ourselves to the joys of everyday life: being overwhelmed by the divine nature of being alive. Psychologist Abraham Maslow wrote about *desacralizing,* a way of thinking and a behavior characterized by not being open and responsive to the simple sacredness of daily living because such awareness might interfere with daily doing. This happens as a survival mechanism; if we did open up to this, we might spend all our days wondering at the majesty of life.[27] The pleasure prescription can free us not only from our addiction to urgent stimulation but also from its cousin, our fear of the power of sacred beauty.

As you will learn in Chapter 5, our brain is simpleminded. Survival is its modus operandi; the powerful sacredness of life a dangerous distraction. It is not only stressful events that flood our system with neurohormonal highs. In those special moments when we glimpse the grandeur of life here on planet paradise, a part of us shudders at its magnificence. It frightens us with its power to transform us. And just as the intensity of a negative stressful event can cause a heart attack, the intense experience of sudden happiness can also kill us.[28] Often, people abuse drugs not to escape a bad life but because the artificial state drugs induce is a predictable diversion from the powerful delight of a good life that can seem too awesome to deal with or demand too much energy and selflessness to live up to.

Western culture often fears divinity or sees it as a distant reward for good behavior and hard work. We practice "weekend worship" rather than regular rituals that revere nature. When the divine comes too close to daily life, we are intimidated by it. Arthur William W. Harwan writes that the need to desacralize the world is a defense against being flooded by emotions of humility, reverence, mystery, wonder, and awe at the amazing grace of being alive.

To live the Oceanic way is to be unafraid of the divine—to feel a part of it, responsible for it, and invigorated by it. Polynesians live a sacred life through connection with the land and sea, valuing the secular only as an expression of the spiritual, and finding the divine in all that they do and see. Rather than meditating to broaden the individual mind, Polynesians cultivate the land to nurture the whole. Polynesians are defenseless against divinity and view feelings associated with it as only a natural part of being alive.

Misappropriating divinity Our built-in need for spiritual bliss is so strong that we cannot deny its power forever. When we do acknowledge greater meaning in life, however, we often stumble upon the third bliss blocker: secularization of the sacred. Altered states of consciousness are sometimes called unity experiences because they make us feel as if all boundaries and separations disappear and we are one with everything. In the West, the state of waking consciousness is considered optimal and claims of higher or altered states are viewed with suspicion.[29] Western psychiatry generally associates reports of unity experiences with psychopathology or regression. This is a form of "scientific divinity defense," avoiding something that most of us feel at one time or another but modern science has yet to begin to understand. As a result of this defensiveness, some modern schools of psychology often seek escape through the formulation of new pseudo-spiritualities.

One example of the weakening of the divinity defense is the recent increase in interest among physicians and patients in the power of prayer.[30] In December 1995, more than 900 physicians, clergy, and academicians attended a meeting on healing and spirituality in Boston, Massachusetts. It was apparent at this meeting that, when the West deals with the power of the scared, it tends to process it through its continental mind and turn it into just another "technique." About one-third of Western psychologists say that their life is based on religion, but more than two-thirds of the public they serve say their life is based on religion. This difference means that many Western healers try to *use* prayer and spirituality as another instrument from their black bag rather than learn its meaning as a way of living.

The Polynesians have a holistic sense of religion, or spirituality. For 2000 years, they have prayed several times a day. Their prayer may take the form of a chant, hula, or song and is a regular celebration of spiritual alliance. They believe that the words of prayer must be motivated by sincere appreciation, gratitude, and grace regarding the sacred and accompanied by behaviors that model that respect. They pray not *to* but *with* their gods, God, their ancestors, the plants, the fish, the rocks, the Spirit, and all that exists or has ever existed. They pray not to bring more happiness to their own life or to ask favors but to express gratitude and promise reciprocity for whatever happiness they have had and the lessons they have received.

For the Polynesian, prayer is the primary communication system that connects all things, not something to be used to heal one individual. Most of their praying is done in groups *(pule 'ohana)* and is intended to enhance and help heal the world. Prayers are motivated by a humble awareness of the immediate presence of the divine rather than a desire to receive divine intervention. Prayer *happens* to Polynesians because they are spiritual; it is not done to be spiritual.

The new Western interest in prayer, however, has tended to look for a subtle, operative "something." This research into Eastern approaches to prayer, often employing principles from quantum physics in order to explain the power of prayer, is now documented in more than 150 studies.[31] A truly "theosomatic medicine" like that practiced in Polynesia easily connects with the supernatural and the immediate presence of the sacred.[32] (For more on this, see the discussion on the four eras of medicine on page 71.) In the Oceanic philosophy there is nothing subtle about the power of prayer. The supernatural is a part of life and prayer is only another expression of it. In fact, to the Polynesian, prayer is the practice of actually becoming "demigods," a public announcement of sharing the inherence of the Higher Power.[33]

The true pleasure of spirituality can only be experienced if the spirituality is genuine and not another "technique" or "movement." The spirituality of Polynesia springs from beliefs about the world as intimately connected with and as an expression of God which are deeply internalized and go far beyond modern pantheism. It is not a satellite hook-up with a higher power or a technique for making miracles that draws on paradoxical phenomena from new physics. It is not the latest meditation or the "relaxation response." These approaches only go halfway. They may help clear the mind, but they do not bring the spirit in to fill the void when the urgency response has died down.[34] One of my Polynesian *kumu* said, "A technique seldom leads to a transformation." And sure enough, research shows that those who "use" spirituality as a way of "achieving" good health do not receive the benefits of spiritual connection.[35]

For the Polynesian, not to be able to pray, chant, sing, or hula would be similar to a Westerner being without telephones. A Polynesian man told me, "I am the ultimate cellular phone. I am made up of cells and I can communicate across time. Prayer just pops out of me. When I feel very good and very much alive in the world, prayer comes over me and I seem to be sending messages everywhere. I don't really do it, it just sort of happens to me. It makes me feel very much at home."

I believe that most Western health-care workers have become interested in prayer not because of some sudden spiritual enlightenment but because something of the divine seems to keep filtering up through their research data. Their own science now documents that spirituality "works." Studies of prayerful healing of human beings and other biological systems, including enzymes, fungi, plants, and animals, now appear in prestigious professional journals. In a culture that measures all things and activities against the motto of Sir Francis Bacon, founder of applied science, who said "useless is worthless," even the most skeptical scientist can no longer ignore what the Polynesians knew about the potential of spiritual connection to enhance and protect well-being in everyday life. To date, 75 percent of 212 studies done and published in professional journals show that prayer and religious commitment have a positive effect on physical health even when the ones doing the praying did not know those they were praying for!

Western scientists seem amazed and puzzled by the power of prayer. Here are just a few of the findings about spirituality that are creating pause—and prayer—among Western physicians:[36]

- Among 232 elderly patients undergoing open-heart surgery, those who were deeply religious were more likely to survive the surgery.
- Eleven of twelve studies showed that religious commitment is associated with curtailed drug use.
- Heavy smokers who attend church regularly are four times less likely to have high blood pressure than smokers who do not go to church, prompting one scientist to say, "If you are going to smoke, take your butt to a church."
- A survey of 91,909 persons who attended church regularly showed that they had 50 percent fewer deaths from coronary artery disease, 56 percent fewer deaths from emphysema, 74 percent fewer deaths from cirrhosis, and 53 percent fewer suicides.
- A study showed that patients receiving heart by-pass surgery who were prayed for had fewer complications than those who were not prayed for.

These findings show that something very powerful takes place in the realm of the spiritual. How is the spiritual affecting and inspiring your life today? The warning label for the pleasure prescription reads, "Take only as directed by your soul and never without living the blissful spiritual life that gives this prescription its power."

Chapter Five

THE RE-ENCHANTMENT OF EVERYDAY LIFE

"I 'okai kai ke aloha."

(Be One, in love with everyone and everything.)

"I'm always one of two ways," said an honor student in my psychology class. I'm either tired and bored or stressed and maxed out. I only have two gears, high and low, and I think I must have burned out my clutch. What worries me most is that nothing seems really wonderful any more. I don't get really excited or really sad. I hardly ever have a good, long laugh or even a nice, cleansing cry. I'm going through the motions but I just don't seem to have emotions. I've been to Disneyland and Disney World. I've jet-skied, bungee-jumped, had wild sex, been drunk out of my mind, and done drugs. Nothing turns me on or off. I'm only 19 years old—I feel like I'm in a pre-life crisis."

My student's statement is typical of many young people in my college courses. They come to class looking tired, coughing, sneezing, and suffering from all sorts of infections from chronic colds to mononucleosis. When I ask what they do for fun, the most frequent answer is "hang." When I ask what they mean by that, they answer, "just hang around looking for something to happen" to turn them on.

They feel suspended in a state of mental, emotional, and, particularly, spiritual fatigue from constantly seeking the happiness that psychology tells them they must have to make them fulfilled, or from trying to neutralize the reactive unhappiness that comes from going to wild parties, abusing alcohol, and having promiscuous sex. Some throw themselves into nightclub "mosh pits"—masses of humanity anonymously grinding, smashing, and tossing against one another to the loud whine of music synthesizers and computerized drums. When sufficient stimulation occurs, they pump their arms in the air and yell "Yes!"—but they seem to have no idea what the question was that they are answering or affirming. They are told by advertising campaigns to "just do it," but they seem unclear as to what it is they are supposed to be doing or why. As the music on stage or the violence and explosions on movie screens escalate, these young people suffer from a real danger of not only losing their sense of hearing but of losing their seventh sense. These young people are engaged in a masquerade of misery, yelling and frolicking anxiously behind masks that hide a tired, jaded boredom.

Psychologist Mihaly Csikszentmihalyi of the University of Chicago says that our apparent preference for intense and threatening stimulation is built into our brain to help us stay vigilant and alert to threats to our individual survival. Because we have remained prisoners of this primitive tendency, we have failed to develop another of our evolutionary gifts, the more moderate seventh sense for healthy, balanced pleasure that results in *collective* survival. Our focus on self-survival at the expense of collective thriving results in an inability to attend to the normal, peaceful, and gentle because of our alert status that is tuned to violence and danger.[1] For a young person who will have witnessed over 70,000 murders on television before he or she grows up, the noise and magnitude of such stimulation creates an addiction to the *urgency response* and a numbing of the *bliss response.* It becomes increasingly difficult to enjoy life when one has seen it so devalued.

Although they often use the term, these young people are not suffering from "burn out," because they have not yet been able to catch fire and glow with the legitimate thrills of blissful joy and shared purpose. They are suffering from not just a lack of happiness but also a lack of understanding that, as you will read in Chapter 15, some unhappiness is necessary to survival and is not a sign of a failed life.[2] They are not bored from understimulation but weary from too much meaningless excitation.

The Urgency Response: Overheating Our Circuits of Joy

The real problem for many young people is their inability to find healthy pleasure because their innate seventh sense for what brings bliss has been contaminated by the flood of urgency psychochemicals that flow on paths made for "tuning in" rather than "turning on." These circuits are so charred by what I call the urgency response that simple, gentle, shared joy is too subtle to alert their numbed pleasure system. They are so consumed by the pursuit of happiness that they run right past it. Parades of the delight-deprived can be seen marching aimlessly through shopping malls in hopes of purchasing what eludes them.

Our nervous system can manage and process 126 bits of information (sounds, sights, smells, and so on) per second, 7,560 bits per minute, or a half-million bits per hour. Over an average lifetime of seventy years and considering sixteen hours of waking time each day, you could say we have around 185 billion bits of information available for mental delight during our lifetime.[3] Too often these bits are more banal than blissful.

As my students have discovered, our society encourages this banality. Our search for continual stimulation encourages an addiction to the urgency response, which is a state of dependence on stress neurohormones for stimulation. How does it work? The system floods with stress hormones that prepare the body to "fight or flee" and take up space intended for the bliss response; as a result you are momentarily occupied and "fulfilled." It is accompanied by prolonged periods of anxiety-induced highs and emotional spurts from the thrill of the chase. When there is no urgency, the result is the Delight Deficiency Syndrome experienced by the persons described in the Introduction. Relying addictively, almost exclusively, on your basic five senses as tools for self-fulfillment results in the urgency response. George Orwell wrote, "Men can only be happy when they do not assume that the object of life is happiness."

The face of a person under the influence of the urgency response has the look of someone in a constant state of fight-or-flight, etched with hormonal "stress signature" lines around the forehead and corners of the mouth.[4] When their defenses are down and they are resting or even sleeping, they continue to wear the mask of urgency, jaws clenched and teeth grinding. If you want to know whether you are following your seventh sense and leading a life of joyful balance, have someone describe what you look like when you are fast asleep. The increasing frequency of TMJ (temporomandibular joint disorder) is one sign of delight deficiency.

When we live by our stress hormones, we are like the donkey with the carrot held just in front of its nose. Even if by chance we do catch it, something strange transpires. We discover we don't really want it; it doesn't make us as happy as we thought it would. In fact, we may even feel sorry because the chase that so invigorated us is over. We immediately begin looking for a new carrot and often wind up experienced carrot chasers but not happy carrot *eaters.* This is why toxically successful people crash, both physically and emotionally. Because they are addicted to the thrill of a high-stress lifestyle, achieving their goal is the worst thing that could happen to them. The urgency response is not just a psychological state, but also a physiological one. A state of prolonged urgency gradually kills us and threatens those around us by weakening our immune system, stressing our heart, and prematurely aging all of our body's systems.

Albert Camus wrote, "If there is a sin against life, it consists perhaps not so much in despairing of life as in hoping for another life and in eluding the implacable grandeur of this life." Such is the plight of the person held captive by the urgency response.

Essential stress Some good stress is a stimulant for health and healing. It is not stress itself but how you learn to handle stress that contributes to or detracts from your health. In fact, if you were to try to predict illness from the stressful events in a person's life, you would be right less than 15 percent of the time. Stress in and of itself has little to do with whether the heart fails or a cancerous tumor begins growing in the body.[5] We need a little urgency response to balance with the bliss response and we need a little unhappiness to balance with our happiness. The pleasure prescription is not a "feel good" program but a "good at feeling" program. It is learning to be a part of life no matter what life gives us and discovering how to find some joy even when we are stressed.

We need our urgency response at times of physical challenge. When we respond to stress, all of our senses become more keen. Experiencing the rush of stress when all body systems go on alert can be great fun if we fully connect with it rather than label it as failure. The danger comes when the stressor is chronic or comes continually from within ourselves and how we interpret our world. The only truly unhealthy emotional or physical state is a "stuck" state, where there are no oscillations.

Healthy Oscillation

Healthy balance and oscillation is the key to the pleasure prescription. Just as too much happiness too often and too long can cross over to psychotic delusion, chronic unhappiness and internal stress from perceived helplessness and lack of joy can cross over to serious clinical depression. Psychoneuroimmunologists often use the metaphor of two elephants on a seesaw to explain the relationship between the "urgent" or *sympathetic neurohormonal system* and the "bliss" or *parasympathetic neurohormonal system.*[6]

Think of two children balanced on a seesaw. Without much effort, they can keep the seesaw in balance, just as we keep our body system in neurohormonal balance between the stress and the relaxing hormones. This is called *homeostasis* and it is our psychophysiological state when we are in what psychoneurocardiologists call "good oscillation" and Polynesians call *pono.* In contrast, when we lead a highly pressured life, it is more like having two elephants on the seesaw. It takes a great deal of effort, and, when one set of neurohormones decreases suddenly, the other flies up much too high. Too much high and too much low is the result.

Another problem with having elephants playing on your system's seesaw is that eventually some damage occurs to the seesaw itself. When we constantly struggle to keep our balance against great highs and lows, our system cannot stand the strain. The wear and tear shows in our faces, hearts, immune response, and emotional character. The pleasure prescription says, "Teeter up with some stressful happiness, but remember that you must always come back down. Totter down with some stressful unhappiness, but remember you can always teeter up again."

Some people become so stressed trying to reduce and manage their stress, trying to constantly have a positive attitude or working hard to achieve happiness, that they take all the fun out of being under pressure and all the learning out of being sad. The five *aloha* principles are the rules for a joyful and balanced teeter-totter ride through life.

The Bliss Response: An Ultimate High

Using your seventh sense to govern your other six senses results in the bliss response. The bliss response is a soothing, healing neurohormonal balance experienced as timeless, delightful gladness. It is our evolutionary instinct for health and long life, where the urgency response evolved for quick spurts of lifesaving agitation. One evolved for escaping saber-toothed tigers; the other for sitting on a hill and watching the sun rise. Unfortunately, both use the same neural pathways. When the urgency response constantly trespasses on the pleasure paths, our lines stay busy and we cannot connect with our bliss.

What are some characteristics of the bliss response? The West views being "high" as being turned on, while the East tends to see it as being totally tuned in. The Polynesians experience transcendence as complete connection. Psychologist Roger Walsh at the University of California Medical School identifies five characteristics of a "transcendent experience."[7]

1. *Ineffability, the experience of such an overwhelming, powerful state so unlike ordinary experience that it defies description.* The Polynesian lives with daily awareness that life is so magnificent and joyful that trying to capture it in written words or numbers is seldom effective. Chanting, singing, and dancing to show such joy is the Polynesian way of expressing the inexpressible. A Hawaiian *kupuna* said, "*Aloha* is feeling so good about being with the *'aina* that you let everyone know how good you feel by just being you and they let you know they know by being who they are."

2. *Noesis, a heightened sense of clarity and understanding of the meaning of life.* Westerners sometimes refer to this aspect of getting "high" as a peak experience, and it is often mistaken for intensity or seen as the top of a pyramid of needs attained after struggling through lower hierarchical needs.[8] The East sees noesis as a self-experienced mental state possible even when

the world outside is in chaos. In fact, most modern versions of Eastern meditative techniques emphasize shutting out the outside world completely. Polynesians see the noetic high as a daily state accomplished by living with and caring for the land and thinking along with the sentient trees, plants, and fish all around them. Polynesians get high by meeting lower needs. A Hawaiian fisherman told me, "Every time I pull out my net and see the treasures put there for me, I know why I'm here and the fish know too."

3. *An altered sense of space and time.* In the West, clock time is the irrevocable measure of life's extent. In the East, clock time is a limiting modern invention that is to be overcome by enlightened, infinite consciousness. For Polynesians, clock and consciousness are less important than the calendar, and they live, love, and play by seasons rather than seconds or internal timelessness. A taro farmer from the Big Island of Hawai'i told me, "I've never had a watch. My clock is all around me. I don't look to see what time it is, I listen and feel for the *'aina* to tell me."

4. *A deep sense of unity.* The individualistic West often seeks in vain for the joy of feeling an intimate connection with the world it works so hard to control. The East seeks a feeling of oneness through contemplation and meditation on the One spirit, but the search often disregards interpersonal and ecological connection. The Polynesian, who sees her soul as outside and among instead of within and owned by the self, lives and experiences oneness every day. After her solo hula, a Polynesian dancer told me, "Did you see all of my ancestors up there dancing with me? Did you see my lei fly up in my face? My *aumakua* were teasing me. Did you see? They were all dancing with me."

5. *Intense positive affect and a sense of perfection in the universe.* The Western model sees nature as something that must be controlled, used, and improved. The East tends to view physical nature as an illusion and an environment for contemplation to pursue self-perfection. The Polynesian sees nature as per-

fect and takes great joy in the privilege of being One with and protecting it.

As you can see, the Third Path can be one of almost constant bliss. Even when Polynesians suffer, they know they are only experiencing what the Earth experiences and what they must experience because they have the honor of being One with the *'aina.*

Recovering the Indigenous Mind

We all have an indigenous mind. No matter where we live now, we all come from ancestors who, like the Polynesians, originally saw the world as enchanted. Your own distant relatives, whether from Europe, China, Ireland, Africa, or the plains of America, saw the world as a joyful, sentient organism in which all things were alive and capable of connecting with us. Your ancient family spoke with rocks, listened to the trees, and moved amid the wonders of a living, breathing planet of which they were a living part. About 400 years ago, when we became disenchanted, warring conquerors rather than caring, enchanted connectors, we lost our indigenous mind. We can find it again by discovering and appreciating the surviving indigenous cultures of the world in all their richness, depth, and wisdom.

I have presented at medical and psychological meetings all over the world. These meetings usually include lectures and workshops on holistic or "world medicine." In more than 30 years of attending these meetings, I have noticed that what health-care professionals call "world medicine" is usually "the continental big six": Chinese, Ayurvedic (Indian), Greek, homeopathic, naturopathic, and allopathic (conventional Western) medicine—and various new age combinations of these. The Oceanic or Polynesian model is hardly ever included. When indigenous medicines like that of Polynesia are on the program, they are seldom presented with the understanding, respect, and deep spiritual connection essential to them. Western medicine is deeply and rightly concerned about the dangers of "alternative" approaches to health care and of people practicing medicine "without a license." However, when indigenous medicines do find their way into Western medical forums, few ask if the modern practitioners of indigenous-based approaches are taking license with these sacred systems.

Dr. Larry Dossey has identified what he calls "eras" of medicine.[9] He refers to Era I medicine as a mechanical, fix-the-patient, "mindless" approach to health and healing. Era II medicine is the currently popular, "one-mind-over-one-body" approach. Eras I and II are the primary domain of Western medicine. Dossey's Era III medicine is a "many minds" approach, focused on the idea that all minds are connected; healing is promoted by tapping into quantum nonlocal and time-free energy forces that are beyond the here-and-now and that constantly influence and connect us all.

Polynesian medicine can be considered Era IV medicine, but it actually came hundreds of years before Era I. It is based on the idea that the spark of the Creator is partaken of by the created—us. It embraces the idea that each of us shares an inner divinity and directly experiences the qualities of God in the form of an inner divinity.

Era I is *somatic* medicine, relying heavily on the laws of Newtonian or mechanical physics. Era II is *psychosomatic* medicine and draws on the principles of modern behavioral and cognitive psychology. Era III is *quantumatic* medicine; it depends on the paradoxical laws of quantum physics and transpersonal psychology to explain the supernatural mysteries and miracles of illness and healing. The Polynesian or Era IV approach is *theosomatic* medicine in that it asserts that we all share, as Einstein pointed out, a common "cosmic religious feeling" that allows for no separation between the Creator and the created.[10]

This Era IV approach to health and healing uses the Oceanic components of *aloha*—patience, unity, pleasantness, humbleness, and gentleness—to allow the sacred breath of the Creator to resonate within the created and to feel the joyful warmth of the spark of creation. It flows easily back and forth between natural and supernatural laws. While the people of the islands understand natural laws, they live their lives in much more easy comfort with the supernatural than their continental cousins. They believe that the perceived distance between the Creator and the created is a modern illusion, derived from the fear of our own divinity, as discussed in Chapter 4. Polynesians see their body and all bodies as a miraculous projection of the Spirit. They see themselves as spirits having a brief human experience, not humans capable of brief spiritual experiences. Islanders are not landlocked or limited by dependence on variations of mechanistic, behavioral, or new physics theories. They are spiritual sailors of and with, not on or apart from, the sea, who are free to navigate the universe as transcendent travelers. Even though we humans are the only animal that sweats and sheds tears of salt, reflective of our oceanic origins, we often forget that we are all gods of and in the sea of sacred natural life.

Western biomedicine struggles with the concept of "mind." While the word "brain" has numerous index references in Harrison's *Principles of Internal Medicine,* the word "mind" has none. Only recently has the concept of mind been openly spoken about by the modern medical establishment. This change is due in part to dissatisfaction with the results of a "mind"-less medicine, recent findings from psychoneuroimmunology that challenge a mechanistic approach to well-being, and a frustrated turning to Eastern paradigms and the recent popularizing of Ayurvedic medicine.

Understanding the indigenous mind requires accepting the concept of Wholeness, or enchantment, and the fact that the mind can use the brain but is not the brain. Western medicine tried to learn about the whole by studying the parts, but in the process lost sight of the whole. Polynesian medicine tries to understand the whole first and then apply those lessons to its parts. In Western medicine, statistical significance is valued over spiritual significance, and repair is seen as more important than relationship. So long as this partialism dominates health care, and even if techniques borrowed from more holistic approaches are used, the power of the Polynesian and other theosomatic indigenous models will not be maximized.

A Third Way to Daily Delight

While many of our physical ills are well addressed by the medicine of the West and the wisdom of the East, our delight deficiency disorder can only be fully understood and corrected by using the Oceanic way.

The generalizations I have made about "East" and "West," the two most commonly traveled paths to well-being, are overstated and oversimplified—they neglect many of the nuances of these systems. Treating these complex and powerful systems in detail and dealing with all their strengths and weaknesses is enough to fill many books, but the following summaries are a good starting point for understanding their implications, and they are a good reference for learning about the Third Way, which is much less a part of modern everyday living and thinking.

Eastern, Western, or Oceanic? Here are a few comparisons among the Oceanic paradigm and continental Eastern and Western life views.

- The Western way to wellness follows a consumer model. The Westerners who first had contact with the Polynesian culture did not grasp the Polynesians' deep sense of *place* because they were in the pursuit mode of *getting* someplace to *get* something, rather than *being* in a place to share everything. Westerners still pursue happiness and wellness by "doing" things to "get" well. As a result they are held captive by a health terrorism that tells them to deny pleasure, work very hard, and avoid death. They compete for physical and psychological space on the planet. They live *on* the earth, but miss the joy of understanding that they *are* the earth.
- The Eastern way of thinking about health and happiness is more personally comparative than interpersonally competitive. The internal landscape, not the earth, is reality. The Eastern orientation is more metaphysical than physical, based on "looking within" for hidden truths to grow spiritually. It is more mindful than mechanical. The Polynesian way is "joining in" with everyone and everything to enjoy everyday life.
- The energy driving the Western way is the push of competition—to have and get more than another. Eastern energy is experienced more as a pull from internal spiritual needs—to become more and more enlightened. Polynesians are influenced by the affiliation motive and are driven to connect. In place of a push to get more or the pull to know more, Polynesians are driven by their profound sense of place—to embrace more.
- The Eastern mind sees the body as a temporary vehicle for the soul, sometimes even a necessary limitation to be transcended. The Western approach has, until recently, viewed the body as a machine and the mind as separate from it. Now, due to Eastern and indigenous cultural influences and the West's own new research, modern medicine is evolving to a "mind-over-body" approach. The Polynesian view does not see

the body as separate from the mind or as an extension of it; it sees the mind and body as one entity connected to all other bodies, minds, and the *'aina.*

- Both East and West see pleasure as a *result* of correct living and as a free choice. Pleasure is the reward for hard physical, mental, or spiritual work. The Polynesians see enlightened, responsible pleasure, shared with all things and persons *now,* as the only healthy approach of life.
- Communication is both necessary for and a reflection of the culture in which it exists. Western communication is fast, efficient, often impersonal; it supports effective competition and assertive self-expression. Except for what is considered a new-age fringe, the West considers communication to be limited to talking to living people, and even the new-age movement tends to rely on subtle expressions of natural laws or physics to explain "supernatural" telepathy. Speaking to the dead, those not yet born, or the ocean and the mountains is seen as a symptom of mental illness and not spiritual strength. Eastern communication stresses connection with the larger Self or a higher power or energy more than with someone or something else. Other people and the environment are seen as settings that may facilitate personal insight, but the idea of being family with a fish is not a key part of the Eastern communication system. The Polynesian way of communication is more rhythmic than assertive or contemplative, and it is based on ecopsychology rather than ego or transpersonal psychology. It is for connection more than self-expression or introspection.
- The West stresses the value of individual *action.* Being assertive, confident, strong, and controlling are highly prized. Self-worth is reflected in accomplishment and is measured by ownership and control. The East stresses *perception,* learning to see and understand more by looking inward. The Polynesian way is through loving, selfless *participation* on all levels with all things and people.
- The West tends to be adversarial and confrontational. The East tends toward passivity and contemplation. As one Polyne-

> sian put it, "A lot of Westerners are passive-aggressive and a lot of Easterners seem aggressively passive." The Polynesian way is one of gentle compliance. Loud aggression and selfish insight are seen as ways in which a person becomes ill because of the disconnection that results from these orientations.

Both East and West have much to teach us and have offered their own miracles of healing and health. In their unique ways, they have dealt well with four of the five basic factors of fitness. The Oceanic way—not surprisingly—is more suited to the fifth. These factors are discussed below.

The Five Factors of Fitness

Most wellness programs deal with five components of physical and mental well-being that can be remembered as the "Five Fs." There are many books that address the Western and Eastern orientations to these five factors in a detailed and complete manner, and most people in these cultures are influenced to varying degrees by the general tenets outlined below. The pleasure prescription goes beneath, before, and beyond these orientations.

1. *Food* (nutrition): Many in the West see food as necessary fuel. To stay healthy means disregarding taste and going for "healthy" food—low fat, high fiber, low cholesterol. What a food is made of is more important than how it is eaten. The East often sees food as an essential inconvenience, something the hedonistic body might enjoy but the mind can do without. Polynesians are more concerned with happy feeding than health food. The sacred food of Hawai'i is poi, made from the taro plant. As with all food, it is to be eaten with joyful ritual and respect. All family meals are to be enjoyed in slow relaxation as a family. No problems should be raised during a meal and the how and with whom of eating are to be relished. Sharing a meal is a way of healing and often takes place after solving problems and restoring *pono* and *pololei* as a way of celebrating the return to healthy harmony.

2. *Flexibility* (exercise): The West views exercise as essential to a long life, a good-looking body, and the stamina needed for the competitive lifestyle. The East views exercise as a way to harness the brain, using movement to develop spiritual stamina and expression, and postures to quiet the body so the mind can do its work.

   Polynesians view body movement as a means of loving the land and demonstrating connection with everyone and everything. All exercise in Polynesia is marked by enjoyment. The purpose is not to build the body, show off, reveal wisdom, or prevent illness but to express and enjoy the connection with the *'aina* and all of its inhabitants by moving in synchronization with the *'aina*. Ancient hula (*kahiko*) is body prayer, not a performance, a way of celebrating one's respect for the *'aina*, the gods, and the ancestors.

3. *Flow* (stress reduction): The West sees stress as a body reaction and tries to "manage" it away. It surrenders to an almost constantly urgent lifestyle while trying various stress reduction techniques. To the Western mind, the body is still essentially separate from the body, so breathing deeply and relaxing the muscles are seen as effective no matter what is on the Western mind most of the day. There is little serious effort to make the difficult choices that would reduce the basic causes of chronic stress. Westerners try to take action against their stress, which derives from their taking too much action, not understanding that true pleasure often derives from the most unmotivated states.

   The East sees stress as a reflexive lower-mind reaction.[11] It deals with stress by trying to mentally diffuse it or at least reduce it by spiritual distraction, going with the flow or doing thoughtful prayer.

   "Polynesian paralysis" is the local name given to the "hang loose" approach to living in paradise. The "hang loose" sign flashed around the islands by tourists and locals is really a modern invention replacing a gesture that symbolized balance and connection. For the Polynesian, stress is essential for life and evidence of a fully engaged life. A native Hawaiian and

Maui radio announcer, Boy Kanahe, sums up the Polynesian way of doing the hula through life by saying, "If things don't go right, take 'em to the left."

4. *Family:* Having largely failed to achieve the sense of well-being it hoped for through exercise, diet, and new-age adaptations of Eastern thought, the West has unleashed a powerful scientific arsenal of genetic manipulation. Emotional and spiritual family ties are seen as important only as a transitional source of support, child rearing, or a place to rest between bouts of success seeking. A new word in the relationship lexicon is *starter marriage,* meaning the first of many relationships to be used for self-fulfillment.[12] Even basic supportive family functions have become institutionalized by the proliferation of daycare centers, quick-neck-massage parlors, and sensory deprivation chambers. While the West talks about the importance of the family, the family suffers from severe neglect.

   The East has long seen the family as sacred and deserving of respect. Like the West, it remains patriarchal, ascribing most power to the male and most responsibility to the female. In the East, the family is highly symbolic but is also often neglected in reality. Like the West, much of the talk about family values in the East is little more than lip-service. Many of the greatest gurus of the East disregarded their primary "intimate" relationships and family units, and most Eastern thought is silent on the point of extremely healthy intimate relationships.[13]

   For the Polynesian, family is not only sacred but, unlike the West which tends to use the family and the East which tends to revere it, the Polynesian family is essential for physical, emotional, and spiritual health. It includes not only people but also rocks, trees, plants, and animals. By caring for the family the Polynesian cares for the *'aina* of which it is an expression. Polynesians view everyone, not just blood relatives, as family. They marry for the welfare of the society, not to make themselves more self-fulfilled, and their children belong to the entire Polynesian family. Children are often given to other family groups to raise in a process called *hanai,* a word referring to the many strands of a fish net and meaning to take in and care for. Even when it comes to family and children, there is no ownership in Polynesia. Perhaps more than any other single reason, this lack of territoriality, ownership, and selfish pride reduces the anger and hostility that derives from the competitiveness, alienation, and loneliness so increasingly common in the West and East.

When anything happens to make the family a place of conflict, a pleasurable environment must be reestablished immediately through a sacred prayerful process called *ho'oponopono,* or bringing back the balance and reestablishing healthy relationships on all levels.

5. *Fun:* Both West and East have wrestled with the concept of pleasure. For both, pleasure is colored with some guilt. In the West, ultimate pleasure is seen as doing it all and having it all and existing in a state of "status happiness." In the East, pleasure is either defined purely in nonphysical and noninterpersonal terms or seen as a distraction from true spiritual enlightenment. Eastern traditions aim for an ultimate state of consciousness called by such names as *nirvana* or *samadhi,* seen as a form of liberation from the physical and transitory.

   For the Polynesian, balanced pleasure is the true nature, process, and purpose of all life. Polynesian myths center around a playful interaction with everyone and everything. Polynesian gods are more trickster than hero. The purpose of life is to find joy in living with the wonderful gifts of nature and in respecting and returning these gifts. A good joke is much more appreciated than a good Western put-down or a profound Eastern aphorism. The bliss of life in paradise is founded on being a part of a wonderful world and being totally free from trying to own, conquer, or protect it.

The pleasure prescription helps you to take delight in eating, moving, sensing, and sharing a love for the *'aina* with your "extended family," which includes all things, finding in each moment the re-enchantment of everyday life.

Chapter Six

CRANIAL "G-SPOTS": THE PSYCHONEUROLOGY OF PLEASURE

"Brain, n. An apparatus with which we think we think."
— Ambrose Bierce

"Wow, you're really hitting the right spot," moaned the young woman. "Keep that up. Don't stop. That's terrific. Oh, that's really splendid," she continued, smiling and then giggling. Although she was experiencing the thrill of a pleasure not unlike intense sexual stimulation, this woman was not engaged in an erotic adventure. She was lying on an operating table.

In a rare and risky procedure, the neurosurgeon had opened this woman's skull and was electrically stimulating different areas of her brain to be sure her scalpel would cut in the precise location needed to reduce the severe seizures that had affected her young patient for most of her life. In the intimidating environment of the operating room, with more than a dozen doctors and nurses peering down at her from over their surgical masks, just after the hum and smell of the saw cutting through her skull had ceased, this patient was having one of the most pleasurable experiences of her life.

The surgeon had placed an electrode in the area of the brain called the limbic system, an area related to potent pleasure sensations. Other patients, when stimulated in the same area during surgeries, have reported the disappearance of negative feelings, the presence of feelings of euphoria or drunkenness, and even multiple sexual orgasms.

For more than 40 years neurologists and physiologists have known that there are pleasure regions in the brain. Just as there is not one spot that elicits sexual arousal, there is not one specific pleasure spot in the brain. Certain patterns of neurohormonal secretions within the brain also appear crucial to our ability to respond joyfully to life experiences. These pleasure templates make up the physiology of our seventh sense, but they are not its cause.

Carrying around electrodes to stimulate our brain's "G"—or glee—areas is not the most practical and safe way of ensuring happiness and pleasure in life. We can, however, stimulate our brain's pleasure paths by using our minds, our consciousness, to tell it how, when, and what to think. We ourselves can create the energy charge that triggers the bliss response.

To access our brain's glee spots it is first necessary to understand how the brain functions and processes sensations. By now you should be well on your way to overcoming the "brain over mind" bias. Both are part of who we are: the brain is of our body, and the mind is of our consciousness, our larger sensibility that makes decisions about how to interpret and act on information our body gives us.

Big mistake, big benefits As often happens in science, a researcher's mistake led to the discovery of the brain pleasure centers. While studying areas of the brain and general arousal in rats, psychologist James Olds accidentally implanted stimulating electrodes not in the hypothalamus, which controls arousal functions, but in the limbic area, which controls the brain's four F's (food, fighting, fleeing, and fornication). Olds noticed that if given the option, rats would stimulate their limbic area all day long, to the point of exhaustion and even death. Stimulating the limbic center seemed far more satisfying than the most tasty food, more gratifying than quenching thirst, more thrilling than sex, and more invigorating than any arousal state such as fighting or fleeing.[1] The popular press seized this discovery and called this area of the brain "the pleasure center."

In another study, physician Robert Heath of Tulane University School of Medicine implanted electrodes in patients with severe brain disorders in order to relieve symptoms of severe mental illness and seizures.[2] He placed the electrodes deep inside the limbic system and then recorded the electrical activity of various brain regions while his patients self-stimulated their brain. Like the woman mentioned at the beginning of this chapter, patients described stimulation of these centers as the "goody place," a kind of G-spot in the brain. Some patients reported general euphoria, while others reported experiencing good memories, feeling intoxicated, or having all "bad thoughts" disappear.

Olds' mistake led to the finding that there is a powerful built-in pleasure pathway within our nervous system. Now, it is up to us to learn how to use it for a more rational, healthy hedonism.

Rational hedonism Neurophysiologist Paul MacLean describes the human brain in archeological terms.[3] The deepest and oldest part is the reptilian brain. About 500 million years old, these parts of the brain regulate the most basic life processes. Higher up is the 300-million-year-old paleomammalian brain. This section deals with our most basic emotions, such as fear, hate, and love. The modern area of our brain, the neocortex, is less than 50 million years old and is the part that thinks. It is capable of keeping a lid on the lower parts, but we have to use our mind—our consciousness—to do so. If we don't, our seventh sense cannot develop, and we are slaves to the ghosts of the ancient brain impulses.

Polynesians, in their sacred approach to the secrets of life called *huna,* referred to the brain stem and limbic system as the lower self, the *unihipili,* the separate hemispheres of the brain as the middle self or the *uhane,* and the integrated whole brain as the higher self or *aumakua,* which is connected with everyone and everything that has ever lived.[4]

When we experience something, signals representing that experience go to the part of our brain called the thalamus, which sorts incoming messages and routes them to appropriate places in the brain. The thalamus communicates with our limbic system and with our "higher" brain. One of the most important decisions we make in our life and a key to practicing the pleasure prescription is the level of our brain with which we consciously choose to lead our emotional life.

Our seventh sense uses but is not limited to our highly impulsive limbic system. Following the pleasure prescription does not mean unabashed, irrational, selfish hedonism. New research on emotional intelligence shows that although emotions are powerful, we do not have to be emotionally hijacked by our lower brain centers.[5] Rather, we can use our higher brain centers to bring about mature pleasure. Author Horace Walpole wrote, "Life is a comedy for those who think and a tragedy for those who feel." The pleasure prescription is based on *thoughtful* feelings: the cerebral cortex overseeing a limbic-based arousal. As you will see in this chapter, our seventh sense draws on and regulates several complex body systems: our emotions, our heart, our hormones, and our immune system.

A Hot or a Cool Head?

The brain is a "hot head" that must be controlled by a cool mind. Signals from the thalamus go not only to the prefrontal lobes of the cerebral cortex but also to a tiny organ in the limbic system called the amygdala. This is the "hot head" of the brain; it attaches meaning to experiences based on prior emotional episodes.[6] The brain's amygdala needs the mind to calm and direct it to healthy balance and to block its maladaptive hyperarousal. We can't emotionally mature if we allow our amygdala alone to dictate the emotional significance of our life experiences.

Another part of the brain that mediates our emotions is the limbic structure called the lateral septum. It has a cooler head and can suppress aversive emotions such as hate and fear. Just a microdistance away from the lateral septum, however, is the medial septum which can escalate negative emotional states.[7] These structures are our built-in emotional seesaw, and only by using our mind to direct our higher brain and prefrontal lobes can we keep the seesaw in healthy balance. The limbic system and its amygdala and septum cause us to be emotional, but our higher brain gives purpose and meaning to our emotions. By being thoughtful, by not impulsively reacting, we develop our seventh sense.

We are made to "emotionally rebound" from whatever emotional state we are in.[8] Signals from our thalamus also go to the left and right hemispheres of the cerebral cortex. While both hemispheres work together, the left hemisphere is more involved with delight and euphoria while the right deals with emotions such as depression and disgust. Because each hemisphere inhibits and helps to moderate the other, we are hardwired for balance. We are made not to feel too much depression or too much happiness for too long. Blissful pleasure comes from being aware of both sides of our emotional self and realizing that life is neither a bowl of cherries nor lemons.

"Addiction" to Pleasure

Addiction is natural. No one has ever cured "addiction" because it is essential for our health and is wired into us to keep us happy and strong. Addiction is adaptive because it can cause us to continue to seek what is very good for us. All animals have addictions. For example, elephants will chew on the coca leaf for hours to make themselves relaxed and playful. They do not, however, leave their herd and give up their life just to chew it. They don't set up factories to synthesize the natural coca leaf into cocaine to get a quicker, stronger high. They do not corrupt or short-circuit their natural pleasure pathways as humans often do.

A mild dose of adrenaline is very pleasing and lasts quite long, yet we humans choose to take large doses of this internal stimulant. We seek increasing thrills to get higher levels of adrenaline, only to crash because enough is never enough. Here are the characteristics of both healthy and unhealthy addiction.

Healthy	Unhealthy
slow, controlled	fast, uncontrolled
no build-up of tolerance	build-up of tolerance
enough is enough	need for more and more
feels "just right"	gets "too high" and "too low"
life-energizing	all-consuming
enhances relationships	destroys relationships
mind-controlled	brain-controlled

The key to the pleasure prescription is not to abuse our natural gift of addiction to it. Addicts abusing the gift of addiction destroy themselves and those around them.

Our DNA is a genetic coil that acts like a natural computer chip, encoding plans for our entire body system. It resonates at millions of cycles per second, sending who we are throughout every cell in our body. We inherit immense pleasure potential from within our DNA, and we are genetically programmed for joy. Our brain and its entire sensory-motor system evolved to support pleasure seeking.[9]

Our brain only "knows" that it and its body are being stimulated. It seems unlikely that our addiction to pleasure was put there, as researcher Candace Pert writes, ". . . just so junkies could get high."[10] We were given this "seventh sense" for healthy pleasure so that we can be directed to what keeps us and those around us alive and well. To practice the pleasure prescription, we must use our mind to tell our brain how much and what kind of stimulation it should be processing. We must show our brain that artificial stimulants such as drugs or urgency neurohormones are not the way to the most fulfilling survival.

Substance abusers are often very high but seldom very happy. They feed the selfish here-and-now brain with a chemical experience but starve it of the emotional states that bring bliss. Real, lasting happiness requires thought and an intensified relationship with the world and those in it, not simply neurohormonal brain masturbation. No artificial high can compare with the natural bliss that comes from the legitimate use of our pleasure potential. We squander this natural gift when we misuse it and fail to see that our "addiction" to pleasure was meant to keep us connected—not to encourage individual escape.

There are now hundreds of scientific studies documenting that those persons who seek and find shared bliss in their everyday life lead the happiest, longest lives.[11] Research shows that our pleasure system is also our most effective health-care system, leading us to what is good for us if we read it correctly.[12]

If we can learn to use our pleasure centers and the neurohormones that flow within them rationally and moderately—to channel our natural addictive tendency—we can almost guarantee not only ourselves but everyone around us a longer, happier, more meaningful life.

How the Body Affects the Mind

Emotions do not just happen to us. We don't feel joy simply because something good happens to us and joyful signals are sent to our brain. We don't just smile because we are happy. We also feel happy because we smile.[13] You may be surprised to know that we can influence our own emotional state. One of the most important things you can do to bring more pleasure into your life is to act joyful. As Shakespeare said, "The play's the thing."

Over 100 years ago, Charles Darwin studied the expression of emotion.[14] He found that emotional expression is remarkably similar everywhere in the world, thus showing that emotions and their expression are evolutionary in nature. Years before Darwin, Guillaume-Benjamin Duchenne studied the musculature involved in smiling.[15] He determined that a legitimate smile required the combined movement of two muscle groups—the zygomatic majors (around the mouth) and the orbicularis occuli (around the outside of the eyes). While these muscles work involuntary when we feel happy, they can also be consciously controlled to let the brain know that you need a little happiness.

Here's a little example to show how you can cause your own emotional state. Look in the mirror, and smile by lifting your lips from your teeth, raising the corners of your mouth, and squinting. The muscles around your eyes are very important pleasure-senders, so pay particular attention to them. Now notice how you feel. Chances are, unless your brain is distracting you with such thoughts as "don't do that, you look silly," you will feel a little better than you did before smiling. If your smile muscles are sore from this exercise, that signals another symptom of Delight Deficiency Syndrome, but you can build them up by "smile-icizing."

Our thinking heart In addition to the thalamus, amygdala, septum, prefrontal lobes, and cerebral hemispheres, there is another organ in our body that does a lot of our thinking—the heart. While we often view the brain as the center of our humanness, romantics have always spoken of the affairs of the heart. Scientists are finally catching up with the poets in discovering that the heart is much more than a pump. When we use such language as "feeling it in my heart" or "my heart tells me," we are foreshadowing new findings from the field of psychoneurocardiology (PNC).[16] PNC shows that the heart actually thinks, feels, and functions in the body much as the brain does.[17] Psychoneurocardiologists at the Institute of HeartMath have shown that the heart and its surrounding areas are rich in biological oscillators that help establish and maintain body rhythms. The heart itself is a master oscillator that produces electromagnetic signals 40 to 60 times greater than the brain.[18] Neurocardiotransmitters such as ANF hormone, secreted from the atrium of the heart, influence our emotional state. They often set off physical responses and emotional reactions even before our brain "knows" we are having feelings—before a full-fledged "thought" can occur in the higher brain. In other words, our heart might react before our brain knows it and therefore before we know it, unless we learn to listen to the messages from our heart.

Practicing heartfulness A modern discovery in psychoneurocardiology called the "Freeze Frame" technique shows how "letting go" or the blissful way to well-being of the pleasure prescription can have powerful health effects. This new technique can be understood as not just "mindfulness" but "heart-full-ness." The approach is similar to the idea we sometimes express when we say, "Be still my heart." The Freeze-Frame technique, however, goes beyond just being still. It involves listening for the lessons from the heart.

Freeze Framing involves asking the heart what it is thinking about a source of incoming stimulation, and is used when experiencing a challenging event. It capitalizes on how, when we experience blissful pleasure and learn to listen to our heart instead of just our brain, healthy electromagnetic energy resonates throughout the body and immune system and vibrates our biosystem to healthy harmony. Try the Freeze-Frame technique and listen for what your heart has to say.

1. Sit down, be quiet, and don't let your brain get jealous and tell you to get up and get going.

2. In a calm, sincere, intuitive manner, ask your heart what's on its "mind."

3. Notice what you are feeling in and around your heart area.

If you are dealing with a stressful situation, ask your heart how it might deal with it differently than your limbic system, amygdala, and septum might do. Remember, your brain is very selfish and may tell you that it alone is in charge of thinking, but there is strong new data that the heart "hears, feels, and thinks" too.

Through the Freeze-Frame technique we can learn to listen to the messages sent by our heart.[19] We can use not only mind-body but heart-body communication to increase our alertness to pleasure. Our heart may sense a source of joy or bliss that our brain cannot see. And there is no reason to assume that our heart's vibrations, or the effects of them, stop at our skin. Oceanic philosophy teaches that each of us resonates with the other and that there is a life rhythm that throbs through every person, rock, bird, and fish. Some people refer to this as "sending out vibes," but Polynesians speak of "becoming in harmony" with the natural rhythms of the world.

Internal morphine In addition to the brain and the heart, our seventh sense employs an infrastructure of neurohormonal pleasure pathways. In response to any type of stress—pleasurable or challenging—our nervous system releases several joy fluids called endorphins. These flood us with feelings of well-being and bliss.[20] These internal opiates (*endo* = inside, *orphins* = morphines) are hundreds of times more potent than external morphines, but just like morphine, they are very addictive and a little endorphin high can go a very long way.

One reason following the pleasure prescription is not as easy as it sounds is because our natural affinity to "endorphinize" can encourage us to seek highs from only one aspect of our life. Since endorphins are so strong, we need only mild, regular doses to feel their blissful power. Science writer James Gorman illustrates the danger of the new fad of endorphin-dependence in his tongue-in-cheek article, "The Man with No Endorphins." He writes, "As near as I can tell, my brain doesn't do endorphins . . . The truth is I'm not even interested in getting high. I'm not greedy. I was happy enough with the mild depression that followed running in the park to continue jogging for years."[21]

Large doses of endorphins lead to unhealthy highs that result in strong crashes, which over time can weaken the immune system. The secret of the pleasure prescription is to learn to sip from our internal fountain of bliss without becoming "endorphaholics."

Psychoneurologist Dr. Edward Diener showed that healthy pleasure derives from brief, moderate, and regular joy rather than irregular, intense highs. He measured mood states in men and women over a six-month period.[22] Each person carried a beeper and recorded their moments of joy during the day. The results were clear. It was not how very happy but how many times a person was a little happy that led to the highest state of well-being.

Emotional rebound Another danger in getting too high is that the brain is programmed to bring you as far back down as you were up.[23] This is called the *opponent process theory*. Our brain has evolved an "emotional thermostat," so that nothing that happens to us is ever emotionally one-sided. The pleasure system pendulum starts to swing when we respond to something in our environment. An opposing emotion always begins sometime after the onset of the original emotion. This is good news for chronic pessimists and bad news for those who constantly strive to be optimistic.

Opponent process theory also says that the second, rebound emotion lasts longer than the first emotion. So if you have been very sad for a long time, you can count on being even happier for a longer time. If you seek to stay happy and be high most of the time, however, you are in line for the emotional boomerang to come back in full force to knock you down. Another aspect of the emotional rebound theory is that if we experience the first emotion on repeated occasions, the opposing emotion grows even stronger. Getting too high too often means you will get very, very low more often.

Polynesian *pono*, or balance, is the key to managing emotional rebound. The pleasure prescription is not about being happy all the time. It is about *being* all the time, and being open to all the emotional colors of life. It is about knowing that, even at our darkest moments, better times will come.

Chapter 15, "Loving and Learning Through the Hard Times," will explain more about how you can do this, but you might want to try this little exercise to note the emotional rebound theory in your own life. Make a timeline listing all the major events of your life from earliest to most recent. On the left side of the line, make a scale going from 0 to 10, to show how happy you were at each time. Every time I ask my patients to do this, they note that every "high period" is inevitably followed by a "down time" and vice versa.

Rivers of reward Some researchers call our natural, internal psychochemicals of joy the "rivers of reward."[24] To flow through life with balanced bliss, you must learn to sail on the sometimes turbulent seas of neurohormones.[25]

Although the neurochemistry of the pleasure-pathway theory is not yet completely worked out, we do know that there are certain synapses along this pathway that use the stress neurohormone, norepinephrine. Too little of this hormone results in a condition called *anhedonia,* or the inability to receive, perceive, and appreciate pleasure. Too much norepinephrine can numb the pleasure senses, polluting the rivers of reward. Just as you stop listening when someone yells at you all the time, intense overstimulation of the natural pleasure pathways may cause you to become deaf to delight and blind to bliss.[26] This is yet another danger of the misuse of our natural pleasure system by drugs or trying to stay too high on adrenaline for too long.

Brain bits all over the body Before 1970 it was believed that the human immune system operated independently from the brain. It did its job on autopilot, somehow recognizing invaders and purging the body of these antigens without any help from the brain itself. In the 1970s two discoveries surprised medical researchers. First, it was discovered that our thoughts and feelings are mediated by the same brain chemicals that regulate our body's immune defenses. Second, it was discovered that these brain chemicals—called neurotransmitters—are not isolated in the island of our brain. Like the canoes of ancient Polynesia, these neurotransmitters circulate from our brain through our body, communicating with every body system, including the immune system. Thus, a neurohormonal template of the pleasure or pain in our life is present everywhere within us as our beliefs become our biology.

PNI has given modern credence to the concept of *aloha 'aina,* for love of the land means love for everything as a whole. Polynesians believe that every thought translates immediately into the land itself and becomes a part of everyone and everything. This is exactly how we have just discovered that our brain, body, and immune and neurohormonal systems work together as one.

Based on the pioneering work of Dr. Candace Pert and many others, the "mind over body" idea is no longer true.[27] Dr. Pert says, "In the beginning of my work, I matter-of-factly presumed that emotions were in the head or the brain. Now I would say they are really in the body."[28] Polynesians would add that they are also in the earth.

The basic line of communication between how we feel and think about our world and our body's biology are our neuropeptides. Dr. Pert showed that a class of our immune cells, the monocytes, have tiny molecules on their surface called neuroreceptors that are perfect fits for neuropeptides. The neuropeptides are the keys that fit into the molecular locks on every cell in our body, opening up the door to our total-body emotional response. In effect, the brain flows into every nook and cranny of our body. Candace Pert says our immune system's white cells are like "bits of brain floating though the body."[29] A key question to answer in learning the pleasure prescription is, "Do you want your body to work like you think?" The immune system talks to the brain and the brain speaks to immune cells all over our body.

A Neurohormonal Hula

The Polynesian healers called *kahuna* (keepers [*ka*] of the secret [*huna*]) have long known that the body, brain, mind, and all of the world are one system, communicating constantly within itself and with everything. It is not just our own cells that communicate with our brain but the entire world we live in reverberating within and among us that constitutes our state of immunity. Every event in our life, others' lives, and the life of our planet is, on some level, a psychoneuroimmunological happening. Every thought and feeling is the drum beat that regulates a neurohormonal hula within and among us as we dance through life.

The ancient Polynesians would not be at all surprised that brain cells can talk to stomach cells and vice versa, or that we can now prove that mind and body are one. They would be surprised only that it took us so long to realize it. They would wonder why we still have stopped short of seeing that it is not just one mind connected with one body but all minds connected and constantly interacting with all other minds and the sentience of everything that constitutes the real "eco-psycho-neuro-immunology."

Whether we call it "sending good vibes" or "getting a good feeling," most of us know that, beyond the brain, the heart, endorphins, and the neurohormones, there is an energy that we feel and send all the time. Something seems to tell us when something is good or bad for us. We often can't find words for it, but there is an internal wisdom that draws us to or directs us away from certain people or things. We must remember that we too are sending out approach or avoidance signals beyond our own awareness. Learning the pleasure prescription means paying attention to the power of our own seventh sense and using it intentionally to send and receive messages of joy in our daily living.

Doctors of Delight or Distress

The phrase "we are our own doctor" is more than a simple comforting statement. The word for doctor comes from the Latin word meaning "to teach," and PNI now shows us that we are teaching our body (and everyone else's body) every second of our life; and our body is trying to teach us, too, if we will only pay attention. The body is an eager student, remembering every lesson we teach it. Like a naïve and trusting child, our body is very literal. Tell it you have a bad back or a weak heart and it believes you. If we open ourselves to the bliss response, our body learns to celebrate it in a balanced, sensual way. If, however, we teach it lessons of impatience, disconnection, hostility, egocentrism, and indifference, it translates these lessons into its internal biology, functioning in a fashion that weakens our defenses against disease. No matter what new "technique" we periodically use to help ourselves, it is our EPNI, our ecopsychoneuroimmunological pedagogy, that determines our fate.

Immunity education and learned lymphocytes In the mid-1970s psychologist Robert Ader and immunologist Nicholas Cohen at the University of Rochester made a startling discovery. They gave laboratory rats a drug that suppressed their immunity and simultaneously fed the rats saccharin-laced water. When Ader and Cohen discontinued the drug, they found that the rats' immune systems had "learned." Their immune systems still responded negatively even when given just sweetened water. Since Ader and Cohen's initial experiment, several researchers have documented that our brain communicates with our immune system; our immune system sends messages to our brain; this immune-brain communication system is all over our body, right into our bone marrow; and how we experience our daily life directly affects our health, immunity, and healing.[30] One lesson of this is that experience is not what happens to us but *what we make of* what happens to us.

As you consider these PNI findings, think about how you want your body's most important defense system to look, work, and feel. The choice is yours: bliss or urgency for every cell in your body. Pressure can be your teacher and urgency can be the lesson your body learns and practices most of the time, or you can faithfully let go of chasing after joy and let it happen to you by living *aloha.*

The new sickness—guilt Psychoneuroimmunology is a complex field, still very much in its infancy. Along with the remarkable advances in PNI and the emerging importance of the bliss response I will discuss throughout this book, a serious downside has emerged. To the threats from Era I medicine, such as high cholesterol or high blood pressure, and the caveats of Era II medicine of too much stress and not enough of the "relaxation response," we seem to be adding Era III self-recrimination and blame. We are not developed fully enough in our collective unconscious, are insufficiently aware of the quantum laws that govern unconscious energy, or have the wrong healing attitude.

Dr. Robert M. Sapolsky writes, "Since the Middle Ages, there has been a philosophical view of disease that is lapsarian in nature, characterizing illness as the punishment meted out by God for sin (all deriving from humankind's lapse in the Garden of Eden)."[31] By misinterpreting the gifts we have been given through the new findings from PNI, we can end up thinking that getting sick was our fault, that we failed to be happy enough, failed to cope with our stress, or violated some quantum principle. This is not only untrue, but such health-guilt can severely interfere with our ability to get well.

There is no physician or researcher in any culture, West, East, or Polynesian, who knows exactly and completely why one person gets sick, why another does not, and why some people get better and others do not. The best we can do is lead our lives and pray together that we will live joyfully and blissfully, allowing as much health to happen to us as possible. We can learn from our suffering, love enough to help others with their suffering, and let go enough to allow all the pleasurable support we can get from the world and the Creator to guide and heal us. Ultimately, *aloha* is not a positive attitude but an attitude of gratitude at being alive in a wonderfully chaotic world.

Pining for Paradise

Every known culture has had its myths of paradise. They are remarkably similar across the ages.[32] These myths of a world in which all people were peaceful and joyful and lived in harmony and with great pleasure with one another, nature, and the Creator seem to tug at the heart of every human being. They may also be indications of our seventh sense, our need for healthy shared pleasure here on earth.

The Polynesian's great creation myth concerns their own "garden of Eden," a long-lost paradisical island home they called Hava-Iki and now call Hawai'i. The Polynesian creation myth is virtually indistinguishable from that of the Old Testament and served as the basis for Polynesian belief systems hundreds of years before contact with the European missionaries and their Bibles.[33] There is no doubt that there is something within all of us, past and present, that remembers and longs to return to a paradise lost.

While anthropology and archeology have failed to prove or disprove the existence of a unitary ancient culture, both fields clearly show that our inability to find our bliss here on planet paradise is due to the brain's selfishness and aggressiveness, our failure to appropriately use our prewired sense of joy and to come to our "seventh sense."

Psychologist Kenneth Ring suggests that the brain's motivation might be a manifestation of a subconscious preparing for a collective near-death experience. Freud's pleasure principle was based primarily on what he called a "death instinct." The pleasure prescription teaches, however, that we do not have to be slaves to our brain's mortality phobia.[34] We can use our minds to play together in the splendor of our daily existence on planet paradise.

I suggest that the pervasiveness of the great myths of paradise around the world is evidence for a circuitry of contentment that is built into our human consciousness and is available to us if we will only slow down, be quiet, and let it speak to us. Perhaps our DNA also carries a neurological template for pleasure, expressed through the hundreds of paradise myths that have been passed down throughout the world. Perhaps, if we keep our brain from interfering with our natural pining for paradise, our mind might help us find it in our ordinary daily existence.

Philosopher George Santayana summed up the difference between the brain's striving and the mind's thriving when he wrote, "A string of excited, fugitive, miscellaneous pleasures is not happiness [the brain]; Happiness resides in a imaginative reflection and judgment [the mind], when the picture of one's life, or of human life, as it truly has been or is, satisfies the will, and is gladly accepted."[35]

A final note before we end this part . . . . Your task in learning the pleasure prescription should be playful, not arduous. The recommendations in this book should be approached with an orientation that easily accepts doing less than you can and celebrating your enjoyment of small, common activities in your daily life. I am not talking about the competitive, intense "I win and you lose" type of play that has evolved from the brain's "victory by me first" orientation. As psychologist O. Fred Donaldson points out, "Play to win and every victory is a funeral."[36]

A Polynesian *kahuna* told me, "Life is a pleasure if you live in kind jest, but it is purgatory if you joust and contest." The pleasure prescription is based on the mind's natural preference for the joyful *pono* and *pololei* that can lead us back to paradise.

Author Richard Heinberg has devoted more than a decade to studying the myths of paradise from around the world, including those of Polynesia. To show how his ideas relate to the pleasure prescription, I have enclosed in brackets the Polynesian words you have read about throughout Part One. Heinberg concludes, "If Paradise is our natural state of being, then the deepest and most compelling force at the core of the collective unconscious is one that is always urging us toward that state of equilibrium [*pono*]. As we deliberately work toward a future characterized by respect and care for Nature [*aloha 'aina*] and toward the nurturing of love [*akahai*], forgiveness [*'olu'olu*], compassion [*ha'aha'a*], and celebration of oneself and in one another [*lokahi*], our conscious efforts resonate with the pattern at the core of our being. Heaven and Nature rush to return to a condition of balance [*pono*] and accord [*pololei*]."[37] Within Heinberg's Western words are the principles of *aloha* and the Oceanic way to paradise on and with Earth.

LEARNING ALOHA

In this section, you will learn . . .
about the five key ingredients of the pleasure prescription, the qualities of *aloha*:

AHONUI: patience, to be practiced with perseverance. You will learn how tolerance and equanimity strengthen immunity and lead to happiness.

LOKAHI: unity, to be expressed harmoniously. You will learn how an intimate and connected life promotes a healthier and happier heart.

'OLU'OLU: agreeableness, to be expressed pleasantly. You will learn that the single greatest barrier to health, happiness, and longevity is expressing anger and hostility.

HA'AHA'A: humbleness, to be expressed modestly. You will learn how selflessness translates directly to physical and mental hardiness, and how it results in healing joy that spreads to everyone around you.

AKAHAI: gentleness, to be expressed tenderly. You will learn that giving and sharing result in powerful "highs" without emotional crashes, and how they help protect you and others from disease.

At the end of each chapter, there is a *ha'awina,* a fun "lesson" or exercise, that will illuminate each quality of *aloha* in your life. These lessons are something you can always go back to when you feel *aloha* slipping out of your life. They are also subtle, conscientious gifts you can share with your family, friends, and coworkers if you see them suffering from delight deficiencies.

Chapter Seven

THE PLEASURE OF PATIENCE—SUCCESS ALOHA STYLE

Ahonui: Patience, to be expressed with perseverance.
"Umi Ka Hanu I Ka Houpo"
(Bear with utmost patience)

On Tuesday, July 20, 1993, with the 1913 Colt army service revolver he had inherited from his father who had died several years earlier, a man who most knew as a tower of strength took his own life.[1] This bright attorney, Vincent Foster, was a very talented and successful man. He was close adviser to the current President of the United States. By his friends' and family's accounts, Foster was an intensely perfectionistic man who valued one thing above all else: his reputation. In his commencement address at the University of Arkansas Law School a few months before his death, Foster said, "The reputation you develop . . . will be your greatest asset or your worst enemy. [Nothing] . . . is worth a blemish on your reputation . . . . Dents to the reputation . . . are irreparable."[2]

Driven by an intense need to be thought of as the very best and plagued by the self-scrutiny, self-doubt, and self-recrimination that inevitably comes with such compulsion, Mr. Foster died from the pain of an urgency that robs life of the pleasure that comes with a forbearance for frailty in one's self and others. He was a public figure killed by the same fatal mistake made by millions of lesser-known people: the failure to realize that we are forever a work in progress and that perfectionism only robs us of the joy of living amidst the chaos of life.

Free-Floating Gloom

We live in a society where we are constantly expected to strive to be our very best and to get what we deserve. We are unforgiving of ourselves and others for failing to meet what author Robert J. Samuelson calls "our great expectations from the age of entitlement." As a result, we are constantly disappointed and disillusioned.[3] Many of us experience what Samuelson calls "free-floating gloom," a chronic, disillusioned impatience with ourselves, our political leaders, and our world.

We have achieved unprecedented prosperity and personal freedom, we are physically healthier, we have more things, and we live longer than ever... yet many of us seem to feel very bad about doing very well. This vague sadness in the face of prosperity is a result of our failure to understand the importance of a patient and serene life, of *wanting what we have instead of always trying to have what we want.*

As long as we continue to live in the "Age of Entitlement" and pursue a "better" instead of a good life, we will remain frustrated and not find the bliss we seek. The Gross National Product continues to increase, but a new national measure currently being developed, the National Contentment Predictor, continues to decrease.[4] Our impatience is destined to lead us into melancholia, a frustration and fatigue that results from the never-ending illusion that "better" or "perfect" is our life's purpose.

Beyond the Age of Entitlement

"Never be less than you can be," hollered the lecturer as he paced back and forth on the stage. "You can have it all if you will be all you can be. If you settle for less than you can be, then you will have less than you are entitled to. You deserve it! You owe it to yourself! Perfection is within your grasp if you want it badly enough and are willing to go after it. Even if you do not achieve it, you must keep going for it. Are you ready to go for it?" The audience of over a thousand stood and cheered.

This pop psychology "go after it" and ego-entitlement approach is the stock-in-trade of hundreds of "motivational" and "success" seminars. It is false prophecy, however, because as long as we are "going for" it we will never be any place long enough to find "it." As I pointed out in Part One, all desire states are transitory. Samuelson writes, "With better as the destination, there was never any arrival and a continual frustration over the endlessness of the journey."[5]

When we feel like a failure because we are not "being all that we can be," we end up impatient and hostile toward ourselves and toward those who we perceive are impeding our progress.

A tolerant, more serene approach to life is one way to lessen the risks of angry impatience. A *kahuna* (healer) summed up the importance of a more patient life when he said, "I have never seen a happy, healthy person who was impatient. Impatience always has some anger in it, and usually a lot of envy. Patience is the key to lowering both anger and envy because it takes away the pressure of trying to control time so you have the time to enjoy living."

The Virulence of Impatience

Because of our illusion of how things should or could be, we become impatient with our work, the conduct of our family members and fellow workers, our spiritual failures, our lovemaking, and even our skill at recreational activities. Our impatience is much more than a preoccupation with time limits and deadlines, although there never seems to be enough time to meet our standards of success or learn from life's inevitable misfortunes. We rush too much to be open to the subtle epiphanies of daily living, and we are too hurried to be available for the lessons of our necessary suffering. A *kupuna* said, "I think we are often in much too much of a hurry to cure. As a result we cannot heal, learn, and become more whole from our suffering."

Impatience robs us of a gentle and forgiving life and often takes the form of Toxic Success Syndrome, which can develop slowly, as it did in Vincent Foster's case, or immediately. Ironically, impatience is considered a virtue, and thus highly rewarded by our culture. Many of the greatest authors, poets, and leaders have been driven by an internal intolerance of being less than their very best and a chronic struggle to be better. Spiritual impatience tells these people that they are not becoming wise enough fast enough. Socialized impatience leads to constant nagging comparisons with others and concern for what others think and appear to have. In both cases, these people are chasing an illusion of perfection. No one can achieve "better" because, by definition, it is always just beyond us. One highly successful person interviewed for this book said, "When I sigh and say 'There, now that's better,' I really mean 'better for now' but never really 'good enough.'"

Is Great Success a Mild Madness?

There is a mental illness called *cyclothymia.* It is a type of "impatience madness," and it refers to a person who is in a constant state of flux between lively, "up" moods and feelings of depression. Cyclothymia can predispose a person to the more debilitating psychiatric disorder, manic-depression. There is now strong evidence that some of the most creative and brilliant people may have suffered in varying degrees from cyclothymia, which may have driven them to poor health and, in some cases, early death.[6] Edgar Allen Poe acknowledged this thin line between genius and madness when he wrote, "Men have called me mad, but the question is not yet settled, whether madness is not the loftiest intelligence—whether much that is glorious—whether all that is profound—does not spring from disease of thought—from moods of mind exalted at the expense of the general intellect."

Cyclothymia has been called "the fine madness," a mood disorder that relates to a sense of failed perfectionism and underdevelopment of the seventh sense resulting in lack of daily life pleasure. Such great poets as William Blake, Lord Byron, and Alfred Lord Tennyson wrote about their severe mood changes, as did modern poets John Berryman, Sylvia Plath, Delmore Schwartz, and Anne Sexton. Vincent Van Gogh, Robert Schumann, and Charles Mingus were also afflicted by this same madness, as were Winston Churchill, Franz Kafka, and Isaac Newton.

Psychiatrists and psychologists recognize a long list of symptoms for what they call the *cyclothymic personality.* It is a condition that hijacks the brain's natural pleasure pathways and numbs them. Unfortunately, persons with these symptoms are often highly regarded by our society, making cyclothymia a highly prized, "clean" addiction to striving for better. The world these influential people have created for us and the qualities in life that their works present are molded as much from this madness as from brilliance.

As you read the following list of symptoms, consider whether or not your favorite artists, poets, authors, composers, musicians, and the very successful people you know may have suffered from some degree of cyclothymia.

Symptoms of Cyclothymia

1. Elevated self-esteem, accompanied by cynicism
2. Abundant energy to the point of agitation, followed by periods of complete fatigue and withdrawal
3. High productivity accompanied by periods of no motivation or direction
4. Distrust, discomfort, and inability to receive compliments, perhaps because they serve as stimulants for even more effort
5. Impatience with others' flaws and with one's own
6. Excitability and quickness to anger
7. Strong convictions about the correctness and validity of their own views
8. Grandiosity to the point of poor judgment, accompanied by destructive impulsivity
9. Chaotic intimate personal and professional relationships
10. Disregard for personal health and safety, to the point of substance abuse, sexual promiscuity, reckless driving, and other life-threatening behaviors

One reason so many of us have failed to find the pleasure we seek in life is that the rules by which our modern world operates and the criteria of great success are in large part formed by these perfectionistic perspectives. To be "normal" in today's hectic world means embracing a form of chronic mental illness. We elect and promote our leaders on the basis of this fine madness, hold them to impossible standards of perfection, and urge them to seek "better" for us and our communities. In our eagerness to pursue more happiness we sacrifice our present happiness. We lead an irritable daily life to achieve the *promise* of a happier life later.

The famous physicist Buckminster Fuller suggested that none of us is a genius, some of us are just less damaged than most. The potential for a joyful, meaningful life rests within each of us, but we often speed right past our own recognition of our pleasure potential. The comments we throw out in casual conversations, such as "What a crazy life!" and "I must be nuts to live like this" are common indicators of our addiction to impatience.

Wandering in the Woods

Are you one of the thousands of people who drive themselves to a near manic-depressive state? Are you very up when you are in the race and very down when the thrill of the race is gone, regardless of whether you win or lose? Are you trapped in your desire for "more"? For many people, "winning" feeds the impatient desire for more wins, and "losing" causes deep dissatisfaction and feelings of defeat that are only overcome by an extreme high (or a "win"). Once this toxic success cycle is established, it is maintained by neurohormonal addiction and social reinforcement. Said one *kupuna,* "I've never really seen a rat race, but I see a lot of humans racing."

The so-called midlife crisis many people complain of is usually just a momentary, reflective midlife pause—a brief contemplation on the absurdity of the chase brought on by the glimpse of one's mortality. With a little therapy, the right motivational tape, a new car, a bigger house, or a younger spouse, these people are ready to head off again in hot pursuit of more happiness. But they miss the point that we are all to varying degrees in a crisis, afflicted with a mild impatient madness.

The opening line of Dante's *Inferno* cries the despair that constant impatience eventually brings: "Just halfway through life's journey, I awoke to find myself in a dark wood far off course, the right way lost." A misplaced emphasis on urgency can in the least result in Delight Deficiency Syndrome and at the worst, cost you your life.

More About Toxic Success Syndrome

In preparing to write this book and to develop the Aloha Test, I conducted a small study of people considered "very successful" by their colleagues. I interviewed seven men and four women who were self-made successes. I call them the "Five-and-Fivers" because each of them had a net worth in excess of five million dollars and had responsibility for work forces in excess of five hundred people. The Five-and-Fivers were at the "top" of the group of 1,465 business leaders who took the Aloha Test.

Each of the Five-and-Fivers granted me a one-hour, anonymous, unstructured interview. They also allowed me to interview someone they identified as a "key person" in their life and/or work. For many this was their spouse, but for some it was their secretary, business partner, or colleague. One Five-and-Fiver recommended his "coach," whom he had hired to call him every morning to provide "structure, support, and motivation." This ministudy of the highly successful and their intimates is the basis for my theories of Toxic Success Syndrome.

The unifying characteristics of all Five-and-Fivers was that they clearly suffered from toxic success. They seemed to have done it all, to have it all, yet were cynical, impatient, agitated, and still looking for happiness. They were unable to fully enjoy and take pleasure in their "good" life because they were so busy going after a better life. On a scale of 0 to 10, with 10 representing "very happy with my life right now at this moment," the Five-and-Fivers' scores averaged 5.5. Most surveys of happiness in Western culture indicate that people score from 6.5 to 6.8—and this includes lottery winners and those with serious illnesses![7] In contrast, the Aloha Test control sample of 100 Polynesians averaged a happiness score of 8.6. Clearly, financial gain and social success did not relate to happiness for the people I surveyed.

Another alarming finding from studying the Five-and-Fivers was that their spouses and other intimates not only scored far below the Polynesians, they also scored below their successful partner. The average spousal score was 3.9, and the score of intimates of Five-and-Fivers without a spouse averaged 4.3. So, despite their immense success, this highly successful group and the person(s) nearest them were actually less happy than the average person—and much less happy than their Oceanic neighbors, many of whom have a great deal less "stuff."

In terms of the Aloha Test, the average *aloha* score of the entire business group was 82 (out of 100), and the *ahonui* subtest score of that group was 17 (out of 20). In comparison, the Five-and-Fivers scored 69 and 18, respectively. Now compare this to the Polynesian control group average of 8 on the whole Aloha Test and 1 on the *ahonui* subtest. How much are we valuing and cultivating the qualities of *ahonui* in our society?

A *kupuna* sat with me during some of my interviews as well as when I gave the Aloha Test to business leaders meeting on Maui. She didn't say a word until all the interviews were over and then, as we walked along the ocean toward my home, she looked out at the sea and said, "You can call it Toxic Success Syndrome if you think they will listen to that name. I have never seen more people with greater natural gifts who were so unable to enjoy them. They are like deaf persons at a symphony. Even meeting here in Hawai'i, they seem busier making deals than making love and too rushed *doing* things to feel the healing *aloha* of this place. I feel very sad for them. I hope you can help them enjoy their journey, because they seem only to look to a destination at which they will never arrive."

Seven Symptoms of Toxic Success Syndrome

There are seven symptoms that characterize a person with Toxic Success Syndrome. As you read through the following sections, consider how these symptoms are related to the urgency response, the seventh sense for pleasure, and how *ahonui* can neutralize them.

1. A hyposensitive disposition
2. A misattribution of the source of one's success
3. A Type T, or time-focused, personality
4. A stronger need to achieve than to affiliate
5. Perfectionism
6. A focus on tangible rewards
7. Living to work rather than working to live

Hyposensitive Disposition Psychologist Jerome Kagan has done research on temperament, a complex and controversial concept.[8] His careful physiological work shows that very soon after birth, babies fall into two general groups: those with inhibited and those with uninhibited temperaments.

While they may be of equal intellect and potential, inhibited babies of only four months old show an overreactive and impatient relationship to their world. They kick and thrash at the slightest stimulation. Uninhibited babies are calmer and tend to require much more stimulation before reacting in the same intense fashion.

My interviews and clinical work indicate that many of the highly successful were uninhibited babies and children. They inherited a physiological predisposition to a higher threshold for arousal and reactivity. They were born inclined to be hyposensitive, and thus tolerate and even require much more intense physical and emotional input than average. Perhaps because of this, toxically successful people may be compensating for their comparative physio-insensitivity by seeking increasingly intense stimulation.

All the Five-and-Fivers said their parents' descriptions of them suggested they were more hyposensitive than their siblings. Like the children and adults in Kagan's study, they said they could tolerate high and multiple stimulations and indeed preferred them and sought them out. During the interview, they were verbally assertive, smiled spontaneously, and even returned quickly to relaxation and resumed almost exactly where they left off in our conversation after what appeared to me to be a stressful phone call or other interruption. The spouse of one Five-and-Fiver said, "I have to practically scream to get his attention."

All said they were risk takers, more so than their siblings and playmates seemed to be. Like the Kagan hyposensitives, they were relatively free of allergies and all but two had dark brown or black eyes. All were mesomorphic (of medium build and height), particularly in comparison to their ectomorphic (thin and taller) or endomorphic (heavy and shorter) "key person." Again like the Kagan hyposensitives, all but one had what might be called rounded and fuller faces than their key person.

None of the above characteristics can be said to prove that toxically successful people were hyposensitive babies who grew to be adults who impatiently and manically desire increasing stimulation. However, the comparisons to the Kagan study were clear in this small group as well as in the entire business leaders' group. This suggests that these people compensate for a hyposensitive temperament by constantly pursuing "more and better," which is more threatening or uncomfortable for those with a hypersensitive temperament.[9] Whether or not hypersensitive babies grow up to be the more withdrawn, codependent spouses of these hot reactors is not known, but I have noted that pattern at meetings where I speak to highly successful women and men who attend with their spouses.

Questions to consider: What stories do your parents tell of your childhood? What stories do you remember? How would your spouse, your close colleagues, your best friend describe you in terms of seeking or avoiding intense stimulation?

Misattributing their source of success Although my interviews were more informal than structured, I asked standard questions in each. In addition to taking the Aloha Test, rating themselves on the happiness scale, and discussing their temperament as a child, each interviewee was asked, "To what do you attribute your success?" Each key person or spouse was also asked, "To what would you attribute your partner's success?" For all of the Five-and-Fivers the answers were radically different than that of their key person. They focused on the potential power, the power "to become," which is the flip side of impatience and imperfection. Their key persons recognized their essential power, the power "of being" or *ahonui*.

Each Five-and-Fiver attributed his or her success to "skill." Other answers were "stick-to-it-iveness," "hard work," "high energy," "knowing how to take advantage of good luck," "being faster and cleverer than the competition," "bouncing back even stronger," and "knowing how to get things done and picking people who can get things done quickly."

Their key associates attributed the Five-and-Fivers' high accomplishments to character rather than performance. Two assistants answered "she cares" and "his commitment to doing the right thing." The nine spouses answered, "I would say his caring about people," "her pride in what she does," "he's basically a very good person," "due to a religious nature and practicing that religion every day," "people really like him," "the kind of person you can trust," and "a very loving person."

Most studies of success in any endeavor indicate that, while short-term success may be achieved by being the fastest, least accepting of imperfection, and the hardest working, in the long run the very effective and successful healthy person is quite different. She usually has her priorities straight, lives by those priorities, and is a humble, gentle, patient person who values family and gives it a high time priority.[10] To the Polynesian, this is to live with *ahonui.*

Toxically successful people misread the sources of their success and tend to almost superstitiously repeat self-destructive behaviors that they believe account for their success. People with toxic success fail to learn the true character of their success because they have not developed their seventh sense for healthy pleasure and the emotional intelligence that goes with it to the same degree they have honed their cognitive skills. Eventually they succumb to what medicine and psychology call "extreme stress reactions"—physical and emotional burnout. A kupuna summed up the misattribution error of very successful people when he said, "Continental people measure success by the personal feeling they think comes from competing or comparing. They think it is a result of individual power or cleverness. We Polynesians view success as very good fortune intended for everyone and coming from collaborating with others. It is not really yours because it could only come from everyone working together and would have no meaning without others to share it with. We are not in a hurry to be happy, but we are very happy to never be in too much of a hurry."

Questions to consider: By what criteria do you measure success? To what would others attribute your success? How has your definition of success changed throughout the years?

Type T personality Every one of the eleven Five-and-Fivers reported that their life was governed by the clock. Even on vacations they tried to "use" every moment, found it difficult to turn off their racing brain, and were often more exhausted after a vacation than before it. One of the interviewees smiled as he said, "God put me on earth to accomplish a certain number of things. Right now, I'm so far behind I'll never die."

This statement about death reflects a common motivation of the toxically successful. Rather than live with pleasure, they try to outrun mortality and its living equivalent, failure. One interviewee said, "I can be in fast-forward or pause, but never in rewind. That would be a waste of my time. I don't even rewind rental video tapes." To test this understanding of time, I asked each group member to close his or her eyes and, without counting, guess exactly when one minute had passed and then open them. Eight opened their eyes in less than 40 seconds, one in less than 15 seconds. The other two started to fall asleep, reflecting the on/off nature of the toxically successful. In comparison, the Polynesian control group all waited beyond the minute and often had to be told to open their eyes.

One of the *kahuna* in my control group lives on the island of Kaua'i. When I gave him the minute test, he did not open his eyes for several minutes and looked to be asleep. When I gently asked, "Are you asleep?" he answered, "No, no. I'm much more awake now than when you asked me to close my eyes." Another *kupuna* doing the minute test explained, "Time does not heal all wounds. In fact, if we let it run our life, time causes most of our suffering. I do not understand the *haole* way of living. It seems based on saving time but I've never met a *haole* who had enough of it."

Questions to consider: How often do you look at your watch during the day? Have someone do the minute test with you and compare your internal clocks. How many of your decisions are based primarily on time? Do you feel rushed and impatient even as you read these words?

Stronger need to achieve than to affiliate Psychologist David McClelland, distinguished professor of psychology at Boston University, is interested in identifying the primary driving forces in human life and has researched the difference between the need to achieve (which he calls *nAch*) and the need to affiliate (*nAff*).[11] He has found that three needs are very important: the need to achieve, the need for power, and the need for connection or affiliation. Healthy success is a balance of these needs, but toxic success comes from a dominance of the need for achievement or power.

I tested my group for their need to achieve (nAch) by having them look at a picture and tell me a short story about it. The picture was of a Polynesian canoe resting half in the ocean and half on the sandy beach and a Polynesian boy looking at the canoe. The theme of every Five-and-Fivers' story was related to achievement and/or the need for power. For example, one man said: "The kid looks at the canoe to see if he can figure out a way to make it faster. He then gets in the canoe and is the first to cross the Pacific ocean in a canoe." A typical Polynesian story was based on the need for affiliation: "The boy looks at the canoe, the ocean, the sand, the waves, the sky, the sun, and listens to the birds. He remembers that his ancestors made and sailed in canoes like this one, so he sits in the shade by the canoe and waits for his family to come for a ride."

In *The Seven Habits of Highly Effective People,* management expert Steven Covey writes about the concept of character over personality.[12] He says that the key to effective and healthy success is a balance between courage (nAch) and consideration (nAff). Toxic success happens when the need for achievement and power becomes the dominant motivation. A Polynesian man in my sample group said, "If you give a Hawaiian a choice between helping a neighbor or winning a contest, he will chose *kokua* (helping) every time. The truly prosperous person is the one who helps the most people."

Questions to consider: How many groups do you belong to? (These can be professional, social, volunteer, family.) How many do not have hierarchical structures? In how many are you a follower, as opposed to being in charge? Would you choose time with a friend or time "getting some work done"?

Struggling for perfection In researcher Frederick Herzberg's study of 200 engineers and accountants, he found that five factors stand out as predictors of feelings of success at work: achievement, recognition, the nature of the work itself, responsibility, and advancement.[13] Unhealthy success is related to the overwhelming dominance of the achievement, recognition, and advancement factors, all of which my success group referred to in terms of perfectionism and impatience.

When asked about their most pressing work-related concerns, each of the Five-and-Fivers answered in terms of the need to avoid failure and being seen as not achieving to the utmost of their ability; not being recognized as skilled, clever, or talented; and not making noticeable advancements. A typical answer was, "More than anything, I want my colleagues to see me as a success. If I thought for one minute they were talking about me as not being really sharp and on my game, I would be really upset." These successful people valued a "perfect" reputation and were motivated to avoid any hint of being less than they thought they should or could be.

A typical answer from the Polynesian control group was this statement by a Hawaiian man, "I would hate it if people thought I was arrogant or that I was only concerned about my own success and didn't care about other people. I know I'm far from perfect and I hope everyone knows I know." These statements illuminate the fundamental philosophical difference about responsibilities and value to community. The Five-and-Fivers believe their goal is to stand out in a group, be an example, a conqueror. The Polynesians seek to be part of the group, to be an agent of change from within an extended family model of society.

Questions to consider: Do you identify more with the Hawaiian man or the Five-and-Fiver? Do you think the Oceanic approach could work for you or is it too "impractical"?

Focus on tangible rewards When asked, "Why do you work?" all Five-and-Fivers stressed tangible rewards. Some masked their answers with platitudes about doing something of value, but when pressed, the criterion of value related to concrete external rewards or ascribed status far more than the intrinsic value of the work itself.

Modern research shows clearly that working for rewards is self-defeating. Studies of success have found that extrinsic rewards for what are intrinsically rewarding activities eventually make those intrinsically rewarding activities less rewarding.[14]

Polynesians shun tangible rewards because they are aware of their dangers. Ask a Hawaiian how much she wants to be paid to dance or chant and you will be met with a questioning look. "Just give what you will; I don't want my performance to suffer because of money" is the usual answer. Polynesians call this orientation *pu'uwai aloha* [heart giving love]—to give from a generous and warm heart. Modern psychology calls this same principle *over-justification theory.*

Over-justification theory says that an external reward will decrease a person's intrinsic motivation when he or she attributes his or her performance to that reward. When the inspiration of a behavior is to seek rewards and to assess the quality of a performance by the amount and extent of the reward, intrinsic motivation will always decrease. In all of my interviews, people talked about the "fun going out of work that used to be fun." I heard fond stories of the "good old days" when "I worked for the hell of it."

Questions to consider: Do you look forward equally to going to work and to going home? Do you long for "the good old days" at work or are most of your days pretty good right now? If at all possible, would you work for free?

Work as life Finally, I asked each successful person, "Do you work to live or live to work?" All answered to varying degrees that, indeed, they had "become" their work. A sample answer was, "I am what I do, and that's all that I am or can be." All their key people agreed. One spouse answered, "If he had no more work, he would have no more life, and he doesn't have much of a life now!"

Psychologist Kenneth Pelletier has studied the impact of work on health.[15] He found that those who can never get enough external rewards never feel successful enough. They lack balance and connection in their life and eventually fail, not just at work. They are also more likely to become physically or socially ill and to suffer in their most intimate relationships.

Researcher J. M. Rhodes studied the issue of overwork and found that those who made work their life failed to thrive. Even if they appeared happy on the outside, their marriages, relationships, and family interactions were in distress.[16] Rhodes identified the following characteristics of the "live to work" orientation:

1. Constant rumination about work problems
2. Adding hours to the work day to make up for diminishing productivity
3. Use of alcohol or drugs as an escape from stress
4. Tendency to postpone vacations and to work on weekends
5. Chaotic family life
6. Focus on independence, a loner
7. Sedentary lifestyle
8. Narrowing interests
9. Inability to laugh at themselves
10. Denial of many of the above symptoms by saying they are the "necessary evils" of a successful life

In Chapter 14, I go on to discuss the *aloha* approach to work in detail, but as you move through this section of the book, keep in mind that *ahonui,* or persistent patience, is the first and most important step to healthy, pleasurable work and joyful success shared with those around you.

This Is to Have Succeeded

There is a well-known Western writer who was in touch with his indigenous mind and who understood the Third Way of patient well-being as the way to healthy success. I end this chapter on *ahonui* with his message.

Ralph Waldo Emerson, in his essay on success, offers an interpretation of the persistent patience that leads to emotional rather than financial affluence and deep pleasure in daily living.

Emerson first writes that success is *"To laugh often."* This is the playful approach to life that Polynesians follow, basking with glee in the wonders of the everyday world. Laughter, or *'aka'aka,* is one of the greatest human capabilities for dealing with the natural chaos of life. If you find yourself sharing many good laughs a day, you have met the first criterion of success *aloha* style!

Next, Emerson adds the ability *". . . to win the respect of intelligent people and the affection of children."* Success is not measured by popularity and prestige but by the respect of wise, healthy, and balanced people. If you are loved and sought out by children, you know you have achieved a measure of healthy success because the very young have the simple internal wisdom to know the real from the phony. Their natural seventh sense has not yet been numbed.

Emerson's third criterion of success is *" . . . to earn the appreciation of honest critics and endure the betrayal of false friends."* Success results from being receptive to criticism without becoming impatient with yourself or with the critic. It also requires tolerance of the petty duplicity and back-stabbing of those so impatient with themselves that it spills over to their closest relationships.

Emerson's next criterion, *". . . to appreciate beauty and find the best in others,"* is one of the most important components of aloha success. When we are governed by our selfish and impatient brain's urgency response, we cannot find enough time to truly appreciate the grace and magnificence of the world around us. This causes us to miss what others have to offer because we look only for their weaknesses or try to impress instead of understanding and caring for them.

Emerson adds, *"To leave the world a bit better, whether by a healthy child, a garden patch, or a redeemed social situation."* The core of a successful life is connection and caring. Giving and loving enough to make the world a better place, and caring for and nurturing the earth's resources, including its inhabitants, is true *aloha* success.

Emerson concludes, *"To know even one life has breathed easier because you have lived. This is to have succeeded."* This echoes the original meaning of *aloha*—sharing the scared breath.

As you continue your reading, take some time to catch your breath and to breathe together with your family and loved ones, for this is the true source and witness to your pleasurable healthy "achievement." A joyful life is one guided by the concept that one does not develop patience because one has time; one has more than enough time because one has learned to be patient.

Ahonui Ha'awina (Patience Lesson)

Try the following "penny for your patience" exercise for a week.

On the first day, place three pennies in a pocket, which you will now call your "patience pocket." Every time you become impatient or irritated with yourself or others, reach into the pocket, gently turn one of the pennies between your forefinger and thumb, and count ten breaths without taking your hand out of the pocket. Then, take one of the pennies from the pocket and give it to someone, or leave it where someone can find it. At the end of each day, see how many pennies you have left. If you still have pennies in your "patience pocket," save them and add them to three in your pocket the next day.

If, as the week draws to a close, you begin to jingle as you walk, congratulate yourself on developing equanimity, and celebrate by taking your pile of pennies and putting them in a charity container!

Chapter Eight

THE CYCLE OF CONNECTION—OVERCOMING THE ILLUSION OF SEPARATENESS

Lokahi: Unity to be expressed harmoniously
"Ho'okahi 'iliwai o ka like"
(One is just like the other)

"If you don't put that stone back where it belongs, we'll never get this truck started," said the Hawaiian man to his visitor from the mainland. His guest had found the stone on the beach while fishing. Taken by its beauty, he had slipped it into his backpack. Now, as the sun sank below the horizon and the palm trees leaned in dark silhouette over the ocean, an early evening shower gently hit the windshield. The Hawaiian and his friend reluctantly prepared to leave, but despite several turns of the key the old pickup truck was silent.

"I don't get it," said the visitor. "What does one little stone have to do with your old truck not starting?" The Hawaiian reached outside, held his hand palm up and said, "Feel these tears? The gods are crying because they don't want the *pohaku* (stone) to leave its home. It does not belong to you. You are breaking its *lokahi* (unity) with the land. Put it back, and the gods will let us leave."

"You crazy Hawaiian," laughed the visitor. He had heard this kind of talk from his friend before and often teased him about it. Not wanting to offend him, he tossed the stone onto the ground. "Start her up," he laughed. "The stone's home." The Hawaiian man smiled and shook his head. "Watch. I'll try it for you, but it won't start." He turned the key but a soft hum was the only sound. The visitor reached over and turned the key himself, and still the truck would not start.

"You must put the stone back where you got it," said the Hawaiian more firmly. "Do it with respect and apologize for disturbing it." The visitor could see deep concern in his friend's eyes.

"You can't be serious," he grumbled as he jumped out of the truck, picked up the stone, carried it several yards down the beach, and placed it where he had found it. "There, stone," he said with scorn, "You're home. So let us go home." The rain intensified and the visitor was soaked as he climbed back in the truck.

Even before the visitor was seated, the Hawaiian turned the key—still the truck would not start. He looked at his friend with more pity than impatience, then removed the key from the ignition and placed his hand on his friend's shoulder. The visitor could see he was not joking. There were tears in his friend's eyes.

"Please go back and apologize again. But say it only if you feel it and mean it. If you don't, we will be here a very, very long time—maybe longer than you can imagine. Even if they find us and tow my truck, nothing good will come of this. You must show your respect for everything here. You may leave this island, but you will always be a part of it, just like that stone. Leave your respect and take the *aloha* of this place in your heart, not in your pack."

The visitor was deeply moved by his friend's sincerity and felt his own tears mix with the rain on his face. He walked slowly to the stone, knelt down, and said without the slightest embarrassment in his voice, "I am very sorry. I didn't understand. Please forgive me. I hope to come back again and see you." At just that moment, he felt the wind blow his hair. The rain slowed and stopped. In the distance, he heard the old truck's engine grind and start.

"*Hele mai!* (come!)," beckoned the Hawaiian man. "But don't forget to say goodbye to the *pohaku*. It will miss you until your return."

Disease and Disconnection

The story of the *pohaku* is true. The Hawaiian man is one of my closest friends and one of the Polynesians who made up my control group for the Aloha Test. I know firsthand that his old truck never failed to start before this incident, and that it has started reliably without repair ever since. For my Hawaiian friend, the concept of oneness called *lokahi* is much more than a metaphor or new-age philosophy. It is a real, fundamental, and powerful daily-life principle that when violated has negative consequences. When respected, it results in great joy and well-being.

For the disenchanted Western culture, the earth and everything on it are here for our "use," or exploitation. So urgently do we live on our planet, using her resources, that the heat generated by our hectic ride is dangerously raising the temperature of her atmosphere. Western culture is one of control and possession more than unity and attachment. In Oceanic culture, there is no separation between the spiritual and the physical worlds. Our world is alive and sentient and must be dealt with in that way.[1] Nothing can be owned or controlled, and deep and complete respect, appreciation, and responsibility for the welfare of the planet are keys to happiness and well-being for everything and everyone.

Western medicine is now learning that all illness and unhappiness are ultimately related to disconnection. Reverend Chris Williamson points out that people who wish to make spiritual progress do not attend more self-enhancement seminars or retire to monasteries to contemplate, they get into and maintain meaningful relationships.[2] *Interdependence,* not independence, is the way of the island cultures.

In a different realm, psychoneuroimmunology is documenting how, whenever we behave in ways that separate us from other people or things, we suffer physically and emotionally: our immune system weakens, our heart becomes walled off from the rest of our body, and our spirit becomes lonely and despairing.[3] To the Polynesian, "self-healing" is not possible because all illness is a matter of relationship breakdown, not individual failure. Self-healing is an illusion of the isolation of the West and the more introspective self-focus of the East.

The First Need

We are happiest and most fulfilled when we feel completely connected. Western psychologist Abraham Maslow wrote about "transcendence" as the highest human need.[4] He saw this need as coming into play only when lower individual needs such as self-esteem and self-actualization were fulfilled. Oceanic thought turns Maslow's hierarchy upside down. It teaches that transcending the self to be and feel totally connected with life is our *basic* drive, and that all other needs are predicated on knowing and behaving in accordance with this central life motive.

To transcend in Polynesia is not to excel, succeed, outshine, surmount, or go beyond. It is to surrender, share, sacrifice, and go within the entire system of the world in order to give of oneself for the good of the whole and to feel the immense pleasure that comes from such unity. Oceanic thought is not *hierarchical* but *harmonious.*

Modern psychologists have done research to show that this harmony-over-hierarchy view is accurate. They have documented how at the most important times in our life we are governed by the need for unity.[5] You can probably think of countless examples of transcendent selflessness. Parents run into burning homes to save their children and martyrs like Mahatma Gandhi fast for the sake of others. Despite the cynical skepticism of developmental evolutionists who suggest that altruistic behavior is only selfish gene-protection, I suggest that we respond to a much more profound and sacred entrenched need to transcend the self, to see ourselves in others, and to live by and for the principle of *lokahi*.

When tourists come to Maui, Hawai'i, they want to see the whales who return to the warm waters there every winter. As they wait on the beach to see these giants play, they yell, drink, eat, and splash loudly in the ocean. As soon as someone cries out, "Look, a whale!" there are squeals of delight, but then the entire beach falls silent as a huge tail slaps the water with vibrations so strong they shake the sand. Even after the whale moves on, there is silence and whispering about the magnificence of what was just experienced. It takes several minutes before there is a return to the hubbub of beach play. For just a moment, the basic need to feel connection with the majesty of nature takes precedence over all else and fills the observers with a healthy, connected pleasure more basic than mere self-enjoyment.

Lokahi, the expression of joyful unity, has three facets: personal, interpersonal, and transpersonal connection. This chapter explores each of these elements.

Personal Connection: Unity with the Self

There is a difference between the pleasure of self-awareness and the isolation of self-absorption. One key aspect of *lokahi* is to be fully aware of your own body, even as you connect with the earth and bodies around you. Living by the pleasure prescription requires being fully aware of our body's language but remaining free of arrogant self-glorification.

Polynesians refer to the bones, blood, and other tissues as the *unihipili,* or lower self. In this case, "lower" does not mean lesser, but refers to the location. The *unihipili* is as revered as the "higher" systems of the mind and the outside world because it is a part and manifestation of sharing life with all of these systems. The Polynesian way is not mind-over-body but mind, body, and world as one. The pleasure prescription involves seeing the body not as something to be perfected, strengthened, and molded but as a conduit between the world and the soul. It teaches that we should pay attention to our body but not show it off. It teaches that we do not *have* a body but, as is true of our unity with nature, we *are* our body.

Our physical body talks to us all the time, sending messages of health, happiness, and needs for remedial attention. Unfortunately, we often try to numb these messages with antacids, headache medications, and bowel regulators. Psychologist Gary Schwartz at the University of Arizona has spent ten years studying the importance of attending to the feedback from our body systems. He describes television commercials as ways of telling you how to turn off your body's language: "The message was: 'Eat all you want. If you get a stomach ache, don't change your behavior and listen to your body. Instead, take Alka-Seltzer. . . . ' We are being taught to say, 'Darn you stomach, don't you interfere with my behavior.'"[6] He has shown that those who ignore their body, cut themselves off from its sensations—be they good or painful, or try to keep their body language inside and not be aware of it and share it with others, are much more likely to have weak hearts and lowered immunity.[7]

Oceanic teaching tells us to listen to our body just as we listen to the thunder and the wind. It teaches that all signals from nature are lessons and that nature talks to us through our body's multiple senses. Our seventh sense helps us listen to our body with a "faculty for feeling" far beyond our five basic senses and even our sixth psychic sense. The seventh sense is responsive to the natural energy that is the poetic language of all natural processes, and our body is one of its key transmitters. When your body "speaks," it is your seventh sense trying to get your attention. Our seventh sense does not just receive. It is constantly trying to send us messages about which way to go in life.

To live more in sync with our bodies, Gary Schwartz proposes what he calls the *ACE* theory, which stands for Attend, Connect, and Express. To "attend" means to be constantly aware of the body's messages as signals for positive action and life change rather than symptoms of breakdown to be masked or repaired. To "connect" means to understand the body's signs as reaction to the nature of our existence as inseparable from everyone and everything, and warnings that we may be separating from our world, not just personal experiences. To "express" means to talk to yourself and others about how your body is working and feeling rather than following "the show must go on" philosophy of self-denial. When we attend, connect, and express our physical feelings, we free our seventh sense to do its job of leading us away from the illnesses of isolation toward the hardiness of connected well-being.

Interpersonal Connection: Unity with Others

We all need periods of being alone. They give us the opportunity to contemplate and reflect. But isolation makes us sick and may even kill us. Isolation is not the absence of people around us; it is a feeling of being lonely and disconnected, somehow left outside the "whole," even when we are among others.

Without the nourishment of social support, a lonely heart hardens and breaks. Like an unwatered flower, it literally atrophies and dies. A study of 2,320 male survivors of heart attacks showed that, more than cigarette smoking, high blood pressure, high cholesterol, diabetes, and other well-known health risk factors, *loneliness* was the leading predictor of early death.[8] The lonely had four times the chance of dying from their heart attack than the more socially connected.

Modern research in PNI (psychoneuroimmunology) continues to show that connection increases longevity and the lack of it shortens life. A study of 7,000 people in Alameda County, California, revealed that early death was much more likely for those who had poor social interactions and social support systems. Western scientists skeptical of a "soft" variable such as *lokahi* or connection offer the "chicken-and-the-egg" rebuttal in response to these studies. Perhaps, they said, loneliness and isolation are a *result* of being sick and not the cause. Using advanced statistical techniques, however, the researchers were able to show that loneliness was indeed the cause, and not the effect, of disease.[9] Another major study of the impact of loneliness on early death done in Tecumseh, Michigan, confirmed these findings.[10]

Oceanic people do not consider *lokahi* as just another way to avoid premature death, but as the way to healthy pleasure in life. They are not surprised that "connected" people live longer and healthier because they know that such persons enjoy the natural, built-in protection of shared joy. Again, the Polynesian elders are surprised that it has taken modern science so long to "prove" what they already believed: unity feels good because it is good for you.[11]

Psychoneuroimmunologists are beginning to discover exactly how loneliness isolates and closes off the heart. When we are stressed by the helpless and hopeless feelings of loneliness, blood levels of hydrocortisone, a hormone secreted under stress, are much higher.[12] Loneliness is also associated with low concentrations of high-density lipoproteins (HDL), the healthy type of cholesterol that protects against heart disease, weakened immunity, and lowered levels of hormones essential to heart muscle strength. When our social relationships are weak, our heart becomes physically weaker too. "Weak social ties cause weak heart strings," one *kahuna* said.

You may be surprised to know that most people in the United States who have their first heart attack before the age of 50 do not have any of the major risk factors—smoking, high blood pressure, or obesity. Most, however, will have experienced loneliness.[13] Western medicine can never effectively deal with heart disease, our leading killer, without taking into account the pleasure of connection and the dangers of social distance.

Transpersonal Connection: Unity with Everything

Polynesians do not live in *lokahi* with their natural environment because they were or are incapable of changing their environment to suit their needs or lacked the wisdom to master and use it wisely. Their hundreds-of-years-old fish farms and aqueducts testify to their skills as ecological managers. They do not seek loving connection with nature solely because of their holistic and reverent attitude toward nature (although that attitude is profound and pervasive). Polynesians strive to live in harmony with respect toward nature because, as one man put it, "We go beyond ourselves by totally being ourselves with everything. We don't seek some extraordinary mystical experience outside ourselves; we just sit in the ocean and be ourselves with it. That's how we connect with God."

The word *transcendence* is often used in modern psychology, most particularly by transpersonal psychologists. In psychology, transcendence frequently refers to a dimension beyond ordinary experience.[14] The Oceanic approach to transcendence accepts it as an everyday immersion in all that daily life has to offer. Polynesian transcendence sees God not as "up there" or "out there" but as "of" everyone and everything. It is not a personal goal, but a shared way of daily living.

The Polynesian transcendence that brings healthy pleasure is not a search for personal enlightenment but taking the time to be with someone we love. It is not a new-age technique but an interpersonal tenderness in living. It is less about going to the mountain top to seek wisdom and more about walking hand-in-hand along a sleepy mountain path with someone to share in the glory of the present moment as the ultimate gift from nature.

The Monk, the Kahuna, and Polynesian Pantheism

A *kahuna* told me, "If you are looking for God, look out at the sea. Look to the horizon. Get in your canoe and go to the horizon. When you get there, you will meet God." He meant that to connect with something more than self, we have to be ourselves with nature but never think we can pinpoint it and draw a boundary around it. Polynesians think of the transpersonal, the Sacred, the Creator, the "something more" as very personal. Another *kahuna* said, "Think of the Creator as closer to you than you are to yourself. If you think you are God, you are arrogant. If you don't know that the sacred runs through you and expresses itself through you, you are divinely dumb."

This same orientation to transpersonal experience is expressed by the philosopher Spinoza, who spoke of *deus sive natura,* or "God is nature." Pacific pantheism, however, is much more than "God is everything." Polynesians are on a first-name basis with the sacred in their everyday life, but they do not just think of God as a metaphorical expression of the combined forces and laws of nature. Polynesians truly believe and behave in a way that shows how the rocks and trees are as real as God is and that talking to them is a way of talking with God. Such is the enchanted world of Polynesia.

Author and Benedictine monk David Steindl-Rast describes this transpersonal unity when he writes, "We experience our innermost reality, that which is closer to us than we are to ourselves, as in some way not simply ourselves but going beyond ourselves, just as the horizon recedes when we approach it."[15] It is interesting that Steindl-Rast uses the same horizon metaphor as the Polynesian *kahuna,* showing that the Third Way of Polynesia crosses paths with the Eastern and Western ways at very crucial junctures. Perhaps the power, wisdom, and effectiveness of the Eastern and Western ways has clouded their central insights about the meaning and purpose of life that the central Oceanic view still clearly embraces. Perhaps the natural truths about healthy pleasure taught by the aloha way can serve as a magnet to draw back together the wise spirituality of the East and the intellectual science of the West. Perhaps Polynesia can be the spiritual and intellectual center of the world rather than just a favorite vacation destination.

Compare Steindl-Rast's statement with that of the *kahuna* who spoke of sailing your canoe to the horizon to look for God. Steindl-Rast says, "We speak about a horizon phenomenon when we speak about God. The horizon belongs inseparably to the landscape. There can't be a landscape without a horizon, nor a horizon without a landscape. The horizon recedes as you go and remains the horizon."[16] The monk and the *kahuna* share a converging view of the transpersonal: that the Creator is the Spirit of all that exists within us and is expressed from within, through, and around us. The spirit of transpersonal connection is not simply a mental process—it transcends matter and thought. It is a view in accordance with the statement by Saint John of Damascus, "God is beyond names and beyond essence."

After spending years learning from the Polynesians about the spirit and the concept of transpersonal *lokahi,* harmonious unity with the Whole, I find that their wisdom is reflected beautifully in a few lines by the poet Walt Whitman. He writes, "Was someone asking to see the soul? See your own shape and countenance, persons, substances, beasts, the trees, the running rivers, the rocks and sands."

Night Rainbows

The island of Moloka'i is one of the least developed in the Hawaiian archipelago. On Moloka'i there are no traffic lights and everyone knows everyone else. When I visit, I am always welcomed warmly, and I have learned much from the quiet, gentle, and knowing people there, who are sometimes called "the people of the night rainbow." The night rainbow refers to a beautiful, unusual rainbow that forms around the moon. It has a rich purple hue with hundreds of shades of blue mixed in, and it is believed that this "moon-bow" is a signal from the ancestors to remember *aloha* and *lokahi.*

As I sat one evening with one of my friends on Moloka'i, she shared with me an explanation of *aloha* which she said taught the lesson of unity, harmony, and transcendence. Here is what she said:[17]

"*Aloha* is being part of all and all being part of me. When there is pain, it is my pain. When there is joy, it is mine also. I respect all this as part of the Creator and part of me. I will not willfully harm anyone or anything. When food is needed, I will take only my need and explain why it is being taken. The Earth, the sky, the sea are mine to care for, to cherish, and to protect. This is Hawaiian. This is *lokahi.* This is *aloha*."

Aunty Betty's Blessing

Whenever I attend a Hawaiian meeting, whether for business, education, or religious purposes, *lokahi* is a focus of the meeting. One of the most revered Hawaiian *kupuna* is Aunty Betty Jenkins, who organizes and directs popular and instructive meetings in Hawai'i. She is a majestic woman and stands tall and proud in front of the group. Even when she is addressing rooms full of politicians and professional people, she speaks with the firm voice and manner of a strict elementary school teacher. If the room is not quiet and ready to begin the meeting on time, she usually shouts, "*hui*," Hawaiian slang for "Quiet down and come be together!" When the room falls silent, she softly says "*ho'i mai*," which means "come back again," and signals the group to come back to their origins and remember the joy of life.

Those who have attended Aunty Betty's meetings know what comes next. Ritual is key to Polynesian life, a way of connecting with the past and bringing it into the present with respect and love. Ritual is the way that all three approaches to *lokahi*—personal, interpersonal, and transpersonal—are integrated. The *hula* celebrates personal unity and awareness of the body as connected to the earth and all bodies past and present, and is often part of the rituals. *Chant* calls people together in interpersonal connection, again not only with one another but with the ancestors and nature. *Pule,* or prayer, promotes transpersonal connection by helping participants retreat inward enough to reach outward to find their soul among all other souls and to connect with God on the horizon of their existence.

As *kumu* (teacher), Aunty Betty facilitates the three levels of connection in a simple gesture followed by everyone in the audience. She closes her eyes, and all eyes in the room close with her. In a clear voice, she holds her hands in front of her, palms up as if welcoming someone, and says, "*Lokahi* is." The participants join her in harmony, almost singing. Though we cannot see because our eyes are closed too, we know that Aunty Betty's hands have slowly formed a Polynesian triangle in front of her heart. We do the same. She sings out, "Unity between God, man, and the *'aina,*" and we sing with her as all of our hands extend upward to God, inward to our heart, and downward toward the *'aina*.

The Unifying Power of Ritual

English scientist Rupert Sheldrake has researched a phenomenon he calls *morphogenic fields*.[18] He says that the so-called laws of nature are not unchanging givens but patterns of occurrence that become stronger as these events are repeated. These "recurring patterns" are like evolutionary habits because the more often an event happens, the more likely it is to occur in the future.[19]

In effect, Aunty Betty is a connection with these morphogenic fields. Her *lokahi* ceremony and the hula, chant, and prayer that surround it are ways of connecting the past with the present and sending it along into the future. Polynesian rituals such as hers are the means of guaranteeing that we never have to be alone—if we follow the cultural habit of sacred ritual, all those of the past can be with us now and forever.

Modern Research in Lokahi

Rupert Sheldrake has proposed seven experiments that he thinks could change the world.[20] I mention these experiments here because each one is an example of the magical power of *lokahi.* Even by proposing these experiments, Sheldrake warns us against being so sure of our Western scientific selves that we turn away from the study of the potential healing power of unity, harmony, and connection in our daily lives.

Sheldrake's seven experiments are designed to shed light on seven known phenomena that reflect personal, interpersonal, and transpersonal connection. They are:

1. The power of pets to know when their owners are returning
2. The homing and migrational patterns of birds
3. The ability of insect colonies to communicate as if of "one mind"
4. The ability of individuals to know when they are being stared at from behind
5. So-called "phantom limb sensations"
6. The everchanging (inconstant), fundamental "constants" of nature that are the basis for all statistical calculations and experiments
7. The impact of belief of scientists on their data and the fact that, despite double-blind studies, experimenters tend to find what they expect and believe

It is possible, of course, that experiments conducted in any or all of these areas will never be able to explain the nature of these events. Sheldrake suggests, however, that if we are wise and open enough to free ourselves from the "useless is worthless," objective constraints of Western science or dependence on the more mystical, introspective Eastern approaches, we may be able to construct simple daily life experiments that do not rely on statistics or mysticism but on our personal senses. These more democratic "in-home commonsense-observation" studies could be added to the "in-the-lab" controlled studies. As a result, we might see that there is indeed a seventh sense that connects and influences all of us. If a few families design and do their own experiments to see, for example, if dogs do forecast the arrival of their owners, and if we are open-minded enough to consider their findings in addition to traditional lab findings, the entire limited paradigm of how things work in our world may be altered forever. Perhaps, as Polynesians believe, all things think, feel, and communicate in ways we have not yet dreamed of, and Eastern and Western approaches are not too separate from one another to embrace.

Lokahi Ha'awina (Unity Lesson)

To personally, interpersonally, and transpersonally experience more harmonious unity in your daily life, take a few minutes to assess your *lokahi.*

Try the following exercises and write down your responses. Check back on your record to see if you are connecting sufficiently to practice the pleasure prescription in your own life.

Personal Connection: Lie down and scan your entire body from the top of your head to the bottom of your feet. Listen for messages from your body. Don't censor your body's reports, just attend to each and every signal it is sending, both pleasurable and negative. Tell someone else what your body has to say to you today and ask if they have received any of the same messages from their body. Then, decide to take some action based on these "body bulletins." For example, if you keep having headaches, don't just take aspirin. Ask your body what is wrong and do something about it. You may find your body needs quiet time alone, a warm bath, some exercise, or for you to stop drinking so much soda pop. If you are eating antacids like candy, ask your stomach what, how, and with whom you should be eating to make it happier and less disruptive.

Interpersonal Connection: Spend at least five minutes a day sitting quietly with someone. Don't try to make a connection, just let it happen. Don't discuss problems, just be quiet together. After your quiet time together, talk about this experience, and you will see just how powerful the seventh sense can be in creating a connection beyond your physical and psychic senses.

Transpersonal Connection: Select one ritual to practice every day, without fail. A prayer, a dance, singing a little song together with your family, saying grace before a meal, and sitting in the same chairs around the table are rituals that others have chosen and enjoyed.

As you put more meaningful rituals in your life, you will feel the presence of all of those who went before and the joy of knowing that *lokahi,* all connections, are forever.

Chapter Nine

THE POWER OF PLEASANTNESS—NO BLISS, NO GAIN

'Olu'olu: Agreeableness, to be expressed with pleasantness
"Puehu li'ili'i ka lehu o kapuahi"
(Ashes fly into the cook's eyes when he blows on the fire)

Your phone awakens you late at night with a wrong number and the caller slams the receiver in your ear. A teenager roars by in his car with the stereo blasting. After taking much too long, your waiter rudely brings the wrong order. A driver cuts you off in traffic and flashes a vulgar gesture. Someone roughly bumps into you in the grocery store but says nothing. After you have been waiting a long time in line, another person cuts right in front of you. What do you think, how do you feel, and what do you do about these and the other annoyances of modern life?

What is your most immediate reaction to frustration? Would the person who knows you best say that you are quick-tempered, fly off the handle easily, and tend to say nasty or mean things? Would that person say that you get angry when you are slowed down by others' mistakes, or become easily annoyed when you are not given credit for doing good work?[1] Are life's annoyances little bothers to you, or total bliss blockers?

Check your *'olu'olu* (agreeableness) subtest score on the Aloha Test. Remember, the higher your score, the *less* you are living by the pleasure prescription. Compare your score to that of the Polynesian control group, who averaged 3, and the Five-and-Fivers, who averaged 17. However, be careful in interpreting this and your other *aloha* scores. We all have a watchful chaperon looking over our shoulder when we take tests, and we often try to impress that chaperon with how "good" we are rather than answering truthfully.

Most of us living in this crowded, hectic, anonymous civilization we call "the rat race" feel angry almost every day. If the situations described above just roll off you, your natural pleasure system can easily bounce back. If they are accumulating aggravations that repeatedly elicit the urgency response (when they happen *and* when you reflect on them), your health is being burned away by the heat of your chronic hostility.

An *'olu'olu* subtest score higher than 5 indicates that you harbor sufficient hostility and express aggression often enough to interfere with your natural neurohormonal pleasure pathways. As a result, you are putting your cardiovascular system at risk, and significantly lowering your immunity and the immunity of those nearest you.

The Components of Hostility

The Minnesota Multiphasic Personality Inventory (MMPI), made up of many subtests, is one of the most widely used personality inventories. The "Hostility" subtest of the MMPI is the most useful for predicting increased risk of disease and death.[2] Other tests of hostility, like the one developed by cardiologist Dr. Redford Williams, from which I adapted some of the above aggravation items and the *'olu'olu* section of the Aloha Test, have been widely used in seminars and workshops.[3] All these tests seem to have strong face validity, in that many who take them report that their scores accurately reflect how much anger they carry with them day to day.

My professional experience with the *'olu'olu* subtest, the MMPI Hostility Scale, and Williams' "Hostility Questionnaire" indicates that there are three components of hostility that put us at risk for illness and loss of pleasure. The word *hostility* refers to malevolence, unfriendliness, antagonism, and feeling that other people are the enemy. Polynesians call hostility *paio,* which means a way of thinking, feeling, and behaving that does not bring joy to anyone and is composed of mental, emotional, and physical experiences of anger.

Hostility is a dangerous combination of cynicism, anger, and aggression. It includes a distrusting attitude, an agitated and defensive emotional state, and the aggressive expression of these thoughts and feelings through internal and external language and behaviors. In short, hostility can be seen as revenging against yourself the mistakes of others.

Wasted Heartbeats

Hostility is the exact opposite of happiness, and the heat of anger is the furthest emotional state from the healthy glow of pleasure. The research is clear: a hot head overheats the heart. Contrary to popular myth, suppressing anger is not a risk for heart disease, but overt hostility increases your chances for a heart attack five-fold![4]

Psychologist Martin Seligman suggests that each heart, like any mechanical pump, has a preset limit or rating.[5] This rating tells how many beats the pump can make before it wears out. Your heart pump rating is determined not only by nature but also by diet and exercise, but basically every heart has it limits. Exceed them and you burn out your pump. While joyful exercise temporarily raises your heart rate, it lowers it over time and actually results in saved heart beats in the long term. Expressing anger, however, uses up heart beats more quickly than any other emotion and only serves to set the rate of beating upward.[6] It is your choice as to how you would like to spend your beats.

Recent research shows that people diagnosed with heart disease who suppress their anger or depression, called the *Type D personality,* may die sooner than people who express their emotions.[7] The "D," sometimes seen as representing "depressed," is a fourth personality pattern added alongside the so-called Type A personality, hostile and time-pressured, cardiac-disease prone; Type B personality, more relaxed, less hostile, and therefore more vascularly healthy; and Type C or "cancer-prone" personality, who supposedly suppress anger and therefore become more vulnerable to body cells growing out of control. Patients who suppress their emotions are almost four times more likely to die of heart disease than those who do not. The key, however, is not to rant and rave in anger but to be aware of one's feelings and confess them clearly to yourself and others. The social isolation that results from being out of touch with one's emotions, being unwilling or unable to share true feelings, or not making the effort to calmly share feelings (including anger) is a major health-risk factor. Reluctance to vent anger is not. Aristotle summed up a balanced approach to expressing emotions when he wrote, "Anyone can become angry—that is easy, but to be angry with the right person, to the right degree, at the right time, for the right purpose, and in the right way—this is not easy."

The choice is yours. You can spend your heartbeats wisely and healthily or you can squander them in angry, ventilating outbursts.

A Profile of Anger

Humans are the angriest of animals and anger is probably one of our oldest emotions. Anger is one reason human beings and not some gentler animal dominates the planet. The great danger in anger is the seductive effectiveness in delivering a sense of short-term victory and protection of one's perceived territory. Unfortunately, to the victor also goes the heart bypass.

Recently I lectured at a meeting of heart transplant recipients, one of the most moving gatherings I have attended. As a transplant recipient myself, I spoke to the recipients, their families, and the donor families, as both patient and doctor.[8] At the end of the meeting a very sad thing happened that illustrates the importance of *'olu'olu.*

After my lecture, a man with gray hair and deep wrinkles in his forehead approached me. Quickly and loudly he told me he was a transplant recipient and had received his new heart four years earlier, after his own severe heart failure. He said, "I got my new heart from her son," and gestured toward the woman standing next to him, without looking at her. I noticed that his face was red, his pupils dilated, and his fists clenched. He said, "I liked your lecture, but these other damn lectures just enrage me. I'd like to kick their asses. They ramble on, waste my time, and they don't know a damn thing. I wish they would all have heart failure like I did. Damn them." He threw his meeting program on the ground and walked away, muttering more profanities.

The mother whose son had donated his heart to this angry man began to sob almost uncontrollably. I embraced her, and through her tears she shared an important lesson about life.

"My son was such a happy, loving, pleasant person. I never heard an angry word from him. The night of his car accident when we had to decide to donate his heart, we prayed that the person getting it would treat it as lovingly and gently as he did. When I see that man wasting my son's gift, it makes me so very sad. That man's heart didn't fail, *he* failed his heart. And now he's failing my son's heart too!"

I consoled the woman and tried to assure her that one angry outburst did not mean the recipient of her son's heart would not treasure and protect his gift. I told her that the heart was new to him and would take time to send the pleasant and gracious energy of her son through all of the man's body systems. I told her that perhaps this was the perfect recipient for her son's heart because, like the Tin Man in *The Wizard of Oz,* he so badly needed a warm and loving heart. I told her about the amazing reports of transplant recipients who often begin to dream the same dreams as a deceased donor and that the joyful, peaceful energy of her son would likely eventually warm the heart of this angry man.

The mother seemed relieved, but I know she still prayed that her son's gift of life and love would not be wasted in a body still governed by an undisciplined, selfish, and hostile brain. I worried along with her about how the angry recipient was burning out his new pump. A new healthy heart placed under the control of a angry brain could fail just as surely as his original equipment.

Despite our efforts to transplant or bypass the heart after we have burned it out, the real secret is to operate our pump as pleasantly as we can. Perhaps, if we all thought of our heart and our body as "transplant recipients" given a second chance, we would take more joy in our gift and find more happy years in our living.

The Anatomy of Anger

The three components of hostility (cynicism, anger, and aggression) can be reduced by practicing the pleasure prescription.[9] Keeping our heart healthy requires distinguishing between these three aspects of hostility, understanding the myths about anger, and following the Polynesian lessons for bringing *'olu'olu* into our daily life. The first step is to understand that anger is a process. By being aware of the thoughts that trigger it and the reactions that express it, we can determine the actions that will alleviate it.

Don't think like an angry ape Contrary to myth, our primate ancestors were not peaceful vegetarian apes whose big brains eventually helped them make better tools. They were more like the monkeys in *2001: A Space Odyssey:* carnivorous apes, the most fit of whom survived because they created weapons and directed their use with explosive, urgent aggression.[10] These angry apes were governed by their territorial imperative—and our modern world reflects the nature of our angry ancestors.

Stress is a result of cynical thinking. When we perceive a threat, our brain's defensive competitiveness tells us that our "territory" is being invaded; this sets off our urgency response. We will never reduce stress by relaxation techniques alone or by just silencing or emptying our brain of its urgent thoughts. We have to learn to replace these thoughts with more agreeable and pleasant ones.

To calm yourself, first recognize how your brain thinks about the world. Take your *'olu'olu* subtest seriously and follow the pleasure prescription for hostility: *don't express it, don't suppress it, confess it!* This is the healthiest way to deal with anger. "Confessing" anger means understanding that you still have an angry inner ape and being alert for the thought that will set it off. This preliminary thought, no matter what its specifics, always translates to "Who do you think you are, trespassing against me?" Those who become easily angry have a short fuse. They slip right past the first thought to quick action.

Our body becomes angry even before we "know" it in our mind. It does this by way of an escalating heart rate, a flood of stress hormones, and a tensing of muscles. Being on the alert for your brain's tendency toward rigid territoriality is a key step in developing *'olu'olu.*

Trespass thoughts are alien to the Polynesian way of thinking. Since they do not think in terms of ownership, they do not have "territory" to protect, and so they are not triggered to fight. Unfortunately, many Westerners mistake the pleasantness of Polynesian people for naïveté or passivity. On the other hand, many Westerners believe that things, and even other people, can be their property, so they are in a constant state of domain defensiveness that easily and quickly translates to anger and aggression.

Let your body calm your brain You don't have to do anything for a trespass thought to get your body ready to fight. Your brain automatically takes charge and tells your body what to do and feel. It will do all aggressive work for you. It will see that your sympathetic, or "hot," nervous system goes into action; your muscles mobilize for assault; your blood pressure and heart rate increase to make more blood available for fighting; and less blood flows to the brain to be used by the mind for non-battle-oriented thinking. Your body's neurochemistry will become one of instant, widespread, systemic hormonal hate. Your brain will shut down your immune system, because it is more concerned with hurting than healing and less about a long life than staying alive now. It will invigorate you with its urgency response, pumping endorphins throughout your body for a hormonal high that suppresses any distractions and keeps you focused on the situation at hand and motivated for meanness.

How can you tell if your angry ape is on the loose?

Watch out for anger ulcers and hostility munchies. To see the extent of anger damage done to our bodies by our brains, count the number of headache, stomach, and bowel medications at your local drugstore. Then count the number of these medications in your home. These anger-signal buffers are "angry ape food"; the greater your supply of such food, the less happy your life will be, and the more likely you will suffer from anger-induced illnesses.

Stomach irritation, gas, and ulcers are manifestations of chronic hostility. Ulcers include holes in the stomach wall (gastric ulcers), the organs around the stomach (peptic ulcers), higher up the digestive system (esophageal ulcers), or at the border of the stomach and the intestines (duodenal ulcers). These are not formed during anger but during recovery from stress. If you are in a chronic state of recovering from anger, you are in a constant state of ulcer formation. No one knows exactly what percent of ulcers are caused by stress, but most researchers are now sure that anger is a leading cause of vulnerability to ulcers or the weakening of the immune system, which in turn helps control the bacteria that cause some ulcers.

When you are angry, your brain doesn't care about digestion. It is more concerned with spitting than swallowing and with mentally, verbally, or even physically killing someone to protect against a real or imagined trespass. The digestive fluid in your stomach is highly acidic, but the lining of your stomach is continually producing layers of protective coating. Like the cells that make up your hair, the cells that make up your digestive system are very fast growing, multiplying in seconds. When you feel very angry and behave aggressively, your brain tells your stomach that it doesn't need those protective cells right now because all your energy is needed for a fight. The neurohormonal alarm is, "Fight, don't feed." So the stomach stops producing the cells for its protective linings.

After the battle is over, your brain may tell your body that it is safe to celebrate its "victory." Meanness-munchies, not unlike the hunger pangs that accompany the use of marijuana, can also follow temper tantrums. So you may have a large and rich victory meal or gorge yourself on junk food. When the strong digestive acids begin to flow again, they encounter stomach lining that has been diminished, so they burn through it and form ulcers.[11]

Don't get your bowels in an uproar. Our bowels are also affected by our anger reaction. Eating is one of our most pleasurable endeavors, and much of what we eat may taste good but is not always completely used by the body. What we don't use is left over in the large intestine after the stomach, bile ducts, and small intestine pick though it. When you get ready to fight for your territory, your brain wants to "dump" all excess baggage so it is lighter and freer to fight.

The language we use when we feel angry reflects what is happening in our body. Yelling out a vulgar word for defecation expresses our brain's desire to jettison the contents of the bowels because they may slow you down in your fight. You can probably analyze your own vocabulary: how often do you use words that express the need to defecate, urinate, or threaten intercourse. You can see the total commandeering of body systems that takes place under the angry brain.

The result of getting your intestines in an uproar is gas, diarrhea, or irritated bowels. Food also moves through the system quickly so the body is not distracted by digestive obligations. This results in an increase of large intestine motility, meaning that everything passes through too quickly for water to be appropriately absorbed. The result is "defense diarrhea." Even more serious results can be irritable bowl disease, which includes colitis, spastic colon, bowel inflammation, constipation, and bowel pain.[12]

Beware people who run hot and cold. As you read in Chapter 6, some of us are born "hot reactors" and compensate for hyposensitivity by seeking intense stimulation, while others are born "cold reactors" who are excitable and try to avoid stimulation."[13] These conditions are states of imbalance, or lack of *pono.* Hot reactors experience many cardiovascular provocations every day. Like traffic that moves over a stretch of highway repeatedly and causes pot holes, the increased and chronic pressure of blood surging through the arteries in response to anger makes tiny nicks in the walls of the vessels. These little scrapes and scratches make good places for the build-up of plaque and, eventually, a clogged artery is the result.

Whether we run hot, looking to pick a fight to turn ourselves on (hot reactor), or fearfully run cold, guarding against conflicts that agitate us (cold reactors), our body's balanced system of oscillation is overstressed by our territorial protectiveness and hyperalertness.

To control your anger-prone brain, pay attention *to* your body, don't medicate away or mask its signals. The body tells you when it is being aggravated by the brain, so use the ACE approach proposed by psychologist Gary Schwartz and outlined in Chapter 8. If you feel your stomach growling in anger, tell your brain you know what is going on. Ask yourself whether or not you want to burn a few holes in your stomach, irritate your bowels, or waste a few more heartbeats defending your physical or emotional territory. If not, sit down, shut up, breath deeply, and tell the brain to calm down.

Don't attack your heart So your brain has told you that what it considers to be your territory has been or might be violated (the thought) and made you emotionally ready to fight (the reaction). Knowing that the body cannot be kept in a state of agitated hostility for too long, the brain encourages you to attack. All your bodily systems made for pleasure are now conscripted for warfare.

The aggression that comes from defensive emotions is seldom modulated. The brain is not concerned with whether or not a threat constitutes a real and present danger. Even if the brain is alerted by a present stimulation resembling a past trespass that took place years ago, it goes through the same motions. The body can be just as aroused by angry reflection as it is in the presence of immediate danger, and our heart and immune system are put at risk not only by present threats but by recollections of past frustrations as well.

No matter how civilized we think we are, what we are doing when we are aggressive is trying to "hurt" or "kill" the trespasser. Unless we have learned the first two ingredients of the pleasure prescription, *ahonui* (patience) and *lokahi* (unity), we quickly abandon *'olu'olu* (pleasantness) in order to attack whomever or whatever is threatening us. And because, as Polynesians believe, all barriers are illusions and we are all one, whenever we attack anyone or anything, we are actually attacking a part of our self.

Aggressive actions follow an identifiable sequence. By simply "putting your mind into" your brain's aggressive cycle, you can interrupt it. So, when you begin to act or speak aggressively, try to remember to stay *F-A-R* from your evolutionary territoriality.

> *F* = *frustration.* Hostility is a reflex of the sense of powerlessness. When we feel impatient and disconnected from the world around us, we feel ineffective. Unless we intentionally practice an abundance of *ahonui* and *lokahi* to increase our threshold of equanimity, we feel completely frustrated. The natural reaction to frustration is aggression.

> *A* = *aggression.* When our brain experiences frustration, it tends to intensify action rather than consider other reactions. As pointed out in Part One, the brain is a reflexive gland and can easily break out in a sweat of toxic hormones that bleed throughout the body. Unless we use our higher consciousness to teach it patience, connection, and pleasantness, it will urge us to exaggerate our actions and lash out at any perceived encroachment on its territory.

> *R* = *regression.* Aggressive behavior never works. Yelling, hitting, and sarcastic put-downs never bring us peace and joy. The frustrated and angry brain causes us to throw tantrums, and we act like children slapping each other in dispute over a pail in a sand box.

The FAR cycle doesn't only take place interpersonally. Our anger-prone brain also gets us into fights with our own thoughts, situations, and things. Consider a simple example: hanging a picture. You begin to hammer the nail, miss, and hit your thumb. At first, you say "ouch." The next time you hit your finger, you begin to feel the frustration of an invasion on your physical territory, time, skin, and picture-hanging self-esteem. So, you grip the nail firmly and decide to hit it even harder. If you miss again, this leads to even more anger and poorer coordination, so you hit your thumb yet again. In irrational, childlike regression, you teach the hammer a lesson by throwing it across the room, swearing at it, and becoming even more upset when it hits a table and damages it. This frustration-aggression-regression cycle takes place on every level of human endeavor from romance to international wars. Remember, such angry living is existing very FAR from a life of Oceanic healthy pleasure.

Ten Myths About Anger

Oceanic thinking results in fewer imaginary boundaries to defend. As any sea-front homeowner will tell you, the ocean is intolerant of barriers. To stop the FAR sequence, try intervening at the first step: the thought. Cultivate thinking about the world in a less territorial way. Ask yourself, "What am I really protecting?" and "Do I want to abuse my body this way?" Clear thinking will reduce hostility. While the hostility response is so rapid that we often act before we think, with practice at patient awareness you will find it easier and easier to overcome angry tendencies.

Here are the ten myths about anger that can lead us to automatic angry actions. Do you believe any of them? After knowing the truth about them, can you put them behind you?

Anger myth 1: Unexpressed anger leads to cancer There is very little research supporting the existence of the so-called "Type C" or cancer-prone personality.[14] It has been speculated that cancer-prone people are unable to express their anger, but studies in this area fail to support this claim.[15] Some recent research shows that "exploders," or persons who have frequent outbursts of temper, have more cancer than non-exploders.[16]

A *kahuna* told me, "Your feelings are not inside you. They are not even yours. They are *ha,* the breath that we all breathe. They are a part of all of us and shared by all of us. You only sample them from time to time. If you ruin them when they go through you by adding anger to them, you eventually poison all of us and everything because you do not live *aloha*."

Anger myth 2: Unexpressed anger raises blood pressure and causes heart disease In fact, the very opposite is true. Expressing anger raises blood pressure and significantly interferes with the efficiency of the heart.[17] The research is clear on this: overt hostile expression is a major threat to your cardiovascular system, and because it drives people away, the resulting isolation also leads to illness.

A Polynesian dancer told me, "I cannot dance if I have been angry. If I have been mean to someone, I will dance meanly, and that will offend the gods. I always *pule* (pray) before I dance and ask to be forgiven for any anger I have sent out to the world and to forgive those who have sent anger to me."

Anger myth 3: Depression is anger turned inward This 80-year-old Freudian fallacy dies hard. Popular psychology still suggests that our emotions work like liquids trapped within our body container. Dam up the flow in any one place and it will flood out in another place. This psychodynamic theory provides a good excuse for aggressive expression, but it is simply not true. Modern research has shown that our emotions are not within us; rather they are a system of interaction with everyone and everything. So when we act aggressively, we are not helpless victims of an emotional plug in our neurohormonal plumbing system. Anger is not depression turned inward or a counter-reaction to poor emotional venting. In fact, PNI research indicates that getting anger out actually worsens depression.[18] Aggression *is,* however, evidence of Delight Deficiency Syndrome. Happy people are not usually aggressive people.

Said a *kupuna*, "I can always tell a very happy person. I just have to look at those around them. I look at the plants in and around their house. Happy people have a happy place."

Anger myth 4: Showing your anger is just being truthful about your emotions Western culture teaches us to be truthful and express our innermost feelings, particularly anger. The problem is that emotions exist to give color to our experiences and often distort and exaggerate them.

Because many of our five basic senses are weak in comparison to those of other species, our brain and our emotions magnify what does get through to us to compensate. Emotions allow us to act powerfully.

How we feel may be honest, but it is not always *truthful*. When we are the most emotional, we can't see truth very well, only the brain's version of reality, and the brain's interpretation is an amplified, biased projection of what it has selected.

A *kahuna* said, "Don't let your emotions be you. They are like the fragrance of flowers, but they are not the flower. They are like music and can motivate you, but they are not the dance. If you were to express your truest emotion, you would always be expressing *aloha*. Don't waste your moments of pleasure by being angry."

Anger myth 5: Showing your anger is how you get justice When we feel frustrated and angry, we are often seeking justice for a perceived trespass. Your brain only sees one side to every issue: its side. As Benjamin Franklin warned, there is always a reason for becoming angry, but seldom a good one. The exaggerated urgency response of anger is not designed to see the world from someone else's point of view, only to protect our personal survival. Anger and the aggression it leads to are self-righteous, not righteous.

A *kupuna* once told me, "The opposite of injustice is not justice; it is *aloha*."

Anger myth 6: You are at your most powerful and effective when you are angry Good, hot anger may help when you are being threatened during a robbery or physical assault, but it is almost useless when it comes to day-to-day life. Anger is an emotion that pals around with guilt, resentment, fear, and hatred. Anger feeds on itself, crippling us intellectually and emotionally when we most need to think clearly. The smoke from the fire of hostility is a neurohormonal haze that blinds us. Saying that we have allowed ourselves to feel angry and upset can be empowering, but accusing someone else of making us angry is an admission of powerlessness.

A *kupuna* said, "Just like the cook who becomes angry with his fire and blows on it very hard, you will get ashes in your eyes and mouth and never be able to see and taste life when you are busy overheating it."

Anger myth 7: Venting your anger prevents violence While the Eastern-Asian mind is not inclined to venting emotions, Western culture stresses expression of almost any feeling, anywhere, anytime. One only has to walk through the corridors of any school and listen to students' language to see how freely emotions, particularly angry ones, are expressed. From our belief in this free expression, we have reaped one of the most violent societies in history. The Polynesian concept that words have *mana,* or energy, is true. Our vocabulary reflects how we live and also helps determine how we live.

A *kupuna* said, "Every word has powerful *mana.* You make the world when you speak, so speak only with *aloha.*"

Anger myth 8: Parents should get their anger out with one another in order to be better parents Social and health researchers know that perhaps the greatest single risk to children's health and happiness is turmoil between parents.[19] When you fight with your spouse, you may get short-term justice for yourself, but the legacy for your children will be injustice. All major studies of family life clearly support one warning: never, never fight in front of your children.[20]

A *kupuna* said, "Parents should show their *keiki* (children) how to live *aloha.* If they fight and argue, they are raising warriors and they are hurting all of us."

Anger Myth 9: A good anger explosion clears the air This is the catharsis theory of anger, which suggests that a good fight once in a while naturally cleanses and revitalizes a relationship.[21] Unfortunately, just the opposite is true. Expressing anger always amplifies it. It contaminates relationships and eventually drains them of their *mana*. Anger leads to contempt, contempt leads to disgust, and there is nothing quite like disgust to prevent a life of shared pleasure.

A Hawaiian canoe paddler said, "We really watch out when we sail our canoes. We know we are creating our own wind, so we don't want to become angry and send out storms that we will have to sail through."

Anger myth 10: Nice gals and guys finish last This myth is about power. It says that the more anger you express, the more success you will achieve through your assertive confidence and resulting competitive edge. The trouble with edges is that you can fall over them; angry people get angrier and angrier in addictive dependence on the urgency response. Assertiveness training courses flourished in the last decade, but the research again contradicts popular psychology. It is clear that those who confess their anger in the most pleasant, appropriate, and socially acceptable way are the most successful in all areas of life.[22]

A *kahuna* said, "If you want to stay healthy, be nice. If you want to heal, be kind. If you want to help everyone be healthy, be very, very tender."

Emotional Bomb Disposal: "Confessing" Your Anger

How much pleasure you derive from your life is in direct proportion to the degree that you do not express anger. The Euroamerican way of dealing with anger is to direct it at relationships. It is based on the "attribution error" that says if someone else is angry it is due to his personality, but if you yourself are angry it is due to the circumstances. On the other hand, the Eastern way of dealing with anger often leads to a passive-aggressive withdrawal from intimate relationships. As you have already read, the Oceanic Third Way is to "confess" anger rather than "express" or vent it.

Confessing anger involves admitting to yourself and those around you that you are not thinking, feeling, or behaving appropriately when you are angry. You can't do this in an emotional vacuum, so learning the principle of *ha'aha'a* (modest humbleness, which is discussed in Chapter 10) is a big part of this process.

If you scored comparatively high on the *'olu'olu* section of the Aloha Test, it may be helpful if you think of yourself as what psychologist Martin Seligman calls an "emotional bomb disposer."[23] You know that you can explode emotionally, and so you try to be aware of the cynical thinking that lights your affective fuse and the body signals that let you know the fuse has been lit.[24] In this way, you can begin to take steps to defuse the bomb.

'Olu'olu Ha'awina (Agreeableness Lesson)

One of the Polynesians in my interview group told of what she called the *'a'i* (neck) anger-control technique, which was taught to her by her great-grandmother.

When your brain alerts you that there has been a trespass, gently feel the side of your neck for your carotid pulse. If your pulse starts to increase, your brain is regressing, your heart is being stressed, and your immune system is at risk. Remember the first of Thomas Jefferson's ten canons of conduct: "When angry, count ten before you speak. If very angry, a hundred."

Next, put your hand down and count out ten slow, deep breaths. Take your pulse again. Don't deal with the perceived trespass until your pulse has slowed.

Although the brain often tells the body what to do, the body also communicates with the brain. Listen to it and let it help you to slow down and stop fighting.

We not only behave as we feel, we can come to feel as we behave. Never deal with anger when your body is in attack mode. If you want to deal with a trespass, write it down, write down what your brain thinks is its source, and then take a break. Come back to the issue days later when your body is calmer and your brain is less defensive. Remember, unresolved anger-states escalate much faster than new anger, so you are best to sleep on it, then discuss it. If you think you don't have time to sleep on it, go for a walk before you get back to the problem. The fuse of anger flickers for a very long time.

Psychologist Daniel Goleman warns that when we are angry, we become emotionally hijacked.[25] When you are not flooded with anger hormones, you can try to be the rational person you are when you're not angry. Polynesians say, "Always act like the person you wish you were instead of the person you say others make you be."

We all "lose it" sometimes. The key to pleasantness is to not get angry with yourself because you get angry. Like unhappiness, we all must have our angry times and can learn from them. Here is the way to pleasantness as expressed by a Hawaiian *kumu hula* (teacher of hula):

"The pleasurable life is a pleasant life. Anger gives no life, it only takes it. It insults the gods. It insults the ancestors and makes the land hurt. Your anger spills onto the soil and rocks and flows out into the ocean and pollutes it and kills the fish. You will end up swimming in your own pollution. Never express your anger, but always learn from it by confessing it. Sometimes the *aumakua* will tease and test you and seem to make you angry, but they are watching to see if you are living *aloha.* When you are angry, you have no aloha because you have no room for it. No one is ever happy that they were angry. You are not important enough for people or God to spend time trying to make you angry. A Chinese sugarcane worker once told me, if you are patient in one moment of anger, you will escape a hundred days of sorrow."

Chapter Ten

THE MAGIC OF MODESTY—SILENCING THE SELF, SAVING THE SOUL

Ha'aha'a: Humility to be expressed with modesty
"Ku'ia ka hele a ka na'au ha'aha'a."
(A humble person walks carefully so
he will not hurt those about him.)

"Wow!" yelled the young Tahitian boy as he splashed to the surface of the sparkling clear ocean. He pushed his swimming mask to his forehead and threw his arms in the air. "I almost forgot to come up for air. I got so close to that shark I could feel his warmth. I lost complete track of time and that I was underwater," he said. "Man, I've never felt so alive. I was really with that shark. That's as near to real living as it gets—a real near-life experience."

In our modern world, unfortunately, such "near-life experiences" receive less attention than so-called "near-death experiences." These NDEs, reports of emotional elation from persons who have been resuscitated after their heart has stopped, should more accurately be called "before-death enlightenment." We often seem to realize the glory of living only after confronting the reality that we may not live for long and that our individual sense of our physical self is not infinite. We struggle to perpetuate the self, yet ironically we seem unable to take full joy in our seven senses, our many selves, and the planet that we are a part of.

Ultimately, we cannot have a pleasurable outlook on life if the only thing we look out for is our self. We cannot see beauty if we only look within our expectations and not for the simple and subtle opportunities life gives. When we are self-involved, we fail to hear the sounds of nature because we only hear the noisy chatter of our brain. When we think only of "me," we miss out on the tender touch of others. We fail to smell the fresh, earthy air or taste the natural nectar of food when we think only of how to avoid toxins and lower our cholesterol and fat levels. We fail to be open to the ebbing and flowing of psychic energies around us when we succumb to the brain's commands to acquire all the physical stuff to which our self feels entitled. When our basic six senses are isolated and employed only for "survival," our natural seventh sense for pleasure, meaning, and connection begins to atrophy.

The Self-Efficacy Epidemic

Researcher and scientist Lewis Thomas believes that the need to fill our days doing something to protect our health and avoid death has become endemic in our culture. He writes, "Americans are obsessed with their health. [The negative side is that it gives] . . . the impression that we are constructed as a kind of imperfect organism—fallible and fragile and likely to collapse unless we are propped up by what it is now fashionable to call the health-care system."[1]

It is no coincidence that one of the best-selling books of the last decade is titled *The Seven Habits of Highly Effective People.*[2] It has sold more than 6 million copies in North America alone and has been translated into 28 languages. Its author, Steven Covey, taps into our pathology of unhappiness and need for high self-competence. Covey states, "It's not nature or nurture; it's our choice. We are a product of our choices. I believe some people have made a choice to follow an evil path."[3] He proudly adds, "I cannot remember any unhappiness in my life."[4] Perhaps because of his own very fortunate life, Covey seems to imply that a childhood without love or familial stability is the choice of the child, and cancer is the choice of the patient. The Oceanic philosophy does not accept such an "all-empowered-self" model.

Ironically, the very unhappiness that leads so many people to buy hundreds of self-help books each year is caused by disappointment due in part to the misleading messages of these books. True, sustaining pleasure comes from allowing ourselves the joy of a full experience—of both the good and bad in our life. Both states are a natural and *inevitable* part of being alive. The Oceanic way teaches that "self-help" is impossible because we are not separate beings. Our best lessons come not from trying to be happy but from giving in and being aware of our human nature and the nature of life, so that happiness and health may happen to us.

Contrary to the popular, so-called "self-empowerment psychology," not all that happens to us in our life is due to the choices we make, any more than a whale beached by a tidal wave chose to swim in the wrong sea. We are a *part* of a naturally chaotic world, not highly effective and all-powerful controllers of it. A tornado is no less beautiful in its majestic power than a quiet waterfall. The pleasure prescription is based on the assumption that we are not always effective, do not always have choices, and are often powerless to do much about what happens to us beyond enjoying it as much as possible

Another paradox of pleasure is that it seems that we are most alive when we are least aware that we are alive. We are never more vitally connected with all of human experience and our world than when we are less consumed with who we are and how we can be more "effective" and "happier."

When I lecture, my audiences are often surprised when I tell them that their greatest fear, the end of their physical sense of self, is actually their greatest pleasure. As I go on to describe the most pleasurable moments of our lives, they begin to agree that losing one's self is indeed the best way to enjoy being alive. Some examples of less ego and more life include making love so tenderly and fully that you become one with your lover; lying on the grass looking up at the vast skies and billions of stars that contain the same elements found in your own bones; laughing so hard that you say the something funny that set you off is "killing you"; or the sudden silencing of your sense of self-awareness when faced with the grandeur and grace of a great beast.

Recall one of your own near-life experiences. Think of one of the best times you have ever had in your life. Recall a circumstance in which you felt so completely connected and involved with what you were doing that your worries and obligations became irrelevant and you lost all sense of self. Think of that time when you basked in the wonder of being alive and felt the wonder that Sir Francis Bacon called "the seed of knowledge and the reflection of the purest form of pleasure." What was the moment of your life when you marveled most at the glory of your opportunity to be alive? I suggest that your own "near-life experiences" are the result of the Third Way, of being less self-aware of the independent ego.

Epiphanies and the Epiorganism

An *epiphany* is the sudden manifestation of the meaning and purpose of the gift of life. It is an "Aha!" experience, an insight into the essential nature and essence of living. It happens when we transcend the urgency response and the strivings of the selfish brain to experience essential connection with everything and everyone. Epiphany causes us to feel wiser and more alive. We may feel that not only have we made a connection, but we, as the created, have become more aware of being One with the Creator.

Loss of self is the key component of epiphany. We are made more alive by the death of the narcissism that our brain promotes in our daily living. We become less a solitary organism and more an *epiorganism.* Epiorganism is a biological term for being a part of a system operating with an energy, meaning, and purpose far beyond the individuals that compose it. During epiphany, the self is silenced, and we become a part of a complex whole experiencing life and functioning as one organism.

Mythologist Joseph Campbell suggests that there are only two paths to enlightenment: suffering and epiphany. Both of these natural and necessary human experiences are profoundly influenced by our willingness to give up self-focus in order to develop our ability to master the fourth element of *aloha*, which is *ha'aha'a* (a Polynesian word which contains the "aha!" factor in it).

As you will read in Chapter 15, suffering is essential to pleasure because it is one of the two ways we learn the purpose, meaning, and potential joys of living. When we seek and find social support and distraction from the focus on our self, which often results from physical or mental pain, the degree of suffering may be reduced and chances for learning greatly increased. Medical painkillers work by artificially silencing the self: numbing the brain to lessen the physical stimulation causing our discomfort. This treatment doesn't promote learning, only anesthesia. Making more intimate connections with others and the world is another way to lessen pain, through increasing feelings of joy and the hormonal changes that accompany it. This *ha'aha'a* approach has the advantage of promoting learning and intensifying awareness.

Polynesians refer to epiphany as *malamalama,* and they call the process of becoming more wisely and viscerally connected with the world *na'auao.* They teach that the wisdom gained from *malamalama* derives from collective consciousness and the ability to feel joy in being totally connected with a present task, thought, or interaction. A Polynesian man told me, "Our *na'auao* (enlightenment) is not 'getting our act together,' it is really feeling like we are acting together."

As you reflect on your own near-life experiences, you may discover that your most pervasive sense at those times was a feeling of loss of your self-awareness. Each of the five components of *aloha* requires the other four to give it its power, so the joy of *ha'aha'a,* the minimal self, can only be achieved by practicing *ahonui* (patience), *lokahi* (unity), *'olu'olu* (agreeableness), and *akahai* (gentleness).

Remember,

> A hurried self (lack of *ahonui*) is too rushed to pause for the simple pleasures of life.
>
> A disconnected self (too little *lokahi*) is too lonely to share and enjoy beauty when it is seen and felt.
>
> An angry self (too little *'olu'olu*) is too adversarial to be open to the subtle invitations to pleasure that surround it every day.
>
> An aggressive self (too little *akahai*) is too defensive to be open to the delights offered up by those around it.

The Pleasure of Flowing

Living in the middle of the largest ocean on earth and floating on the sea for many of their days, Polynesians have learned the art of flowing. In order to survive in their island communities, they have to live together as an epiorganism, to "go with the flow" of their everyday island existence. They cannot afford to be selfish because ego-centered independence can destroy their island home. They lead a life characterized by what Mihaly Csikszentmihalyi calls *flow,* the same characteristics of behaviors, thoughts, and feelings that are most likely to lead to the epiphanies or *malamalama* that bring a meaningful, joyful, healthy life.[5]

Csikszentmihalyi identifies eight factors that lead to maximal pleasure. Compare each of these eight "flow factors" with your own near-life experiences and you will probably find that you were much nearer to being truly alive because you were in a state of flow.

1. The fun of finishing You have a sense you can complete the task. A common complaint is that our work is never done and there is no end in sight. We look at the piles on our desk, search through our daily planners, and feel that no matter how hard we work, there is always something waiting to be taken care of. A flow experience is free of these endless goals and is characterized by an understanding that whatever we are doing has a clear end point.

A Polynesian woman explained this in terms if her work making leis: "When I am making my lei, I enjoy seeing the end before I begin. As I work around the circle and add each flower, there are sometimes hundreds of blossoms to thread with my lei needle. I know that I will finish my lei, but I don't work just to get done. The lei finishes itself when I come back to where I started. I get lost in my lei and we sort of finish together."

2. The fun of focus You are able to concentrate completely on the task. Because much of modern life requires we do many things at once, we often find our brain interrupting our train of thought. While we knit, dance, or make love, the selfish brain interrupts, saying, "Don't forget you have to get up early tomorrow" or "You have more important things to do." When we allow ourselves to tune into what we are doing while we are doing it and without distractions, we fall into an enjoyable life rhythm.

The role of total concentration on a given activity is epitomized by this Hawaiian man's statement: "When I make my fishhooks, I think only about my fishhooks. I think about how smooth they are becoming, how the angles are coming out, and what color they are taking on. I don't think about how I will use them or how many fish I will catch. When I'm a hook maker, I'm a hook maker. When I'm a fisherman, I fish."

3. The pleasure of purpose The task at hand has clear goals. When we begin to flow and lose our self in our activity, joy comes from realizing exactly what must be done and how we will know when it is finished. On the other hand, working hard with no clearly definable goals or end point results in stress.

The fishhook maker shared his joy of clear purpose in this way, "You can rub and rub on your fishhook, and in a way it is never done. But somehow you know when it is done enough. You feel it, and that feeling always guides you. My goal is to help the fishhook get out of the bone I am carving, and it will let me know exactly when it is ready if I listen and look. That's what keeps me going for hours. I rub and carve until it is as finished as that hook can be, not as finished as other hook makers think it should be or other hooks may seem to be."

4. Joyful physical feedback The task provides immediate sensory information. In our age of electronic communication, direct, immediate physical and personal feedback is rare. Those activities that directly stimulate the six senses lead to a pleasurable seventh sense manifestation of flow that make activities enjoyable.

The floral lei maker poetically offered an example of this physical aspect of flow. "I can feel each petal caress my fingers when I place the flower on my needle. I can smell the beautiful scents and I can hear the flower tell me how to put it on the string. I talk to the flowers the whole time. I sing and rock and let the lei help me make it. Making a lei is like a hula. You have to dance with it."

5. Being in comfortable command You have a profound sense of control. One of the greatest threats to the bliss response and the sense of flow is that it can be blocked by the feeling of being out of control. Much of our life seems to be under the control of forces we cannot see. How often have you heard someone explain, "There's not much I can do about it"? When we flow, however, we feel *in control* without being *controlling,* because we have cut our task down to size and are alert for our impact and efficacy in that limited framework. Our accomplishments and failures are like children for whom we cannot take full credit but for whom we are still responsible and accountable.

The Polynesian fishhook maker addressed his understanding of this control issue: "When I make my hook, I feel that I have complete control of my whole life, because I am not trying to be the boss. My hands move in their own way as I pray, chant, or sing. I never feel so much in charge as when I am working on my hooks. That's because I am part of everything, going with the flow and not just trying to direct it. I feel the power of nature through me, but I don't feel like I am the one who is powerful. I'm like a palm tree bending in the trade winds."

6. Recreational work Your actions seem effortless. Flow activities are never hard work, but they are often very intense work. In a state of flow, the person seems to "become" the task rather than trying to "do" it.

The Polynesian lei maker you have been hearing from also works as an airline desk clerk. She finds her lei making effortless, but not her airline work. "I don't even know the lei is finished until my fingers tell me that I have come full circle. It's funny, but I feel much more rested after I have worked for hours with my lei than if I just did nothing. I feel much more calm and energized after I have worked for hours than if I just sit or when I work at the airport counter selling tickets."

7. Timeless pleasure You lose all sense of time. When we flow, minutes seem like hours and hours like minutes. We may forget to eat or even to go to the bathroom. Those around us may have to remind us of our obligations as we drift blissfully into whatever it is we are doing.

The fishhook maker is no stranger to the timelessness of flowing, "A tourist asked me how I could work so long on one hook. He said he had driven by in the morning and seen me and there I was still working in the same place on the same hook when he drove by at sunset. I told him I had never thought about it. When I make my hook, there is no time. Only the darkness stops me, and sometimes the moon allows me to go on."

8. Selfless pleasure Concern for self disappears. Silencing self is a key part of the ecstasy of flowing. *Ha'aha'a* is the result of flow because the activity or interaction totally engrosses us and banishes all feelings of selfishness. After the flow activity, your sense of an authentic, connected self emerges again. You are even more profoundly centered and aware of your interrelated attachment than before the activity.

The lei maker showed her *ha'aha'a* when she said, "When I'm with my lei, I'm never hungry, sleepy, or thirsty. A whole other sense takes over [her seventh sense] and I myself don't seem to exist. When the lei says we are finished for now, I feel refreshed and like the lei has woven me into a new person. I feel very good about the lei because the lei seems to feel good about me."

Csikszentmihalyi's Western research on flow and its positive effect on health goes hand-in-hand with what the Polynesians have taught for centuries: We get something out of life when we are least aware of trying to get the most out of it. We get the most for ourselves by giving of ourselves. This is the lesson of *ha'aha'a*.

The Joylessness of Selfing

Now that you have read about flowing and feeling the joy of *ha'aha'a*, consider the other side of flowing, which I call *selfing*. Think of the worst times in your life. Which periods of your life would you not want to go through again? These times are likely to be ones in which you were most profoundly aware of your individual self.

Austrian psychiatrist Victor Frankl pointed out that happiness cannot be pursued; it must ensue as the unintended side effect of one's personal dedication to a course greater than oneself.[6] Our cultural focus on self-development and one of our greatest hopes—the wish for a better and longer life—have resulted in one of our greatest fears: the loss of the effective self. We try to get an edge on competitors, get a step ahead of others, get a piece of the pie, and urgently pursue what we are entitled to.

Selfing is the exact opposite of flowing. While flowing leads to great satisfaction, it is primarily characterized by a sense of submersion of the self in activities that enhance the community. *Ha'aha'a*, or humbleness, is based on the *lokahi* (unity and connection) that happens when you lose awareness of the self and get lost in your activities or environment. One sees dozens of lei makers, wood carvers, and fishhook cutters working as groups around the Hawaiian islands. They are flowing in their work, talking among themselves, enjoying one another's company, and are keenly aware of the working group even as they get lost in their task. Their seventh sense for pleasurable activity keeps them connected.

Egotistical selfing is reflected in our distrust of social and political institutions and diminishing frequency of joining and being an active part of social organizations. Robert D. Putnam, Harvard professor of government and international affairs, wrote a popular essay titled "Bowling Alone: America's Declining Social Capital."[7] In that essay he identified the dangers of what will happen as Americans become less and less likely to join groups of any kind, and lead lives essentially alone. As an example, Putnam points out that more people than ever are bowling, more people bowl than vote, and yet leagues of teams have decreased by 40 percent. Instead of playing their sport in relationship to others, bowlers are going alone to the lanes, throwing their balls, and sitting down to wait their turn as they stare at the television set suspended above each lane.

Selfing can be understood as trying to enhance the ego, being totally self-sufficient, and working hard to get one's perceived entitlements. You know you are moving away from a pleasurable life when much of your time is spent in activities that have the following eight self-focusing—or *selfing*—factors.

1. Endless days You feel your work is never done. This is often shown by trying to do several things at once, making careless mistakes in the simplest tasks, and feeling emotionally fatigued though you are not physically tired. Energy seems to come and go in rushes or spurts.

2. Distraction and forgetfulness You feel a general sense of agitation. You may be continually bothered and diverted from a desired task by what feel like distractions and ever-new obligations. You try to do many things at once and seem unable to fully concentrate on the task at hand. Pressuring thoughts spurt in and out of your awareness.

3. Busy going nowhere You feel that your task has no clearly definable goals. You tend to move here and there mentally, physically, and emotionally, but you have little clear direction and meaningful purpose.

4. No idea how you're doing You feel you are getting too little tangible feedback about your efficacy. Except for financial reward or social prestige, you feel that no one really cares and that you are unsure of the ultimate purpose, outcome, and meaning of your behaviors.

5. High responsibility with little power You believe that you have high accountability but little control to do what you should or would like to do. You feel pressured at work or at home by constant accountability, not only to projected high standards from others but to your own perfectionism. At the same time, you feel that you have little authority or control over what you are doing.

"They all want to be their own boss," said a Hawaiian fishing boat operator. "You try to make suggestions, but they always try to take control. You would think these rich, powerful people would already have too much responsibility in their life, but they always want to take on more. Maybe they are really feeling powerless even though they seem to have all that power. Maybe that's why they try to be in charge on the boat even while they are on vacation. And you know what? The more they try, the less fish they catch. It seems that the person who isn't really trying very hard and who listens and smells and feels for where they are always gets the most bites."

6. Everything is a big effort You feel pressured, work hard, and do more than you need to just to get simple things done. Your life feels like you are lifting heavy weights. You prepare, strain, rest, and prepare again. Like Sisyphus, you feel like you are pushing the same boulder up the same hill each day, only to have it roll back down again and again.

7. Never enough time You feel that the clock is always ticking and you check your watch several times an hour, trying to save time or feeling afraid your time will run out. You complain that the years are rolling by and that time is flying. You feel like the Type T (or time-driven) personality described in Chapter 7.

"You just can't fish fast," said the fishing boat owner. "*Haoles* try to do everything fast. They pull on the line and it pulls right out of the fish's mouth. They ask how long it is before the fish will bite, but they don't understand that the fish are in no hurry."

8. The weight of the world on your shoulders You feel under pressure to live up to your own or others' expectations. You feel "on the spot" and resentful that you have to be on the alert for attacks and criticisms from others or from your own perfectionistic brain. An endless string of problems seems to recycle in and out of your life.

"Maybe they feel the weight of the world on their shoulders because they have claimed it for themselves and tried to carry it away," said a Polynesian tour guide. "If your life is a burden and you think you have to do it all yourself, you climb under the world and try to lift it. Nobody puts the world on your shoulders. You pick it up and put it there."

To learn to flow with *ha'aha'a,* there are two steps you must accomplish. First, as emphasized above, you must learn to silence the self and the brain. Second, you must learn to diversify your central self and broaden your identity into several adaptive selves.

A Less Selfish Self

In a very few years, we have gone from a society with a social code of self-restraint and humbleness to one of arrogance and self-gratification.[8] We have become such consumers that we have developed all-consuming selves. Like spoiled children, we become angry at politicians who fail to meet our narrow and selfish needs. Our personal debt has followed along with the national debt. The consuming, entitled self has filled its house and garage with everything new. If we wish to see the selves, we have only to look at our houses and what we put in them. The more the self gets, the more it thinks it has to protect and the more nervous it becomes. Americans now spend more on private security guards and burglar alarms than they spend in taxes that go toward public police forces.

Psychiatrist Thomas Szasz says, "Happiness is an imaginary condition, formerly attributed by the living to the dead, now usually attributed by adults to children, and by children to adults."[9] The happiness attained through the pleasure prescription is not "out there"—it can't be purchased. The goal of a humble, modest, unadorned life is not ascetic self-denial. The way of *ha'aha'a* is an unembellished simplicity. The Oceanic way teaches that human wants are insatiable and human needs are socially defined rather than stemming from the soul. The non-egotistical self knows that the true resources of human happiness are all around us in the loving people and beautiful places of the world.[10]

The Midas mistake Like King Midas, the selfish self sits amidst its world turned to cold, lifeless gold. We are now four times richer than our great-grandparents, but the data shows that we are also at least four times as depressed.[11] While it is difficult to know exactly how many of us are very, very happy, most research shows that less than one in five of us are leading lives of joy.[12] Author and priest Father John Powell writes, "One-third of all Americans wake up depressed every day. Pollsters estimate that only 10 to 15 percent of Americans think of themselves as very happy."[13] Regular surveys by the National Opinion Research Center of the University of Chicago reveal that no more Americans report that they are very happy now than in 1957.

Like the lonely King Midas wishing for more and more, we seem compulsively driven away from the true delight of living by what I call the "Rule of Two." We seem to naturally want about twice as much as we have. *Harper's* editor Lewis Sapham has been asking people how much money they would need to be happy. He has found that, no matter how much money they have, Americans feel they need about twice as much. Economist Juliet Schor points out that we can now reach our 1948 standard of living in less than half the time it took then. Instead, we have chosen to work twice as hard to get twice as much . . . and ended up half as happy.[14]

The narcissisms In psychotherapy, there is a concept called *narcissism,* of which there are two types, primary and secondary. *Primary narcissism* is a state in which a person exhibits a relatively innocent, childlike love of self that is almost oblivious to others because of the joy in the person's newly emerging individual identity. Childish narcissism is not a choice. It is necessary for the way a child develops through the overwhelming tasks of taking care of the immature self.

Secondary narcissism is not so innocent. It is egotistical and reflects a decision to enhance the self regardless of others. It means choosing to care for the self over caring for others, choosing to be effective rather than connective. Secondary narcissism obstructs the bliss response because it creates a barrier to the joy of being with others, which is essential for healthy pleasure. It is a narcissism fueled by acquisitions, wealth at others' expense, and the grandiosity of effective independence.

The natural pleasure system is constructed to warn us away from the consuming, secondary narcissistic self, so that we feel best when we are giving, sharing, helping, and caring, and worst when we are taking and hurting. If we pay attention to our need for joy, we will learn that getting a lot of things almost always means losing a lot of pleasure. The more things people have, the less they are able to find joy in what they say they want most—loving, happy interactions with others.

Researcher Jeremy Seabrook interviewed several older, working-class people and asked them about the rising prosperity in their lives. One of his interviewees illustrated the impact of secondary narcissism when he said, "People aren't satisfied, only they don't seem to know why they're not. The chance of being satisfied we can imagine isn't by getting more of what we've got now. It's what we've got now that makes us dissatisfied, so getting more of it only makes us more dissatisfied."[15]

Studies show clearly that the main determinants of happiness are not related to possessions but to a happy family life, strong marriage, good work, leisure time to enjoy these things, and friendships. Few people list "getting more things" as their happiness goal, and yet their lives appear dedicated to that pursuit.

Author James Ogilvy identifies yet a third type of narcissism he calls *tertiary narcissism.* The primary narcissist innocently loves herself in self-absorbed lack of recognition of "other" selves also busy trying to develop. The secondary narcissist makes a decision to love himself instead of the "other." The tertiary narcissist is someone who is preoccupied with the self without any appreciation of a core, authentic self. Ogilvy says that this type of narcissism brings all the negatives of both primary and secondary narcissism, but none of the innocent delights of childhood or appreciation and pride of adult narcissism.

The primary narcissistic sings his own song oblivious of others'. He doesn't seem to know others are within hearing distance. The secondary narcissist sings her own song because she has chosen not to listen for others' singing and doesn't care if anyone likes her song or not. The tertiary narcissist is furthest from *ha'aha'a*, or healthy humbleness. His song remains unrecognized within him; he is too distracted getting and doing. He is too busy to listen for the songs of others and may be frightened by the sound of singing. For the tertiary narcissist, childish joy and adult pride give way to chronic dissatisfaction.

Mythology and Multiple Selves

There is another alternative to dealing with the compelling selfishness we feel daily. Primary, secondary, and tertiary narcissism are dominated to varying degrees by the urgency response. The bliss possible from following the pleasure prescription comes from having one strong, authentic self surrounded by many other ever-changing, evolving, and adaptive selves. This "many selves" theory is what researcher Patricia Linville calls "the complex self" and psychiatrist Robert Lipton calls "the protean self."

One sign of developing maturity is when a person stops trying to determine "who he is" and, instead, works hard at developing many "whos." One woman put this idea as follows: "When I was young, I used to think I was having trouble finding my self. Then I spoke to one of the *kupuna* in Hawai'i who told me that looking for one self was like looking for one grain of sand. I know now that I am a mother, a doctor, a lover, a daughter, a wife, a creator, and on and on. My great challenge and great joy comes from nurturing many 'me's' and not just trying to protect one 'me.' If I screw up as a mother once in awhile, I don't get all down about my self-concept because I have a 'many-selves concept.' "

Linville and Lipton provide Western-based approaches to what Polynesians have understood for over two thousand years—the complex changing self. *Ha'aha'a* is realized through the enjoyment of the birth of many new and ever-learning selves throughout our life and through encouraging the evolution of new selves in those around us.

Author Henry Dreher uses the Greek myths of the Hydra and Proteus to illustrate lessons about a healthy self. The myth of Hercules and the Hydra relates to Patricia Linville's theory of the complex self.[16] In this myth, Hercules does combat with a many-headed beast, the Hydra. The battle is complicated because every time Hercules cuts off one of the Hydra's heads, another two heads grow back in its place. Only when Hercules cuts off the one immortal or "authentic" head and buries it, is the Hydra defeated. The lesson of the Hydra is that many "selves" prevent us from "putting all our cognitive eggs in one basket," as Dr. Linville states.[17] While we all need one central, healthy, genuine self to keep us in mental balance, we will never find the bliss we seek without a set of ancillary selves developed to deal with life's natural chaos.

A Polynesian *kahuna* described his version of the complex self by saying, "We have to know who we are, but that is never enough. We have to know all that we are and can be and help others know and be all the selves they can be. We have to send out many selves from our center self. If we are consumed with finding and protecting one self, we stifle our potential for happiness and healing that comes from our diversity of selves. You don't have to just be yourself, you have to learn to be your selves and help others be their selves. That is the *aloha* way."

The myth of Proteus also contains lessons that illustrate the healthy pleasure that is derived from having the dynamic, adaptive self proposed by psychiatrist Robert Lipton. Proteus was an old, prophetic man of the sea. He knew all things but did not want his secrets known. When anyone captured him to learn his secrets, he would escape by assuming different shapes—a leopard, a lion, even a fire. If a captor managed to hold him fast, Proteus would assume his old man image and share his secrets. Once released, he would escape back into the sea. Dr. Lipton suggests that Proteus is a good metaphor for health and happiness in our fragmented times. Lipton writes, "Though variation is the essence of the protean self, that self has certain relatively consistent features."[18]

Lipton's idea of "consistent features" agrees with the Polynesian view that, while humble modesty requires many diverse selves instead of just one strong self-image that is rigid and vulnerable, it also requires a base of sturdy centeredness around a core of stable, key identity features. These include general acceptance of one's appearance through life, acknowledgment and respect of one's familial origins, and a consistent, explanatory system strong enough to carry one through difficult times of loss and change. Polynesians know that humble selflessness is not weakness or self-confusion. It is a sign of a strong core identity in which the individual knows that who she is is tied to who everyone else is. It makes one able to fill several roles, survive and grow through failures in some without diminishing efficacy in others, and avoid the reactive compensation of arrogance or shame when the extended selves encounter distress.

Ha'aha'a, or selflessness, then, requires that we accept that we have many selves so we can enjoy our varied world. It requires having a core self which is rendered authentic by its connection with and respect for all other selves. This humble and modest self can be both a Hydra and Proteus. Ultimately, *ha'aha'a* is revolutionary and liberating because it is based on the idea that while we do not choose our destiny, we do choose how to view ourselves.

Ha'aha'a Ha'awina (Humbleness Lesson)

To help you monitor and avoid the constant control of the selfish brain and to practice *ha'aha'a* in your own life, try this "Polynesian pronoun" exercise. Try to spend one entire day without using the pronouns "I," "me," or "mine." Be alert to situations in which you would use such words and substitute another pronoun, or just don't say anything.

If you are like most people who have tried this Polynesian pronoun test, you will notice it is very difficult to go an entire day in our society without self references. During this day, you will probably stumble in conversations and search for words, but after a few hours, you will discover new ways of speaking—and thinking. You will start asking others about how they feel, what they want, and how you might be able to help them. You will notice that people feel much more relaxed around you. Listen for others' "self" vocabulary and you will notice many selfish pronouns. You will also notice that, as you decrease your self pronouns, they will too.

At the end of your "Polynesian pronoun day," spend some time thinking about your experiences and feelings. You may find that it was one of the most enjoyable, pleasurable, stress-free days you have spent in a very long time. You will become more patient, feel more connected with others, and experience more pleasure. You might also feel a more compassionate orientation to the world in general, which is *akahai*, or the gentle tenderness that is the fifth and final *aloha* ingredient in the pleasure prescription.

Chapter Eleven

THE GIFT FROM GIVING—TRY A LITTLE TENDERNESS

Akahai: Gentleness, to be expressed tenderly
"E wehe I ka umauma I akea"

(Open up the chest so that it may be spacious
—have a warm and open heart)

As we sat on shore watching the humpbacked whales play, my old Hawaiian friend pointed to a group of what he called "aunty whales." "See how gentle those monsters are," he said in a whisper as if trying not to disturb them. "All the other females whales are helping the mother whale. They helped position the male and female for sex, acted like midwifes at the birth, and got the mother in position to nurse her new baby. Now they keep circling around to keep the sharks away. They even play with the calf like babysitters while the mother whale rests. They know *akahai.* The biggest mammal is also one of the most gentle creatures on earth."

The sensitive, nurturing play of the whales exemplifies the last of the five *aloha* ingredients: *akahai,* kind, considerate, tender relationships with everyone and everything.

How Do You See Your Body?

Western medicine takes an aggressive and defensive approach to health. It speaks of "winning the war" against disease and preventing illness by "strengthening the body's defenses" and approaches the body as a machine of muscle and bone, driven by a fluid pump (the heart) and coordinated by an electrical organ (the brain). Medical diagnoses often refer to conditions such as "cogwheel rigidity," "hammer toes," "sickle-cell disease," and "piston pulse."[1] One scientist went so far as to put a price on the body, as if it were a bag full of salable stuff. He calculated the cost of purchasing the body's compounds from chemical companies and concluded the market value would be in excess of $200,000.[2] His estimate was at 1980 prices and did not include the value of transplantable organs. Another author reported that there is enough water in the body to fill a ten-gallon keg, enough fat for seven bars of soap, and enough carbon to make 9,000 lead pencils.[3] Such mechanical thinking about the body implies an objective, static view that ignores the unquantifiable, natural dynamic of our thoughts, feelings, and intentions.

The Oceanic view of the body is more musical than mechanical. It sees the body as a rhythmic representation of the spirit of life and a result of all things resonating together to create a harmonious system.[4] In Oceanic culture, the body is referred to with respect, kindness, and love, and it is not seen as an entity separable from its environment. It is viewed as one of many manifestations of the human soul and therefore must be dealt with as sensitively and caringly as possible.

As you have learned, to the Polynesian the soul is not *in* the body, it *is* the body. It is also merged with all souls outside the illusory boundary of one of the body's largest organs of immunity, the skin. For the island people, just as there are no physical boundaries of property owned by any one person, there are no boundaries of individuality, so it does not make sense to speak of a separate body controlled by a separate brain.

Both Eastern and Western medicine and philosophy often see the body as an essential limitation of the soul. The Polynesian view is that the body is a great gift to be enjoyed, relished, and sensually shared with the world through loving, dancing, singing, and chanting. Many old Hawaiians keep all fingernails and hair clippings, and the bones of the dead are seen as very sacred and powerful.

The Third Way to wellness teaches that a long and joyful life derives from the loving experience of connection with all the bodies around us, including people, plants, and animals. Total Polynesian fitness means not just keeping the body in shape but taking pleasure in keeping the whole world in good health. The body is a primary communication system for maintaining and experiencing connection. It is a part of the ecosystem and should be cared for just as one cares for the plants and fish. This chapter on *akahai* is about how gentle concern is expressed in our intimate relationships, our relationships to others in our communities, and our relationship to the environment and world.

The Power of 'Ohana (Family)

As the Hawaiian man and I continued to watch the whales playing, we saw the *'ohana* (Polynesian family) in action. Chapter 8 presented the principle of *lokahi* (unity) and described the family as a central and inclusive component of Polynesian life. The word *'ohana* comes from the word *'oha,* the taro corn which comes from the root and the stalk of the taro plant. *'Oha* refers to the offshoots, or "offspring," from the taro plant. Adding *na* on the end of the word makes the word plural, so *ohana* means many healthy shoots growing and developing from a healthy root.[5]

One of the key pleasure principles of the Polynesian culture is to take and give great respectful joy from within the extended family. Mary Kawena Pukui, one of the greatest Hawaiian scholars and teachers, taught that the family is the world, and like a vulnerable, growing plant it must be protected and nurtured as the healthy root of all life. She wrote, "Members of the *'ohana,* like taro shoots, are all from the same root."[6] Oceanic tradition teaches that there are no boundaries to delineate our mission of concern and tender care. It teaches that there is only one sin: to harm another soul. Since souls dance everywhere in the environment, tenderness must be practiced on a grand scale, not just with the self, close friends, and family. Polynesians are emotionally "at home" in the world because they enjoy *being* it instead of trying to *have* it. They strive to treat everyone and everything like family.

Polynesians also practice *ho'okipa,* meaning caring generosity, as a daily responsibility. This generosity has often been practiced to a fault, as other less gentle cultures who do believe in ownership and have a narrow definition of family and what constitutes "us," have taken advantage of *ho'okipa* by plundering the island lands and waters. The Polynesians cultivate a caring heart to protect and nurture everything and everyone in a practice they call *malama,* showing a respect and love for the macro *'ohana*, the extended family of life.

My wife Celest Kalalani once complimented a Hawaiian woman's beautiful hat. The next time they met, and much to my wife's embarrassment, the woman gave my wife the hat as a gift. My wife and I have since learned to be cautious in praising our Polynesian neighbors' possessions for fear we will take advantage of their *ho'okipa* and appear to be coveting their property. Many Indian and Middle Eastern cultures also have this tradition, again indicating that the three paths to well-being intersect at important junctures.

Love Polynesian Style

The first and most basic meaning of the word *aloha* is "love." Oceanic love is based on *akahai,* which is a constant, conscientious, gentle and caring behavior. *Akahai* is not an automatic or impulsive feeling; it is not a response or a reaction. In the West, "romantic" love is an exaggerated, impulsive, sexualized loving that glorifies the self in erotic and passionate fulfillment. Western culture encourages us to think that love is a spontaneous feeling that "happens" to a person, one that can overwhelm with its power. It says we helplessly "fall" in and out of a state of love, and that finding "true" love is a matter of finding the right partner instead of doing the right things and being the right person. Western culture sees interpersonal love as a romantic way to self-fulfillment.

The Eastern tradition's take on love has been more abstract and spiritual and less secular and romantic. In turn, loving behavior in a relationship with another person is often interpreted as a sign of human weakness, of succumbing to temptations of the flesh at the expense of an enlightened spirit. If you listen carefully to the teachings of Eastern medicine and philosophy, you will hear surprisingly little about making a good marriage and more about becoming a wise individual who has tuned in to what one of the modern teachers of this orientation calls "the inner wizard."

The Oceanic way says love is something you *do,* not feel. It is based on the action of being a loving person. It is not a surrender to the seductive power of another person who promises great rewards for the self. It is not a barter, or erotic exchange. Love is volitional, not emotional. It means *being* the right partner more than *finding* the right partner, being compassionate instead of passionate, and helping, healing, and giving through life's difficult times. It is based less on self-enlightenment than on lightening another's load.

In Polynesia, marriage is based on the idea of extended *aloha*. The purpose of marriage for most island people was summed up by Leo Tolstoy when he wrote, "The goal of our life should not be to find joy in marriage, but to bring more love and truth into the world. We marry to assist each other in this task."[7] For those who follow the Oceanic way, all love is world love.

A key to Polynesian loving is the concept of *pana'i,* which we have mentioned before and which means "reciprocal rebound." Polynesians believe that every word we say has great power and that saying bad things about someone or something will inevitably come back to the speaker. The same holds true for the good.

By its nature, this holistic understanding of love applies beyond interpersonal relationships and includes our relationships with ourselves and our surroundings. In the Oceanic mind, you cannot have one without the other. Author Riane Eisler differentiates between a "dominator" and "partnership" model of love.[8] The dominator model refers to intimacy predicated on controlling another for the good of the self. It works on fear and force, and Eisler points out that cultures that embrace the dominator model of "using" a lover for enhancement of the self also tend to place humans in control over nature. The result is more pain than pleasure. The Polynesian culture is one of the oldest partnership cultures and has often struggled with the painful impact of the dominator cultures.

The Danger of Criticism

To put *pana'i,* or reciprocal rebound, into your daily life, criticize as little as possible. Criticism sends out what Polynesians call bad *mana*, and that energy will come back at you sooner or later. Criticism is a personal attack that never leads to pleasure; it almost always leads to feelings of withdrawal, anger, dread, and disgust. Polynesians believe that "criticism creates," meaning that the more we disparage others, the more they behave as and become that for which we castigate them. Complaining, on the other hand, can be very helpful. Complaints focus on actions and can help make persons aware of and more able to correct behavioral problems.

A complaint is not a whine of victimization or misery. It never accuses, only identifies problems. It is a statement of willingness to invest time and effort into making a relationship better for both partners. "I wish we traveled more. We have to figure out something to do about this together" is a complaint. "You don't take me anywhere" is a criticism that leads to more trouble than problem solving. Current research shows that constructive complaints that point out nonpersonalized problems in a relationship lead to the best and most enduring relationships.

You can also see the difference between criticizing and complaining in the following example from my clinic:

"You never want to have sex," said the wife. "You've lost your sex drive because you care more about your work than about me." The personal attack this wife launched on her husband surely led to what researchers call physiological, emotional, and mental *flooding* by her partner. Flooding is characterized by accelerated heartbeat, increased blood pressure, diminished immunity, increased stress hormones, and the inability to think clearly.[9] While there are gender exceptions, men generally flood more quickly than women and react by stonewalling, shutting off their emotions in order to quiet their flood.

Women often react to male stonewalling with their own flooding, which may lead to intensified criticism. This in turn leads to more stonewalling by the man, and a dangerous emotional tango ensues.[10] Carefully conducted research now shows that, with some exceptions, women tend to be the emotional managers in relationships. They are better at detecting interpersonal problems and more sensitive to subtle signs of trouble. Men, again with some exceptions, tend to be fix-and-repair oriented, and much less alert to early signs of trouble. Men more easily stonewall and avoid problems when they feel they cannot fix them, while women tend to want to go right after problems and discuss them. Psychologist John Gottman's research, described throughout this chapter, clearly demonstrates that when a woman's early warning system leads to complaint and a man fails to hear that complaint, the woman then escalates to criticism, to which the male reacts by flooding and stonewalling. Despite protests of "sexism," the data clearly show that women tend to be much better at the relationship game than men are, and that awareness rather than denial of this basic gender difference (again with many exceptions) is the way to better and more healthy relationships.

Lethal Love

Because of lack of *akahai,* or gentle, uncritical relating, we are failing to meet the challenge of the most difficult and demanding of all relationships: marriage. Statistically, almost all of our most intimate relationships are failing. While the divorce rate per year has more or less leveled off at just under 50 percent, the risk of divorce—the chance that a new marriage will eventually end in divorce—has increased dramatically.[11] About 10 percent of couples marrying in 1890 later divorced. Almost 70 percent of the marriages that started in 1990 ended in divorce. If this risk factor continues at its present level, by the year 2000 less that two of every ten new marriages will survive.

Marriages are microcosms of *aloha,* the capacity to love on a broad scale. They magnify our loving strengths and weaknesses, so they provide a good laboratory for testing our capacity to practice *akahai* or tender caring.

One reason almost all of our intimate relationships fail is Delight Deficiency Syndrome. We lose our ability to take and give great pleasure in our marriage, and our selfish loving becomes lethal to our relationship. We end up consuming our marriage as we consume most things, and casting it away when it is used up. We fail to practice *akahai* and the crucial principle of *pana'i*. To help bring more *akahai* into your life so you can relish the pleasure of lasting loving relationship, remember the following rules:

Putting More Pana'i into Your Life

1. *Give five compliments for every criticism.* For some reason researchers do not yet understand, a five-to-one ratio in favor of compliments over criticism keeps relationships alive and healthy.

2. *Watch your flooding level when you are in conflict.* Use the *a'i* or "neck pulse" method discussed in Chapter 9. Flooding involves a rise in heart rate from your resting pulse rate. Women average about 82 beats a minute at rest and men average about 72 beats a minute. Flooding technically begins at an increase of about 10 beats per minute over your resting, bliss rate. When your heart accelerates above ten beats per

minute, the urgency response has kicked in and you become love-blinded by stress hormones.[12]

3. *Watch for the "disgust dimple."* When we flood, we feel defensiveness instead of tenderness. We react with a nonloving expression and contract the "dimpler muscles," the small, powerful muscles that pull the corner of the mouth to one side. Since the right side of the brain is primarily involved in our negative emotions, such emotions are typically expressed more on the left side of our face. In addition, our eyes may roll up and we may sigh in disgust. Polynesians call this "giving stink-eye," and they know that love is likely to end up on the rocks when this look of contempt and disgust begins to appear on a regular basis. Research shows that when a partner sees the disgust dimple, his or her heartbeat automatically increases two to three beats per minute and mild flooding begins. When the disgust dimple is in a marriage, women are more likely to experience immune system depression and are much more likely to develop bladder and yeast infections as well as colds and flu. Men are very likely to leave the relationship quite soon. New research shows that, when the disgust dimple is present, the relationship tends to end within four years.[13]

4. *Watch for the "anger lip."* When we are feeling contempt, we usually are feeling that we are much better than someone else or that our territory has been violated. We may show our destain by curling our upper lip and looking off to one side.[14] Modern research shows that putting on an unhappy face can also depress our immune system, drive people away, and lead to the end of an intimate relationship.

5. *Try the "Saturday List."* Remember the lessons presented in Chapter 8 about dealing with anger. Don't express it, don't suppress it, confess it. Write down or tape-record an anger list and plan one day a week to deal with your list. By the time you get to your list, many of the sources of your anger will have diminished.

6. *Remember the "F Index":* When couples monitored the number of acts of sexual intercourse and arguments in their marriage, researchers discovered what they called the "F Index" which they expressed as "the frequency of fornication minus the frequency of fights."[15] If a couple fights and criticizes eight times per month but engages in sex twelve times a month, their F index is +4, meaning that their relationship is likely to last. If a couple has conflicts four times a month but only has sex once a month, their F Index is –3, which means their marriage is likely to fail. I don't mean to imply that you should keep arguing and just add more sex to your relationship, but criticizing less can set the stage for more sensual tenderness and create a more erotic ecology in your relationship.

The Risks and Rewards of Love

Cathexis is a psychological term meaning to channel life and loving energy into someone. Confiding is the process that makes cathexis possible. In Chapter 9 I explained that cathexis is a key part of *lokahi* (unity), and it means to invest ourselves in a person, place, or thing.[16] One of the most necessary aspects of the pleasure prescription is to have someone in whom to invest loving energy and who also invests energy in you.

There are great health benefits from having one close person with whom you confide your innermost secrets, feelings, and fears. Those who have such a "cathexis" or investment in their life live longer and happier, but those who lose it and do not replace it with another are extremely vulnerable to weakened immunity.[17] The danger in getting very close to someone is that you can end up feeling very alone when that relationship ends. This is why a broader experience of loving *aloha* is necessary as a buffer against the inevitable physical end to intimate relationships.

Talking Story

Polynesians refer to the Western concept of confiding as "talking story," which essentially means to sit down and talk about anything and everything. Talking story is a loving energy exchange essential for perpetuating a relationship as well as for keeping the society and culture alive. Sharing constructive and pleasurable confidences maintains connection not only with people in our life now but with our ancestors. It is a ritualistic way of generating the energy fields and "morphic resonance" of scientist Rupert Sheldrake, discussed in Chapter 7.

A Polynesian *kumu* summed up the importance of talking story when she said, "I think that if more couples talked story more often, they would have happier and longer lasting marriages. Too many couples don't talk story, they just give messages about surviving day to day. They don't talk together like partners. Instead, they are always trying to dominate one another. They don't spend enough time talking about the past and going over the joys of today. They are always solving problems, but they forget to enjoy the fact that they have lived. They don't see that they are always creating memories and that they ruin and waste these memories if they only talk about getting things done rather than enjoying things they have done together."

Here are some ways you can enjoy "talking story" and bring more *akahai* to your important relationships.

How to "Talk Story"

1. *Catharsis is not enough.* Catharsis is often venting emotions—ranting or raving and "getting it all out." Confiding is an organized, thoughtful sharing of both feelings and facts. It is a long, rational, calm, slow, process that contains complaints but never criticism. It requires balancing the urgency of your feelings with the reality of the facts related to them.

2. *Writing it down helps.* Putting your thoughts and feelings on paper can help organize them, and research shows that such writing promotes insight, not just expression.[18] When students wrote down their concerns and feelings, they stayed healthier than other students who reflected but did not write down their thoughts.[19] "Talking story" with yourself on paper is not just keeping a diary. Diaries are daily records that often exclude confessions of true feelings and reflective thoughts. Talking story is sharing, admitting, reflecting, and accepting.

3. *Confess what you are trying to keep inside.* Inhibition not only takes mental energy, it takes an immense amount of physical energy and weakens the cardiovascular and immune systems. Polynesians call confession *ha'ina,* meaning to acknowledge one's fears, faults, and failures and to take responsibility for hurting another soul. Polygraph experts report that people become nervous when first attached to their monitors. They begin to flood: their heart races, stress hormones flow, and their breathing accelerates. If a person confesses during this test, another polygraph test is always given to confirm the results of the first. Although the confession now means the person faces jail and financial loss, the second, post-confession polygraph shows that the flood is over. Heart rate, blood pressure, breathing, and skin conductance (another sign of stress) all come back within normal limits. Even as the convicted confessor is handcuffed and taken to jail, most offenders stand up, shake the polygraph examiner's hand, and thank him. Having talked their story, they apparently find more balance and relax.

4. *Before disclosing in a talk story with someone else, confess and confide in yourself.* Even professional therapists unknowingly give subtle cues that may condition certain expressions. Because others may influence our confession, it is best to talk story with yourself first so you are not influenced or censored in your expressions. And remember, you have many selves to talk with, including your ancestors.

5. *Use negative words as well as positive ones.* Don't make your story to yourself or another person an exercise in affirmations or a demonstration of your degree of positive attitude. Research shows that those who used negative words in their personal written "confessions" strengthened their physical health.[20]

6. *Make a commitment to talk story at least four or five days in a row.* Rather than keeping a diary, in which you may forget or choose not to make entries, decide you will write at least an hour or so for four or five days in a row. Most people are inconsistent with their diaries, so making a decision to write for

several days consecutively for a short period of time is a better way to talk story to yourself and to get ready to talk story with someone else.

7. *Take plenty of time to talk—and listen—story.* Talking story is not one-way therapy. It is an interactive, *lokahi* (unifying) process, so you must listen as much as you talk. There is no psychoanalytic "fifty-minute hour" for talking story; it can and should go on for hours if it needs to. If your selfish brain gets bored, ignore it. Keep going.

Commitment: Lessons from the "Termites"

For the Polynesian, there is no such thing as a divorce. All commitments are forever. While there may be legal separations, the Polynesian concept of infinite oneness means that there is no way to declare a relationship over. In Western culture, divorce has become the "marriage-after pill," taken when "things don't work out." Research shows, however, that divorce is not a panacea: it is the single greatest social problem in our society.[21]

One of the classic studies in the history of psychology was conducted by Lewis Terman. Beginning in 1921, he began a long-range study of 1,528 very bright children to see how high intelligence related to success.[22] These bright young people called themselves the "Termites," and a recent look at this 75-year study, which is still in progress, reveals shocking lessons from the dead Termites.

As one would expect, a large number of the Termites have died since the study began. The surprise is that, as much as smoking, high blood pressure, and other well-known health-risk factors, having a divorce or being a child from a divorce was a leading cause of early death. Studies show that children of divorce face a one-third greater mortality risk than people whose parents remain married until they reach age twenty-one.[23] And parental conflict and separation is a greater influence on psychopathology and physical illness than is parental death.[24] Divorced people themselves are three times more likely to kill themselves, and divorce ranks as a major factor linked with suicide rate and physical violence.[25]

The illusion that there can be a quick, easy termination of relationships is causing serious negative health and happiness consequences in our society. The Oceanic concept of permanent bonds teaches that, even if a physical distance occurs between persons, every effort needs to be made to behave, think, and feel in ways that demonstrate that a relationship never ends and that all relationships have an impact far beyond the two persons who compose them.

The Big Five of a Mighty Marriage

Those who are able to stay married and reap its mental and physical benefits show what psychologists call the "Big Five" traits that parallel the qualities of *aloha*.[26] The Big Five of a strong and healthy character are also the five elements of a loving person: conscientiousness *(ahonui)*, agreeableness *('olu'olu),* connection *(lokahi),* cooperation *(ha'aha'a),* and trust *(akahai).* Terman's research shows that in the race toward early death, good guys and gals finish last.[27] The authors of a study examining Terman's data for life health risks associated with troubled relationships conclude, ". . . if such patterns of findings were found concerning toxic association with insecticides, electromagnetic fields, or diet . . . it is likely that a public health emergency would be perceived."[28] Ironically, because this biggest risk factor is relational, we don't acknowledge the crisis—or the prevention.

Unless you plan on practicing the pleasure prescription and the five components of *aloha,* don't get married! Marriage is for adults only, and for those mature enough and willing enough to behave lovingly over time in order to feel love. One marries to learn to love, not because one is "in it." You have learned that the data is clear that there are key gender differences when it comes to intimacy, and practicing *akahai* or loving tenderness is the way to keep creating love and to bridge the gap between the genders. If your marriage is in trouble, start practicing *aloha* right away! It is not just better sex and communication that can save a relationship, it is patience, intimate connection, pleasantness, selflessness, forgiveness, and tenderness. Unless you practice the pleasure prescription, getting married may be one of the major risks to your and your entire family's health and happiness.

Caring: The Value of Loving Strangers

The ancient Polynesians knew what Einstein meant when he wrote, "A human being is a part of the whole called by us the universe." Our happiness depends on realizing that we cannot find joy alone and without bringing joy to others. Einstein went on to say that we must free ourselves from the prison of the delusion of individual separateness by widening our circle of compassion to embrace all living creatures and the whole of nature in its beauty.

I end our discussion of the five principles of *aloha* with *akahai* because gentle, loving kindness is a public announcement that you have decided to bring more *aloha,* and therefore more joy, to the world as your means of bringing bliss to your own life and the life of your family.

Author Allan Luks has dedicated his life to the study of altruism. He has found that there are immensely powerful health-enhancing rewards for giving to and caring for others. He refers to the "helper's high," a natural endorphin rush that rewards tender, selfless giving. Polynesians taught that there is no more powerful and sure way to pleasure than to help.

Luks and others who have studied allocentrism suggest that the biochemical rewards of altruism have their roots in our human evolution. As I mentioned in the discussion of *lokahi* (unity), we ultimately survive only through cooperation. We are wired to be giving because giving allows the world to survive and provide for us.

Psychologist Jack Panksepp at Bowling Green State University has shown that fulfilling the need for social contact and showing supportive behavior to others are accompanied by a strong endorphin rush in all animals.[29] What clearer message could there be from the Creator than the fact that we are constantly biochemically rewarded for helping others?

Not only empathy but sympathy is built into the Oceanic mind. Empathy involves trying to feel what others feel; sympathy is accepting these feelings, caring that they exist, and trying to do something about them. Polynesians believe it is not enough to say "I know how you must feel." *Akahai* requires saying, "I care deeply about how you feel and I will try to help you."

You have seen that Polynesians believe that the unifying principle of their life is Oneness, and all acts that promote that oneness promote hardiness, happiness, and health. The word *waiwai* means wealth in Hawaiian. *Wai* means water, and the island people believe that all life comes from water. *Waiwai* is the highest prosperity, sharing, caring for, and protecting with and for others all the water and the land, plants, beasts, and people who are a part of it. One cannot buy the *wai* or own the *'aina* (land) no matter how much financial wealth one has. Only by giving to people and the planet can one find a blissful and balanced life.

Allan Luks and others have shown that our indigenous altruism can wither away like an unused muscle if it is not exercised regularly. Based on the research by Luks and others, and the Polynesian lessons of *kokua* or helping, here are six suggestions for exercising your inner helper.

Altruistic Aloha Aerobics

1. *Help complete strangers.* While helping immediate family is important, there is a down-side to such giving. As often happens to family members caring for relatives with chronic diseases, fatigue and depression can result from the constant and often unrelenting giving and sacrifice that is required. In keeping with the concept of *'ohana,* or broadly extended family, health and happiness benefits come to those who give to complete strangers.[30]

2. *Make personal contact.* Don't send a check, be there yourself. The helper's high comes from a one-on-one relationship, not impersonal donations.

3. *Give from your extra energy, not your core.* We can overdo any exercise, so be sure that you care for your own family and your own health first. This will free you to have the energy to give to others. Your central, authentic self must be protected so that your multiple selves can spread out to the community to offer comfort and aid.

4. *Give about two hours a week.* Luks' research shows that to derive the health and happiness benefits of altruism, we need to put in as much time giving per week as we need to exercise. So worry less about making "buns of steel" than having a heart of gold.

5. *Don't work for high effectiveness.* Helping is giving, not fixing. Don't assess the worth of your loving kindness by measurable outcomes. Remember Einstein's observation that not everything that counts can be counted and not everything that can be counted counts. Don't compete to be the "best" or "most effective" volunteer or try to "fix" those you are trying to help. The benefit to others and ultimately to you and your family comes from just being there for someone who needs you and who, until you reach out, you see as a stranger.

Caring Humor

The 17th century physician Thomas Sydenham pointed out that "the arrival of a good clown exercises more beneficial influence upon the health of a town than 200 asses laden with drugs." As you end your reading of this section on the *aloha* elements, there is no more pleasurable *ha'awina* for spreading *aloha* than dispersing delight by sharing humor.

You will find that laughter is the perfect way to combine patience, connection, pleasantness, humbleness, and kindness into one joyful behavior that brings pleasure to those around you. Laughter is a happy explosion of your seventh sense. Laughter shows you appreciate what is joyful and want to share your joy with others. Laughter signals that you have been patient enough to see the ridiculous in the natural chaos of life and to wait for the good times when you are going through the bad times. It shows you are willing to reach out and connect, even at the bad times, and to share the good times. It indicates that you are agreeable and pleasant enough to share a good laugh with someone else, and modest enough to laugh at your own foolishness. It shows you are humble enough to know how foolish you can be. Finally, sharing laughter is a way of casting delight to the wind so it blows everywhere and to everyone.

Overall, people with a good sense of humor experience less stress and better health.[31] A few minutes of laughing lowers stress hormones and raises the number of circulating antibodies that fight off disease for almost 36 hours. It is no coincidence that our most hardy and intense laughter is social laughter. Research also shows that laughter can make stressors seem less negative and may evoke social support from other people.[32] It can defuse interpersonal conflicts, contribute to effective teaching, promote the survival of marriages, improve social relationships at work, and even provide a means of confronting the existential reality of death.[33] There is now evidence that a good sense of humor is associated with enhanced immune efficiency and that mothers who laughed and expressed their sense of humor during their pregnancy had fewer illnesses and their babies had fewer infections.[34]

A word of warning about the use of humor: while kind and tender humor is very good for you, people who use hostile, derogatory humor are prone to poor health and unhappiness.[35] Humor can also be used as a weapon. C. L. Edson, a 20th-century American newspaper editor, commented, "We love a joke that hands us a pat on the back while it kicks the other fellow down the stairs." The humor that connects us is the humor that heals us. So remember "AT&T"—be appropriately timely and tender in your joking.

Akahai Ha'awina: Tenderness Lesson

To put *akahai* to work in your own life, try this daily exercise. Commit yourself to helping one complete stranger every day. That help may be as simple as doing someone a favor while driving in traffic, helping someone carry packages, paying someone else's highway toll, letting someone move ahead of you in line, sharing a silly joke with a stranger, or some other gesture of benevolent consideration. Your *akahai* gesture may also be as meaningful as offering a prayer for a stranger you saw during the day. If we are to live *aloha* and receive the great pleasure, healing, and health it brings to everyone it touches, we must lead a much more kind and caring life than is common in our modern civilization.

Hawaiians say *malama pono,* meaning literally, "to take care." *Malama pono* also means to *kokua* (help) to keep things righteous—the way they were meant to be, in loving balance. The pleasure prescription requires a life of taking care to help make and keep the world in better balance. Leading a gentle, noncritical, giving life, being a partner rather than a dominator, confiding in and helping others, and finding the humor in the common problems we all encounter is the way of *akahai*.

LIVING ALOHA

This section applies the five *aloha* principles and the research presented in Parts One and Two to intimate relationships, raising children, and working, healing, and caring for our planet. Each of the five chapters in this final section is based on my interviews with the *kahuna* and *kupuna* of Polynesia as they taught me their Third Way to happiness and health. Each chapter contains a Pleasure-Ability Test, which will help you assess how much you are using your seventh sense in the areas of familying, parenting, working, healing, and living. Each test is followed by Pleasure Prompters, reminders of how you can apply the pleasure prescription every day of your life.

In this section, you will learn . . .

How to make your most intimate relationship happier and stronger

How to raise joyful children—the art of "pleasure parenting"

How to find joy on the job, despite the many changes in the nature of the workplace

How to learn through unhappy times in life

How to make the world a more cheerful and healthy place

Chapter Twelve

MAKING A PLEASURABLE PARTNERSHIP

"We often think that when we have completed our study of 'one' we know all about 'two,' because 'two' is 'one and one.' We forget that we still have to make a study of 'and.'"
— A. Eddington

It is often assumed that marriages are failing at an alarming rate because of increasing social violence, financial difficulties, changes in the law that make divorce easier, and other social factors that stress our intimate relationships. Both modern research and Oceanic wisdom stress that marital problems are less the *result* of such factors than the *cause* of them.[1] The lack of unity, connection, and a cooperative, tolerant approach called *lokahi* is *the* major social problem of our time, and the inability to maintain lasting, loving relationships accounts for most of the unhappiness and poor health in our lives.

In Chapter 11, I explained how the popular notions of "love" are limiting and, to a degree, unhealthy. These views are fed by contemporary myths about what love is and what it does to us. Many of our current ideas regarding love are derived from popular psychology, which was formulated by Western minds that value self-fulfillment over "us survival," focus more on dysfunction than joy, and are invested in the individual therapy model of healing relationships.

To what degree do you understand the true nature of love? Take the following "true/false" test and see.

1. Opposites attract . . . . . . *True / False*

2. Love is a feeling. . . . . . . *True / False*

3. Your lover should be your best friend .... *True / False*
4. Life crises can destroy a relationship .... *True / False*
5. Good sex is important for a lasting relationship .. *True / False*

Current research shows that all of these statements are false. Choosing an intimate relationship with someone as much like you as possible is what makes for the longest lasting, healthiest, happiest relationship.[2] Contrary to romantic myths, love is the way one treats another person and not a feeling-state in which one finds oneself.[3] While it is often said that liking is a prerequisite for loving, research shows clearly that liking and loving are only mildly related.[4] Liking is easy and is based on appreciating the qualities of another person that make us feel good. Loving requires us to make someone else feel good and to feel very good when doing so.

What researchers call the "Romeo and Juliet Factor" shows that relationships more likely to do well and last long are those that suffer though many crises together, not those that revel in a splendid, romantic world.[5] There is something about a crisis that generates unique, powerful energy. When this energy is tapped constructively by two persons who understand the necessity of suffering, the result is a gift of lasting and growing love.

Last, and perhaps surprising for many, is that too much good sex actually interferes with the development and maintenance of lasting intimacy. Sex can become a shortcut for passion and can allow us to avoid the hard work, time, and personal vulnerability spent talking, listening, and understanding. When asked to rate what matters most in their relationship, most respondents indicated that ninety-nine percent of it was unrelated to sex.[6]

This chapter shows you the pleasurable Polynesian way to a lasting, loving, joyful relationship. It also shows how our modern emphasis on love as an individual feeling and on relationships formed to gratify the self are a leading cause of Delight Deficiency Syndrome.[7]

Polynesian Partnership

Researchers have identified three types of marriage.[8] The *volatile relationship,* characterized by frequent conflicts and emotional outbursts, and the *conflict-avoiding relationship,* in which one partner surrenders to the other in order to avoid conflicts, are related to the dominator model of relationship discussed in Chapter 10. The third type, the *validating relationship,* is similar to Oceanic intimacy and has a pleasure-partnership orientation. It is characterized by putting the family's welfare before individual concerns, having frequent compromise and collaboration, and calmly working out problems. In Oceanic tradition, this primary intimate relationship is first and foremost a *compassionate* coupling.

New research is documenting that Oceanic tradition has had it right all along. Marriage is strong and lasting when it is made up of two persons who have learned to suffer together in addition to being drawn together by romantic attraction. It is perpetuated by the partners' mutual effort to "do" love, to "make" love, rather than to "create" love. Shakespeare honored this love in *The Two Gentlemen of Verona:* "They do not love that do not show their love."

Applying the pleasure prescription to an intimate relationship requires much more than good communication, exciting sex, and romantic gimmicks. It is based on knowing how to be patient, connected, pleasant, selfless, and tender enough to keep the relationship together through the bad times. It acknowledges and accepts differences between partners and is founded on the premise that there will be mutual effort to make the relationship a joyful place to be for both partners—*and* for everyone influenced by the relationship.

Differences in what constitutes intimacy, adequate sexual frequency, and sufficient romance are natural. Relationships fail when one partner clings to his or her view and is unwilling to form a new, collective view. In the Oceanic orientation, two selves become one with an entirely new "us" orientation to the many faces and expressions of love.

While it can be erotic, an Oceanic partnership is based on tolerance and patience. It is predicated on permanence, the assumption that the relationship *will* never end because, like all natural connections, it *can* never end. It deemphasizes self-fulfillment in favor of doing and sacrificing for the partner and, by extension, the family. It is often a relationship established more for the good of the community than for the individuals in the relationship. It is a two-person hula, a dance of loving tenderness that celebrates unity with and protection of the world.

The quality of an Oceanic relationship is based on the pleasure it generates within itself and from itself for everything around it. It is the core of the *'ohana* (family) and therefore must be like the sturdy root of a growing plant. Here is the Pleasurable Relationship Test based on Oceanic intimacy. Both you and your partner should take it, then discuss your answers together.

The Pleasurable Relationship Test

That's us = 2
Sometimes that's us = 1
That's never us = 0

1. Do you look forward to seeing each other every day and start and end the day with kind words for each other?
2. Do you enjoy playing together—cards, chess, board games, golf, tennis—or engaging in other recreational activities together?
3. Do you compliment each other at least five times more than you criticize one another and speak positively about your partner to others?
4. Do you laugh together frequently and enjoy one another's jokes and humor?
5. Do you easily forgive and forget?
6. Do you share almost everything and live free of territory, possessions, and attempts to dominate the relationship?
7. Do you sit quietly with one another just being together without watching television or reading?
8. Do you make love much more than you argue?
9. Do you respect each other even when one of you is behaving in an immature manner?
10. Is your family and the world a better place because of your relationship?

Total Pleasurable Relationship Score ____

16–20 = A merry relationship
12–15 = In need of more shared pleasure
11 and below = In urgent need of shared pleasure

Here are five suggestions—what I call "Pleasure Prompters"—for cultivating a more lasting, natural, pleasurable relationship.

Relationship Pleasure Prompter 1: Happy, Healthy Relationships Are Based More on Patience than Passion

Remember, both you and your partner married both a fool and a sage. Tolerate each other's weaknesses as indicators of unique potential and of your need for each other.

Patient partners: Ahonui in relationships Don't marry for love, marry when you are ready to love. Marry slowly, rationally, carefully, and compassionately, not quickly, romantically, impulsively, and passionately. Create love day by day by doing it, not trying to feel it. Remember that good marriages depend on being the right partner, not finding the right partner. A joyful relationship requires that you try every day to be exactly the person you would want to be married to.

I cannot emphasize this enough: marriages are failing today because they cannot fulfill the purpose we have assigned them—to provide a way to achieve more self-fulfillment. If both of you are taking from the relationship and not giving anything to it, soon there will be nothing left to sustain it and it will disappear. A healthy relationship requires a mutual choice to work together to enhance each other.

Lust never lasts. While courtship involves eroticism and physical attraction, these feelings are transitory. They serve as the force initiating the formation of a relationship, but because they affect us in an intensely personal and vulnerable area, they will never be strong enough to maintain the relationship through the turmoil of an exciting, chaotic, meaningful life. If you think you are in love, go someplace and rest until the feeling passes. Then return to your relationship and start behaving lovingly.

Research shows that long-lasting relationships require about seven years to develop their "love legs" and establish an intimate momentum, so the principle of *ahonui* (patience) is crucial to strong relationships.[9] If we are loving enough to allow time for this bonding to take place, such a bond can actually reduce the chance of serious illness and help heal damaged hearts.[10]

An intimate partnership evolves through the following three stages:

1. *The Thrilling Romance Phase.* This is the time of "attraction": you feel strong physical fascination with a new partner. It is excitement, but not commitment. This phase always passes.
2. *The Addiction/Dependency Phase.* This time is characterized by feeling consumed by and trying to consume the partner. You may think of him or her almost constantly and feel a temporary, childlike, complete dependence on your partner.
3. *The Choice: Detachment, Attachment, or Bonding.* There always comes a time when you must make a choice: to end it, surrender to it as an adequate place to be, or continue to create and nurture it as a growing system.

Unless you are patient, your union will not make it to and through the choice phase. Your need for a family and to have children may be displaced into extramarital affairs in order to recapture the illusion of high eroticism, and your relationship will suffer.

One *kahuna* offered me this view of an intimate relationship: "When you think you are in love, you are being directed only by selfishness. Love is not a feeling, it is a choice. It is how you treat a person, not just how you feel about a person. It is what you do everyday with and for a person, not how urgently and strongly you feel about a person. Once you learn to *do* loving, loving is forever. It takes many, many years to learn how to love someone, so you must be persistently patient with your partner and with yourself. If you think you are falling out of love, you are getting love lazy and not doing enough real loving. Only very patient persons should marry, because lasting love is very hard work for a very long time. Anyone can fall in love, but staying in love is a way of daily life led between two persons."

Relationship Pleasure Prompter 2: Relationships Are Forever, So Ending Ours Is Not an Option

The more you speak of ending a relationship, the more you are in crying need of one.

Permanent pairs: Lokahi in relationships Once married, try to stay married at almost any cost. There are, of course, times when divorce is essential. I tell my patients to follow the "triple-A" theory of divorce: end a marriage only if there is adultery, abuse, or addiction. Even in these three circumstances, seek professional help first and do your best to make a marriage out of a mess. The physical, emotional, and mental sideeffects of separation and divorce are almost always worse than staying together—even in a far from optimum relationship—and it may take less energy to solve the problems in the relationship than to prepare for and cope with its end. I have rarely met a person whose own life and the lives of others were made healthier and happier in the long run by ending a marriage relationship.[11]

Most of us embrace the idea of "parenting" and are concerned about raising healthy and happy children. Unfortunately, we have yet to vigorously and selflessly consider the art of "marriaging" or raising, protecting, and developing our most intimate relationship. Raise and develop your marriage as you would a growing child, for a relationship is an entity formed by and larger than the two of you. Only end your relationship with the thought that you are throwing away that child.

Relationship Pleasure Prompter 3: Avoid SAADD Language: No Sarcasm, Accusations, Assumptions, Demands, or Demeaning

Words have power (*mana*) and how you speak is as important as what you say.

Pleasant partners: 'Olu'olu in relationships Opposites attract, but they soon and almost inevitably repel. To form a strong relationship, look for someone who is very much like you and the image of your "perfect" self, and then try to become more like that person once you find her or him. If you are already in a relationship, work harder to become more like what you admire in your partner than you do to get your partner to become like you.

We often take the most liberties and are most careless with those we are closest to. Some of this may be behavior that is carried over from our relationships with parents and siblings. Some of it may be sanctioned by power imbalances between partners that are accepted—or taught—by society. But even in healthy relationships, the comfort that comes with familiarity and trust can easily lull us into loving laziness. We may become careless in our speech, forgetting to say "thank you" or "excuse me," or to extend the most common courtesies to the person most deserving of uncommon courtesy. Perhaps because of fatigue from the high of the initial stages of an intimate relationship, we fail to work hard to be kind, and are sometimes more kind and polite to strangers than to our own spouse. Many marriages simply suffer from bad manners and rudeness that would never be shown to a complete stranger or colleague at work.

To make a joyful union, avoid sarcasm, because it leads to withdrawal. Avoid accusations, because they lead to rebellion. Avoid assumptions, for they render meaningful communication irrelevant and create self-fulfilling prophecies. And avoid demands, because they lead to confrontations and counterdemands. Never demean your partner, for it leads to surrender and feelings of helplessness or a pattern of counterattacks and emotional retreat.

Relationship Pleasure Prompter 4: Give Five Compliments for Every One Criticism

Criticism always leads to negative physiological reactions, which block rational thinking, loving feelings, and caring behavior.

Praising partners: Ha'aha'a in relationships As you read earlier, when criticism is used to create change in a relationship, it eventually destroys the relationship because it leads to flooding and stonewalling, which have physical, emotional, and mental repercussions. Relationships can adapt and grow when partners complain constructively about specific behaviors that need changing for the good of the system. Obliging relationships are joyful relationships. They feel pleasant because the partners work hard to behave in a congenial and amiable manner. They are free of hostile negative attacks and selfish efforts focused on getting one's way. Instead, these relationships are characterized by helping one another to find a new and better way to love. They are collaborative efforts to find a creative way to live, instead of competitive or domineering efforts to get the most out of or from someone else.

A *kahuna* said, "If you put your partner down, that is exactly where they will stay and how they will feel. Always try to put your partner up, make him or her feel very good, and try to make their life better because they are with you."

Relationship Pleasure Prompter 5: Try a Little Tenderness

If you behave lovingly, you will feel love.

Pleasing partners: Akahai in relationships A *kahuna* said, "Westerners speak of codependence as an illness, but we see it as the ultimate healthy way to relate. Every relationship should be codependent, with each person taking care of the other, trying to please the other, and protecting the other." Our Western culture often sees "sticking it out" as "codependent" and struggling with natural developmental crises as "dysfunction." The Oceanic way is to be "creatively interdependent" by working hard to help your partner when he or she is down, knowing and accepting that all of us struggle with life's challenges and are not "dysfunctional" when we argue, get sad, or can't seem to cope too well. When healthy dependency of love goes only one way is when our relationships get in trouble." Make what is important to your partner as important to you as your partner is.

Sex can be one of the most exciting and fulfilling aspects of a relationship, but it can also be one of its greatest risks. As pointed out earlier, sex offers a shortcut to intense interaction. It can be a quick and easy physical excitement that bypasses or becomes a substitute for other, more intimate ways of communicating.[12] Too often, sex becomes a stress reliever, a way of relaxing at the end of the day, a means to self-gratification, or a way to make up after an argument. When sex becomes more release, escape, or therapy than expression of connection and caring, it robs the relationship of its vital *mana* or energy.

Take the time to just be together, touch and hold one another, and connect with each other beyond the physical. Your seventh sense can be your most erotic sense because it coordinates and maximizes all of your other senses, but it will not emerge without time and focus. When you are together, feel how the presence of your partner gives you pleasure and sense how your presence gives pleasure to your partner. This time of communing is very tangible. Do you feel it in your skin, your gut, or your mind? Can you almost "smell" it? Does it run like an energy from your fingertips to your heart? One of my patients called this technique "having silent sex."

A *kupuna* who had been married 57 years summed up the Oceanic way of relating intimately when she said, "My husband and I see our marriage as our most treasured gift. We are so lucky to be together and to have one another to remind us about the sunsets and sunrises, that we would never do anything to ruin that gift. Without each other, there could be no pleasure."

Chapter Thirteen

RAISING BLISSFUL FAMILIES IN PRESSURED TIMES

"I take my children everywhere, but they always seem to find their way back home."

— Erma Bombeck

What one lesson above all others do you want your children and the children of your relatives and friends to learn about life? The Polynesian response to this question is always immediate and clear, as typified by this Hawaiian mother: "I want my *keiki* (child) to learn *aloha*—how to love. I want her to live *aloha* every day and to be able to teach her children to live *aloha*." The health and the happiness of our world depends on the children we give to it, and many researchers are concerned that the modern answer to this question is less about selfless love than accomplishment, acquisition, and autonomy.

As you read in Parts One and Two, depression among our children is increasing at an alarming rate. It is shocking to learn that suicides and attempted suicides among children *under age ten* are increasing. As hard as we have tried to give our children everything, we are failing at an alarming rate to give them the one skill that would bring them the most happiness and health: the emotional intelligence to live a patient, joyful, sharing life.

The word *parent* used to be considered a noun, but popular psychology has turned it into a verb. Adults used to "be" a parent rather than "do" the job, but today "parenting" has become a skill to master that results in successful children who are able to compete with other children. Our ancestors did not "parent"; they created a mutually responsible family based on reciprocity of caregiving. Children were not "raised"; they lived, worked, and absorbed their values from within the family system. They were expected to contribute to the family and were obligated to help their parents, grandparents, and siblings to develop even as they themselves were cared for into maturity. In Polynesia this is still the approach to parenting. Hawaiians call it "family-ing," or *'ohana.*

The Institutionalization and Computerization of Families

Here on the mainland, we have divested ourselves of the meaning of family and the family system. We have turned our families over to institutions. The most important and difficult task in life—helping someone grow up in a pressured and changing world—has become a lost art. Divorce, separation, single-parent (which almost always means single mother) homes, day-care centers, and long days in increasingly violent schools that end with return to an empty home are increasingly the norm. As one twelve-year-old boy alarmingly told me, "It isn't any fun growing up. And I'm not sure it's worth it."

Despite our politicians' expressions of concern for family values, many of them are themselves divorced and ignore their own babies to kiss those of strangers. Distant extended families and a fast-paced lifestyle have resulted in an emotional "homelessness." Families seldom eat or play together, and much of the joy of growing and learning has been replaced with trying to provide things for children to give them a "competitive advantage."

Rather than taking the time to select television programs to watch with our children, we are developing the V-chip, a computer system that will censor our children's television viewing in our absence. Our children spend more time on the Internet than in our laps. Day-care centers, computers, and shopping malls are the "home" we offer our young people.

Like it or not, computers and institutions cannot teach *aloha* or raise joyful children. Caring for children is too complex a task for any one person, and draws on love, instinctive responsibility, and spiritual investment. Stable, long-lasting pair bonds evolved so that two people would care for the very dependent young that we mammals have during their long years of development. Tribal structures and close-knit communities meant that husbands and wives were seldom separated for long periods of time, and even when separation was necessary, the entire community was small enough and connected enough to keep a collective, protective eye on the children.

With *'ohana,* the Oceanic approach to "familying," the child or *keiki,* is treated like a seedling (*keiki* also means a young plant). As they develop, *keiki* are to be protected and cared for by everyone, but their development also involves caring for other *keiki* and *makua* (parents). *'Ohana* stresses a steady, leisurely, joyful approach to child-care. Mealtimes are sacred rituals during which lessons of respect are modeled and taught. Ancestors and living elders are revered, and children are expected to help and care for the family. Failure to provide a child with the opportunity and privilege of caring for and showing respect not only for the immediate family but for all elders and the community is considered the ultimate child abuse.

Ho'oponopono: Oceanic Family Therapy

The *aloha* way of familying involves singing, dancing, fishing, playing, and walking together as a family—not chauffeuring children to ballet classes, soccer, and little league. When family problems and conflicts take place, they should be addressed immediately, in a sacred ritual called *ho'oponopono,* meaning to make right again, to bring the family system back in balance.

Ho'oponopono involves hours of talking as a family, to return balance to the family. First there is *pule 'ohana* (family prayer), followed by time spent talking story to identify the person or people who violated the family code of *aloha*. Tangible restitution must be made in the form of apology, making amends for a transgression, replacing a broken object, or making a commitment to more loving and caring conduct. Once *ho'oponopono* is over, there is to be no more talking about the problem by anyone in the family. A *pule 'ohana* is said, and a celebration is held to signal the end of the conflict and the reestablishment of *pono* (balance).

The entire process is based on a scared commitment to live family life by the five principles of *aloha*. Praying for the family is not just a nice thing to do but a key way to bring healing energy from ancestors and God to bear on the problem. Would your family benefit from its own form of *ho'oponopono?* Do you have personal, learning, and peace-making rituals that should be practiced more often? Happy families spend at least as much time in the home "setting the family right" as working outside the home to get the right things.

To assess the healthy pleasure in your own family life, take the following test. If possible, get together and take this test as a family and discuss the results.

Pleasurable Familying Test

That's us = 2
Sometimes that's us = 1
That's almost never us = 0

1. Does your family eat at least one happy, peaceful meal together every day?
2. Is there a lot of laughter in your house?
3. Are older relatives respected and treated with patient kindness?
4. Does your family have its own rituals and customs that have been practiced for years and continue to be practiced joyfully today?
5. Does your family operate by the principle that no one is finished with his or her household chores if another family member is still doing chores? Does everyone chip in and help with any and all tasks?
6. Does your family play games together as a group, with everyone taking part voluntarily?
7. Does your family watch very little television?
8. Does your family share everything; do all family members feel they can tell any family member anything?
9. Would your family support and stand behind all of its members, no matter what?

10. Is your family free of bickering, name-calling, and put-downs?

Total Family Pleasure Score ____

16–20 = A merry family
12–15 = In need of more shared pleasure
11 and below = In urgent need of shared pleasure

Here are some suggestions to help boost your family pleasure.

Family Pleasure Prompter 1: All Family Members Make Up Family Members' Minds

The family psychological ecology and every member of the family constantly molds the brains of every child and adult in the family—so form a more patient state of mind.

Making a patient mind: Ahonui for the family

Psychoneurological research now proves what Polynesian *kahuna* knew centuries ago. Our brains are not formed at birth but continue to grow new cells and connections as long as we live. The brains of the youngest child and the oldest grandparent are constantly reconstructed by the atmosphere of the family, by a kind of "connective cerebral ecology." Whether we form happy love maps with well-established glee centers, or etch angry, temper templates depends on the atmosphere the entire family creates together.

Psychoneuroimmunological research shows that it is possible to sculpt the brain for patient pleasure. We can directly influence how the brain grows by creating a steady, dependable environment in which reasonable risks can be taken without fear of rejection. This works even when we are adults, but the brains of children are particularly ripe for what might be called "pruning for pleasure."

Children are born with millions more neurons, or brain cells, than their adult brain will ever need. Through a process called *neurological pruning,* the brain loses the neuronal connections, or synapses, that are less used, and forms strong connections in the synaptic circuits that have been utilized the most. This pruning allows the brain to focus more on what has been called for by early experiences. So if these experiences have been characterized by a calm, even-tempered family life, the brain forms itself into a patient brain. If there has been hostility, criticism, and physical or emotional violence in the family setting, only the angry, selfish, impatient brain paths remain.

Pruning is constant and occurs very fast. Old synapses disappear and new ones form in a matter of hours or days. In effect, a person's brain is sculpted from birth to adulthood and even late into life.[1] If we teach and model the pleasure prescription in our family life, we nurture a beautiful garden in which children grow into loving, caring parts of the family system.

As parents and as a society we are the gardeners of the next crop of adults. If we nurture with *aloha*, we will reap a world of balance and patience. If we neglect our vulnerable crop or expose it to impatience, aggression, and hostility, we will reap a generation of intolerant, selfish, hurried people and, by extension, a combative, violent world.

A *kahuna* said, "Our *keiki* are our flowers and we are their roots. They will be roots some day, so we must nurture them and let them learn to nurture us too. We must be patient with our *keiki*. One would not yell at a flower to make it grow."

Family Pleasure Prompter 2: Get Out More Together

The recent trend toward "cocooning," or staying inside the home with only a few "vacations" or sorties out into the natural world, is starving families of the light of their life.

Lightening up together: Lokahi in the family How much time does your family spend together outdoors? This simple question tells much about the healthy pleasure your family experiences. Lack of full-spectrum light, which is the light of sunlight, is now known to relate to a condition called Seasonal Affective Disorder (SAD).[2] Symptoms include anxiety, reluctance to go to work or school, withdrawal from social interaction, self-criticism, tossing and turning at night and trouble falling asleep, inability to get out of bed in the morning because of lack of sleep, and *anhedonia* (the lack of the ability to take pleasure from daily life).

About 20 percent of people are vulnerable to SAD because they are extremely light sensitive. The symptoms usually begin in the early teens and may last throughout life. Unlike clinically depressed people, SAD people do not tend to lose their appetites; instead, they gorge on food. My clinical work indicates that not only SAD individuals but their entire families suffer from lack of healthy light.

While many explanations are possible, I find that families who get outside together tend to have less conflicts, resolve their conflicts more quickly, and feel more energized as a group. Research shows that the fluorescent lights found in homes and schools are particularly deficient in ultraviolet illumination. Students in schools with broad spectrum ultraviolet lights have almost half the illnesses that students in schools with fluorescent lights experience.[3] And the families in my clinic who experience more natural light also reported less illnesses.

Lighting at 2,500 lux, an amount similar to standing by the window on a bright spring day, actually stimulates the brain for pleasure. The pineal gland, a tiny organ in the middle of the brain just behind the eyes, secretes a substance called *melatonin.* Light stimulates the secretion of this hormone and, as a result, sleep comes more easily and a natural, calm life cycle results.

With more rest, our mood elevates and pleasure comes more easily. A "non-moody" family is a less agitated, more united family. Polynesian families have the luxury of natural sunlight almost every day of their lives, and many families take full advantage of this by swimming, fishing, boating, and picnicking together several days a week. If you are concerned about your family mood, try spending a weekend outdoors together and watch for the household tenor to improve in the following week.

There is also a reverse form of SAD in which people become depressed in the light of summer and more agitated and manic in the winter. This may be caused by staying inside in darkened rooms with humming air conditioners, or by a particular heat sensitivity.[4] Playing with children outdoors in mild temperatures, in small doses of sunshine, will actually train the brain to think with *aloha*.

Don't forget that the concept of *'ohana* includes the community, plants, animals, fish, rocks, and trees. So a "family outing" is a connection with nature, not a trip to see it. Helping to heal the earth by doing community cleanups or planting trees will make your family—and the world family—stronger.

A *kahuna* said, "The family must be with the whole family. The whole family is the land. Go to the land as a family and you will grow together like the *'ohi'a lehua* flower that sprouts from the rocks of the volcano. The *'ohi'a* flower comes in many forms, but it always grows in clusters as the sun pulls it from the warm rock. It has leaves of various shapes and blossoms of many forms and hues, but all flourish with the sun and rain. Your family is healed by the *'aina.*"

Family Pleasure Prompter 3: Cool It—Feelings Are Not Facts, and You Don't Always Have to Express Them

Contrary to popular psychology, there is little therapeutic value and potentially serious health consequences from "letting it all hang out."

Coaching for coolness: 'Olu'olu in the family The areas of the brain that can override our more impulsive lower brain are also the slowest to develop. Anyone can raise an angry, impatient, hostile, selfish child because the lower brain (which deals with these emotions) has a head start over the calm, patient, loving areas of the brain. As parents and educators, we can influence whether a brain develops blissfully or urgently from childhood right through adolescence and into adulthood.[5] By coaching our children and young adults not to let their urgent lower brain instruct their actions, by talking with them about and—more importantly—modeling pleasant and agreeable ways of living, we can help the prefrontal lobes and brain circuitry related to such behaviors to develop and begin to exercise control.

Perhaps one of the most important brain-training tasks for children is showing them how to calm themselves when they are upset. When a child is upset, a caretaker usually soothes and rocks the child. This not only comforts the child, it teaches the child how to comfort himself and others.[6] Polynesians teach that allowing a child to comfort elders is another way to teach the art of calming. If you spend some time observing modern "parenting," you will note that many parents seem uncertain about how to deal with an unhappy or ornery child; perhaps this is because they themselves were too seldom calmed and never taught how to lovingly and tenderly soothe another person.

Psychologist John Gottman's research illustrates the importance of calming, which can elicit the bliss response in both the "calmer" and the "calmee." It involves the *vagus nerve,* which is connected to the heart, the adrenal glands, and the amygdala. All of these interact to create what Gottman calls *vagal tone.* When this tone is one of anger, the result is the urgency response. Neurological vagal temper can be trained to calm down.[7] Gottman has shown that talking gently and patiently with children about their feelings and showing them how to understand them rather than just express them is coaching for calmness and for being a pleasant family member. Living one's own life with a modulated vagal tone provides the best role model for a developing child.[8]

A *kahuna* who conducts *ho'oponopono* for troubled Hawaiian families said, "When there is sickness, I always look at the family to see what their tone is. Sometimes I can feel an angry tone and I know that no one will be healed until everyone calms down. We do *ho'oponopono* and try to put things right. We do not just express our feelings. We discuss them and teach everyone that they are not just their feelings."

Family Pleasure Prompter 4: Look for How Other Family Members Feel

Try to read the emotions of your family and be sensitive for the subtle cues that express a need for support.

Emotional literacy: Ha'aha'a in the family We spend much time and money promoting literacy. We place great emphasis on when a child learns to talk but little emphasis on when he learns to listen. Our families and schools neglect *emotional* literacy: the ability to read others' emotions, care about them, and deal sensitively with them.[9]

Educator Karen Stone McCown developed what she calls the "Self-Science Curriculum," what might better be called "a less selfish science curriculum."[10] McCown uses the language concepts of life skills, social development, and emotional learning, but she is actually teaching the five components of *aloha*. Instead of stressing competition, self-expression, and power, she teaches children how to see the hurt in others and how to read the need for joy and the fear of loneliness. She teaches children how to perceive nonverbal signs that someone is angry, in distress, or afraid.

To have a happy, healthy family life, we must get out of ourselves and into others. We must be less worried about "codependence" and work harder at fostering interdependence. An excellent way of developing your own and your child's *ha'aha'a,* or emotional literacy, is called the *perceptive pause.* One *kupuna* explained this perfectly: "It is a way of making contact before making a communication. Before you say a word to someone, always pause for several seconds and be quiet. Look before you talk. Read how a person seems to be feeling before you talk, rather than just assessing how that person reacts to what you say. Try less to influence and more to unite. Connect with your eyes before you use your mouth. Never begin talking without looking and never say anything without scanning first."

Family Pleasure Prompter 5: Never Stop Rocking, Cuddling, and Comforting

Everyone knows how much comforting contact babies demand, but many of us forget how much touching, holding, and gentle caressing we continue to need throughout our life.

Staying in touch: Akahai in the Family While the brain exercises much control over the body, the body also constantly forms the brain. Tenderly touching, gently handling, and rocking newborns helps develop those centers of the brain that bring us the most pleasure in adult life.[11] In a very real, psychoneuroimmunological sense, our eroticism, tenderness, and sensuality (our *akahai*) begins and ends in the rocking chair.

Located just behind the limbic system is the part of the brain responsible for balance and coordination. This three-lobe structure is the *cerebellum,* which means "little brain." It controls the timing of well-learned movements such as driving a car, swimming, and other activities that we say once learned are never forgotten. The cerebellum also controls the timing of movements that are too rapid to be controlled consciously, such as playing the piano or doing the hula. Researchers are now discovering that this little brain is much more than a timing, balance, and rote-activity center.

Dr. James Prescott, a developmental neuropsychologist at the National Institute for Child Health and Human Development, hypothesizes that gentle cuddling, rocking, and singing to a child early in life results in the development of the cerebellum and thus a more balanced and joyful person.[12] He suggests that lack of such gentle rhythmic rocking produces confused and fearful overreactions to similar motions in the future. Angry and even aggressive compensations may take place in order to adjust to what seems like a strange tenderness—a type of emotional hyper-reactivity.

Too often, just when our teenage children need gentle comfort and rocking, we pull away from them physically as well as emotionally. Our modern society has developed eroto-phobia to such an extent that claims and diagnoses of sexual abuse often extend beyond reason. This erotophobia denies the various powers of touch. Just as it narrows the touch of marriage partners to sexual, it limits the touch of parental nurture to infants. We are often afraid to hold and comfort our maturing young people. But in trying times, we need to hold and rock them . . . and we need to be held and rocked by them. If we hope to find harmony in our loving, working, and playing, we must return to a more gentle and tender life rhythm.

A *kahuna* summarized the *akahai* element of a pleasured and pleasing *'ohana* with this story of a family, "Grandpa is very, very old and weak. He is over one hundred years old, but nobody knows for sure his exact age. Grandpa has lost control of his bowels and we have to change his diaper several times a day. He needs to be rocked and taken care of now. Nobody minds and we all take turns—the kids, the parents, the uncles, and the aunts. Why not? We have a new little baby in our *'ohana* too, and we have to rock him and change his diapers. The baby needs it and grandpa has earned it. Grandpa has done a lot more for us than the new baby has. Sometimes we rock grandpa and the baby together in the same rocker that rocked our *aumakua* (ancestors). That is the true meaning of *'ohana*."

Chapter Fourteen

LABORING WITH LOVE: HEALTH AND BALANCE IN THE WORKPLACE

"I love work. It fascinates me.
I could sit and stare at it for hours."
— Jerome K. Jerome

Almost all of us work or want to work. In fact, most of us spend more time working than playing or with our families. Whether working is a source of great pleasure and health or a harbinger of stress, burnout, anger, or depression depends in large part on why you work. Before learning about the Oceanic way of working, take the following "work motivation" test. Put a check next to the item or items that most describe the basic reasons you go to work every day.

The Work Motivation Test

1. *Productivity.* Do you work because you feel like you have to get a lot of things done or made? Author Isaac Asimov said, "If my doctor told me I had only six minutes to live, I wouldn't brood. I'd type a little faster."

2. *Knowledge.* Do you work to add to the wisdom of the world? Anthropologist Margaret Mead said, "I was brought up to believe that the only thing worth doing was to add to the sum of accurate information in the world."

3. *Justice.* Do you work to make the world a safer and more equitable place for others? Civil rights activist Martin Luther King, Jr. said, "I have a dream . . . that my four little children will one day live in a nation where they will not be judged by the color of their skin but by the content of their character."

4. *Autonomy.* Do you work to gain independence? Artist Georgia O'Keeffe said, "I can't live where I want to, go where I want to, do what I want to. . . I decided I was a very stupid fool not to at least paint as I wanted to."

5. *Power.* Do you work for status, recognition, and control? Former Secretary of State Henry Kissinger said, "Power is the ultimate aphrodisiac."

6. *Duty.* Do you work because you believe everyone should work? Stateswoman and humanitarian Eleanor Roosevelt said, "As for accomplishments, I just did what I had to do as things came along."

7. *Excellence.* Do you work to achieve distinction and superiority? Olympic gold medalist Florence Griffith Joyner said, "When you've been second best for so long, you can either accept it, or try to become the best. I made the decision to try and be the best."

8. *Money.* Do you work to get more, have more, own more, and do more? Surrealist artist Salvador Dali said, "Liking money like I like it, is nothing less than mysticism. Money is a glory."[1]

9. *Victory.* Is working similar to a contest in which you must engage? Former professional football coach Vince Lombardi said, "Winning isn't everything. It's the only thing."

10. *Fun.* Do you work because you love it? Noel Coward wrote, "Work is more fun than fun."

11. *Obligation.* Do you work because you have no choice? Aristotle wrote, "All paid employments absorb and degrade the mind."

12. *Ecology.* Do you work to heal the planet? Jeannette Armstrong, an ecopsychologist and activist for indigenous people throughout the world, writes, "We are responsible for the Earth. We are keepers of the Earth because we are Earth. We are all Earth."

What motives did you identify as central to the reason you go to work every day? No matter what other motives for working you identified, if you did not put a check by "ecology," it is likely that your work is not bringing you, your family, and the world in general the happiness and health needed.

Polynesian Excellence

When Sigmund Freud was asked to identify the keys to a healthy life, he responded, "Lieben und Arbeiten," to love (*aloha*) and to work *(hana).* He meant that a balance between laboring to make a living and loving to make life worth living is the way to a joyful and healthy existence. Polynesians found that balance in what they called *po'okela,* excellence in working based on valuing the earth over meeting personal objectives.

In our modern world, we are literally working ourselves to death. The average person beginning his first job today will have at least ten job changes in his life. Stress on the job continues to be a leading cause of illness and accounts for billions of lost dollars because of worker inefficiency, despair, tardiness, and absenteeism. If there is joy available on the job, many of us seem too busy, overwhelmed, distracted, or numb to recognize it.

Polynesians, on the other hand, view working as the sacred opportunity to express respect for the world and connection with the community. The number one criterion for assessing their work is whether or not it brings them and others happiness and health. Success is achieved by living up to the five principles of *aloha*.

Informal Surveys on Work

I asked 300 of my undergraduate students at Henry Ford Community College, "What do you want to do for a career when you graduate?" One hundred and seventy answered that they had no idea and the rest were uncertain. Most reported that they were in college because there was nothing else they could do at this time in their life or because their parents expected them to be there.

When I asked the highly successful people I interviewed for this book if they were happy with their work, they gave valuative answers that reflected financial satisfaction or the achievement of status. When they took the "Work Motivation Test," only a few checked the ecology item, but almost all checked the items for productivity, autonomy, power, duty, excellence, victory, and money. They did not say that they were doing what they desired, only that they were doing what brought them tangible rewards. Some called themselves "SOBs" or "sons of the boss," working because their successful parents expected or required them to go into the family business.

When I asked the children of some of these highly successful people what they wanted to be when they grew up, all but four of the ten boys and nine girls aged 4 to 16 answered that they didn't know. The others all answered that they thought they would probably do what their father or mother was doing because they would be expected to enter the family business.

The aspiration of doing something as an adult that brought joy and significance to one's life and the lives of others was far down on the list of reasons for working. The one answer that fit the pleasure prescription approach to working came from a four-year-old girl who answered my question by smiling and saying, "I want to be very, very happy and help make everyone else very, very happy." When she gave her answer, the other children laughed at her.

To assess your own happiness with your work, take the *aloha* work test below. Like all of the five *aloha* tests in this last section, this test is an "us" test and not a "self" test, to be answered in terms of your family (or intimate community).

The Pleasurable Work Test

That's us = 2
Sometimes that us = 1
That's never us = 0

1. Does your family look forward to your return home at the end of the work day?

2. Does your family enjoy happy reports about wonderful experiences at work when you bring them home?
3. Does your family know, understand, and appreciate what you do at work?
4. Is the whole family interested in what you do at work?
5. Would your family say you love your job?
6. Would many in your family like to do what you do for a job?
7. Does your family think that what you do is very helpful to others and the world?
8. Is your family free of worries about your job security?
9. Would your family say they are as important to you as your work and that you put in as much time with them as you do at work?
10. Would your family say you work by your values rather than objectives, and work more to make life better for everyone than to make a better life for a few people?

Total Pleasurable Work Score: ____

16–20 = Joyful, healthy work
12–15 = In need of healthier, more joyful work
11 and below = In urgent need of a healthier, happier job

Based on the Oceanic Third Way to wellness and the pleasure prescription, here are five suggestions to help boost your pleasurable work score.

Working Pleasure Prompter 1: Work to Live, but Never Live to Work

Working is for keeping you, your family, and the world alive and well. It is essential to life but it is not the purpose of life.

Patient working: Ahonui in work When your job becomes the sole purpose of your life, it is only a matter of time before your life will have no purpose. Throughout this book you have read that balance *(pono)* is crucial to health and happiness; it is never more true than in this instance. When working crowds out time for loving, it eventually consumes your love. You become so distracted and busy that those who would love you become afraid to "bother" you with their needs, fears, hopes, and dreams. When work is your purpose in life, your work is never done. When you work to enhance your self rather than the world, those who should matter to you become obligations, bothers, and distractions. You end up isolated, alone.

A *kahuna* said, "When you find that your job is on your mind almost all the time, then you know you are working at losing your mind. When you live to work, all of life becomes work. When you work lovingly and work hard to love, the world is made a more loving place by your work because it is accompanied by loving energy."

A grave danger in our society is that we are now working twice as hard as our great-grandparents with half the joy and half the time to be with our families. We often see work as a way to define the self rather than to give of the self. To work in a way that brings happiness and health, you must see your work as only one of the ways you share your love of the world.

Working Pleasure Prompter 2: Your Job Isn't Yours, It Is Ours

Claiming your task as yours alone will only lead to very high responsibility with very little control.

Unified working: Lokahi in work Collaborative working is the most joyful working. The number-one health risk of working, high responsibility combined with low power, can only be reduced by seeking the power of the group rather than autonomous control. When work becomes a means to achieve status and control or to carve out territory, it is a contest not a contribution. Whether or not we choose to acknowledge it, we can never work alone. All tasks are collective tasks, even if we do our work at home or communicate by computer. Modern research and Polynesian wisdom teaches: if at all possible, work in face-to-face groups.

Our need for connection is exemplified by the information highway's most popular online subjects. More time is spent on the Internet communicating about two things: sex and the paranormal. One reason these subjects attract the most interest is because they are things that matter most to us—intimate connection and the meaning and mysteries of life.

A *kahuna* said, "Never think you are your job or that your job is yours. You are just filling a role much like an actor takes on a role in a play. Others have done it and will do it. When you swim in the ocean, you are not the only swimmer. You are probably not the best swimmer. It's not your ocean. And whether you know it or not, there are millions of creatures swimming all around you. You are just a human fish in a school of fishes. You are a person enjoying what everyone and everything enjoys. But if you try to claim a part of the ocean for yourself or take in the whole ocean, you will drown. If you work hard to be the best swimmer, you will just miss out on the joy of swimming."

Working Pleasure Prompter 3: Don't Work at Your Job, Enjoy Your Job's Purpose

To be happy and healthy at work, remember the reasons you are working and try to make one of those reasons ecological.

Pleasant working: 'Olu'olu in work Researchers have identified something called the Black Monday Phenomenon.[2] More fatal heart attacks occur on Monday morning at around 9:00 A.M. than at any other time of the week. No other living creature dies on one day more than another, but we humans seem unhappy enough with our work that it breaks our heart. Research shows that sudden death occurs at the beginning of the work week not only because of the extra physical exertion that comes from the stress of transitioning from the weekend couch to the Monday rush hour but because of the emotional distress of returning to a job that brings and gives too little happiness.[3]

To reduce the Black Monday factor in your own life, sit down every Monday morning before leaving for work and remember why you are working. If you drive a delivery truck, try to think of doing so because others need the food or the services that you bring them, not because your boss will fire you if you don't show up. Ask yourself, "Who is ultimately helped by what I do, and how does what I do help them?"

A *kahuna* said, "Fishing and taro farming are very difficult, but they are never really work because they are the way we connect with the land. They are more joyful working than hard working because they give the opportunity to be one with the land and to help the land. What else could be more fun? We look forward to every morning because it is another chance to be with the earth. Even if we are exhausted and feel the pain in our back at the end of the day, we think of these as love pains, like those you have after vigorous lovemaking. They are your body's signs that you have loved the *'aina.*"

Working Pleasure Prompter 4: Define Your Work and Describe It to Yourself and Others by Its Purpose, Not Its Task

When someone asks what you do for a living, answer in terms of the ultimate purpose of your working and not your specific job description.

Humble working: Ha'aha'a in work In a society that values status, achievement, and measurable signs of success, it is tempting to brag about what we do. The power of the helper's high is that giving and sharing brings much more healthy happiness than does self-recognition. Keeping in mind the values and the higher purpose of your work—not the specific task objectives—is the best way to avoid burnout.

Humble, or *ha'aha'a,* working is conducted with little concern for receiving "due credit" and more with concern with doing our best to fulfill the objective of our working.

A *kupuna* said, "You can only burn out if you are really, really hot. If you work for and by values such as love, caring, fairness, and *aloha 'aina* (love of the earth), you cannot burn out, because you are cooled by the natural breath of the earth. That is what *aloha* means. You feel the healthy, fresh breath of the *'aina* when you help it breathe."

Working Pleasure Prompter 5: Work Gently, Not Hard

If you are working hard at your job, your job is working hard on you.

Tender working: Akahai in work Pay attention to the effort you put into your work. Do you keep a "work stress pharmacy" of aspirin and antacids in your desk at work? What is your body telling you about how you are working? Hard and fast work almost always results in inefficiency and even injury. By reading your body's signs about the impact of your work, you can discover ways to make the circumstances of your work more enjoyable.

Don't just attend to what happens on the job but also to how hard you seem to be working or how much effort you expend just to get to and from work. How many of your aches and pains at the end of the day are due to your tasks and how many to your hours spent gripping the steering wheel of your car during rush hour?

Many of us spend almost one full workday a week in traveling to and from work. If this is a necessity for you, make the best of it. Make this time some of the most relaxing, enjoyable time of your week. Leave early for work so you are never pressed for time. Listen to relaxing music or an enjoyable book or tape, carpool so you can talk with others about life (not work!), and try to flow with traffic rather than fight against it.

Here are six other suggestions for softening up your work.

1. *Return calls immediately.* Pressure builds up with the number of unanswered phone calls, and those calling are likely to become more impatient and angry as they wait. Don't say you will get back to someone if you don't mean it. If you say it, do it.

2. *Always take time to inquire of callers and office visitors as to how their day is going.* Do this with real interest that reflects your concern for the welfare of the other person. Even if you don't feel concern at first, remember that motivation is preceded by behavior. Do it to feel it. Respond to the person's answer honestly and legitimately. Talking about life issues is not a waste

of valuable work time; it is crucial to effective, efficient, and meaningful work.

3. *Follow the OHIO rule: "Only Handle It Once."* Cut down on the piles of files that accumulate around you by making decisions at once about filing or throwing away correspondence, phone messages, and memos. Your in-box should almost always be running on empty. The repercussions of making a mistake and throwing away something that might be needed are usually far less negative than the buildup of "ought-to-do" and "maybe-will-do-later" pressures that eventually bury you and make your task overwhelming.

4. *Phone home.* At least once a day, give your family a quick call to say you care and to ask how things are going. This helps slow down the pace at work and strengthens your feelings of connection with your family. These calls also reduce the reactive stress of emergency "problem calls" from home.

5. *Don't spread rumors at work.* Whether true or not, rumors almost always involve talking about someone who is not present and unable to offer a defense. Words have power, so keep your discussions immediate and positive.

6. *Compliment as much as possible.* Modern work is often based on faultfinding or blame-avoiding. Speaking positively about the work of others is one way to counter negatives in the workplace, and it helps create a mindset of looking for what's right.

A *kahuna* summarized this approach when he said, "The harder and harder you fish, the less the fish will come. They sense the stress and they do not want to give themselves to someone who has so much negative energy. Enjoy the ocean, the sky, the clouds, and those with whom you are fishing. The fish will come to work with you in making everything *pono* (balanced). Their job is to be nice fish who come to nice fishermen. Your job is to try to be a nice fisherman."

Chapter Fifteen

LOVING AND LEARNING THROUGH THE HARD TIMES

"It is not the threat of death, illness, hardship, or poverty that crushes the human spirit; it is the fear of being alone and unloved in the universe."

— Anthony Welsh

To the island people, suffering is an essential part of pleasure. They realize that there are only two ways to find meaning and purpose in living—epiphany and suffering. The sudden revelation and enlightenment of an epiphany is a wonderfully powerful experience. Epiphanies usually happen to people who are open-minded and open-hearted enough to learn from the miracles that occur every day. If we stay alert to the joyful wonders of daily living and overcome our fear of the sacred, we can find great wisdom and joy in the natural and spontaneous epiphanies of our life.

The second path to joyful enlightenment, suffering, is the more difficult but profound. The heartaches of life can be powerful lessons in why we live and the joys to be had from our living. The first of Buddha's "Four Noble Truths" is "Life is suffering."[1] The Third Way to well-being teaches that there is a big difference between healthy suffering that comes naturally *from* the illness, loss, and the universal catastrophes of life, and the unhappy suffering that comes from resenting adversity, falling short of "having it all," being disappointed at not getting "our full share," and feeling treated unfairly by the cosmos.[2]

I noticed the difference when I experienced cancer. As my hips were eaten away by the disease, the pain was unbearable. I suffered terribly and often became angry that I was "being put through" this horrible experience. Around the same time that I was sick, one of my dogs also became very ill. Desi was a sad-looking basset hound who was also in extreme pain. As I complained, whined, and protested the unfairness of my situation, Desi would slowly walk to the window, lie down in the sun, and let out a loud groan. She would whimper whenever she moved, but otherwise rested and wagged her tail when I looked at her. Like me, Desi was in pain and suffering terribly from her illness. Unlike Desi, I worsened my suffering by a selfish and martyred view of life. Desi did not question her situation, but I spent hours asking why *I* should be the one bearing this burden. The healthy suffering I finally learned from the *kahuna*, which I write of in this chapter, acknowledges that suffering is inevitable. Suffering is a mandatory requirement of the gift of being alive. Misery, on the other hand, is optional and comes from not working to understand the catastrophes of living.

While no one likes to be in emotional, physical, or spiritual pain or to go through the chaos of deep loss, we all must. Great suffering can be a powerful learning tool for insight into joyful living. Practicing the pleasure prescription involves being open not only to the glory of epiphany but also to the challenge of suffering.

We often shy away from the crises that cycle through our lives and seek only to return to what we see as normal, happy, and problem-free. Just as we must overcome our fear of the sacred in order to practice the principles of pleasure, we must also overcome our fear of life's new challenges.

A *kahuna* said, "We are afraid of fear, depressed by our sadness, and unhappy with our unhappiness. This only makes us too afraid to learn from our challenges, too despondent to learn from our losses, and too dejected to learn from the natural and necessary times of sorrow. The way of *aloha* is to learn and grow through all of our experiences and to see whatever we are given by the gods and our ancestors as required courses in learning why we live."

A Canon of Catastrophe

There seems to be a bitter rule of life that might be called "magnetic misery." People who have a lot of problems seem to attract even more problems. In your own life you may recall times when something went terribly wrong and then several other things also went sour around the same time. One reason is that when we are challenged, distracted, and weakened by a crisis, we become more vulnerable to other crises. However, beyond the reactive vulnerability, the fatigue, and overextension we experience at difficult times, why is it that problems have a power to attract more problems?

In my clinical work, I have noticed that those experiencing what I call "serial suffering" are often rejected by some of their closest friends. Despite the fact that their problems are very real and not their fault, many people in their lives just don't want to hear about them. They often pull away, as if saying, "I just can't hear any more of this. I feel sorry for you, but it bothers me to hear all these negatives. I'm even beginning to get a little angry with you, and that makes me mad at myself for being so insensitive. In fact, I'm even a little afraid your problems may begin to rub off on me, so please let me get away from this. Good luck and good-bye."

The canon of cumulative catastrophes not only teaches that problems seem to attract more problems but that others' pulling away because of these problems causes an isolation that results in more problems. One way of minimizing this is to work hard to maintain social connection during times of distress. Diffusing negative energy through social support is a key way to deal with suffering, but the challenge is that few people want to be around people with problems. Sending out pleasure to others even when you are suffering is an effective way of dealing with the strain and pain that fills our lonely brain. In other words, trying to send out a little pleasure even when you yourself are in pain is the best way to reduce the pain for yourself and others.

To assess the degree to which the pleasure principles are neutralizing the influence of the misery factor in your own life, take the following test. Like the other tests in Part Three, the following is also an "us" test and not a "self" test. The Polynesians teach that all pain and pleasure is a matter of the Whole and a system reaction. This is because of the *mana,* or unmitigated, unmediated, immediate energy generated during times of turmoil.

The Growth from Pain Test

That's us = 2
Sometimes that's us = 1
That's never us = 0

1. Do your family and friends joke with you about your problems even when these problems are very serious?
2. Does your family avoid the blame and accusations that come with life's problems?
3. Does your family start talking together more and more when problems strike instead of pulling away from one another?
4. Is your family free from self-pity, feelings of victimhood, or the martyring of one extremely and seemingly constantly needy member?
5. At times of crisis, does your family consider itself lucky to be together rather than sulking and distancing from one another?
6. Does your family pray, reflect, or contemplate together when problems strike?
7. Can everyone in your family tell every other family member anything and express their true fears and worries?
8. Does your family cry together?
9. Is your family "real"—facing and experiencing problems head-on rather than trying to put forth a good front and positive attitude?
10. Is your family made stronger by their pain instead of being weakened and torn apart by it?

Total Pleasurable Pain Score: ____

16–20 = Your family thrives through suffering
12–15 = Your family needs to share more during times of suffering
11 and below = Your family urgently needs more sharing and support during times of suffering

Psychiatrist Victor Frankl wrote, "Even the helpless victim of a hopeless situation, facing a fate he cannot change, may rise above himself, may grow beyond himself, and by so doing change himself." The pleasure prescription for dealing with suffering emphasizes this "changing through challenge" approach to crises.

Here are five suggestions that can help you and your family weather life's natural crises.

Healing Prompter 1: With a Little Grit, a Little Grace, and a Lot of Love, This Too Shall Pass

There is no fooling our seventh sense. Try as we might to adopt a positive attitude or use visualization, unless we practice the patience to let our true spirit emerge and lead us, we only fool ourselves and block our natural healing powers.

The law of impermanence: Ahonui and suffering Nothing lasts. No person, place, thing, or emotion is forever. At those times when life begins to feel not worth living, the most important thing to remember is that "this too shall pass." How we help in that passing, however, determines whether we are passive victims, fatigued fighters, or loving healers.

None of us can completely control our destiny. The idea that we can exercise such control is a distinctly middle-class, Western idea.[3] Those in poverty do not see this possibility for control and often feel that no matter what they do, nothing works out as they desire it. Nonetheless, our culture clings to the "dominator model" mentioned earlier in Chapter 12, or what psychologists call the *primary control orientation,*[4] in which we constantly try to modify reality by changing other people, situations, or events. This is a "fight" orientation.

Psychologist Warren Berland works with people with cancer and has studied why some cancer patients with grim prognoses outlive their doctors' predictions for recovery or survival. His research indicates that a "fighting spirit" is not always what determines unexpected survival. Berland found that about 16 percent of those in his "miracle" survivor group could be classified as "determined fighters" who exercised the primary control or dominator approach to personal crises.[5] But the unifying characteristic among all the unexpected survivors was that they had *managed,* in their own unique ways, to find more joy in life *because of* their cancer and were able to *share that joy with others.*[6]

The Eastern cultural model embraces a *secondary control orientation* to life and illness, in which reality is dealt with by changing one's own attitudes, goals, or emotions, not by battling against disease. This is an effort to develop a new, more accepting attitude. Berland's research shows that about 30 percent of successfully healing persons adopt an (Eastern) "go-with-the-flow" or "learn-to-live-with-it" orientation to life's problems which accepts the fact that crises are facts of life and one must get used to them. This approach is symbolized by Japanese proverbs such as "To lose is to win," "Willow trees do not get broken by piled-up snow," and "The true tolerance is to tolerate the intolerable."[7]

The Oceanic approach may be called a *tertiary control approach,* a combination of Western fighting and Eastern flowing with a strong emphasis on reestablishing partnerships and maintaining connection with others and the world. It includes seeing suffering as a necessary part of life, but it does not involve a passive surrender to misery from such suffering. The *ahonui* (patient) way of dealing with suffering is to try harder to connect with the immediate family, *aumakua* (ancestors), and *Ke Akua* (the Supreme Being), while working hard to reestablish balance and connection with the earth.

While Polynesians do not believe they can control everything, they also do not believe that they have no control at all. Healing power rests in connection. Polynesian miracle-making is part grit, part grace, and a lot of group.

A recent study of women coping with breast cancer showed that those who used the tertiary control approach to healing did much better in their long-term prognoses. They did not blame themselves for their illness or feel that they should have fought harder to avoid sickness. They did not go with the flow, but felt that they could do much to alter the course of their cancer. They reached out to others to continue to find joy and love in daily life. They fought their illness enough to avoid being a victim, flowed with it enough to avoid self-recrimination, and related and loved enough to attract the social support crucial for healing.

Those who do best in times of crises use *aloha* in their healing, combining patience, pleasantness, connection, tenderness, and selflessness. One woman from the above study who used this approach summed it up by saying that her life was now more satisfying and happier than she had ever thought possible. She concluded, "Love of life? I'm just having the best time of my life."[8] Berland's study of those who healed from cancer shows that the largest number of the miracle makers, more than 54 percent, employed this partnership approach.[9]

A *kahuna* summarized the Polynesian tertiary control approach by saying, "We don't fight the crises in our life, but we don't give in to them either. When we surf, we don't fight the wave or it will wipe us out. We don't give in to the wave, or we won't have any fun surfing. We ride and enjoy it as best we can, and learn how to ride waves better. We see all healthy suffering as a shared process with the grit provided by the power of the *'ohana* (family), the grace (*aloha*) provided by *Ke Akua* (God) and the *aumakua* (ancestors), and the *ahonui* (patience) to let all these things come together in *pono* (balance) to make suffering collectively meaningful so it can make us more *holo'oko'a* (whole). When you are whole, you are healed, whether or not you are cured. If you want to be healed, you must not only find your own life meaning at times of challenge but also teach and share that meaning with others."

Healing Prompter 2: When You Hurt Inside, Go Outside. Reach Out. Self-Healing Is Not Possible.

Pain can be the ultimate isolator. The selfish brain worries about its own source of life and doesn't care about anyone or anything else. It becomes annoyed and annoying, but we must make our strongest effort to keep reaching out instead of turning in.

Sharing suffering: Lokahi and suffering Sophocles said, "One word frees us of all the weight and pain of life; that word is *love.*" Epiphanies most often take place on an individual level and tend to "just happen." While many things we consciously and unconsciously do increase our openness to them, there is something spontaneous and reflexive about epiphanies. Sometimes by just sitting alone and watching a sunset, some great lesson about the meaning of life can spark our soul. Enlightened suffering, the other path to healing wholeness, requires much more reaching out than turning inward and cannot be achieved alone.

Connection is the catalyst of healing power. Without it, suffering turns quickly into the more intense pain of isolation. As you have read throughout this book, Polynesians taught and modern psychoneuroimmunology now proves that social support is essential for health and healing. Whenever you suffer, take that suffering as a sign of your need for a deeper connection with others, God, and the Earth, but never as a sign of failure for not having reached out enough. Don't consider it the need for a fighting spirit, more positive attitude, or a personal philosophy. Don't blame yourself for not connecting enough. See your suffering as a call, however painful, for a higher level of connection, which many who suffer less may never know.

The more you suffer, the more you should try to give. If you are in the hospital, send flowers to loved ones at home who are worried about you. All illness is caused by disconnection on some physical, neurohormonal, emotional, and/or spiritual level. All healing and most curing requires reconnection in the physical realm and the reestablishment of biophysical balance, emotional connection with your family and friends both present and past, and spiritual reconnection with your invisible means of support.

One *kupuna* summed up the *lokahi* aspect of suffering when she said, "See your pain as a push by the gods over the edge of security. Don't blame yourself, but know that somewhere in your life you have to make more and deeper connections."

Healing Prompter 3: Don't Be a Pain When You Are in Pain

You need as much social contact as you can get, and doing your best to be nice even when you feel rotten is the best way to keep life lines connected.

The pleasure of pardoning: 'Olu'olu and suffering When I was in the throes of cancer, going through chemotherapy and a bone marrow transplant, I could see clearly that something was going terribly wrong around me. While my wife, sons, mother, and brother tolerated my self-pity, many of my closest friends began to pull away—in part because I pulled away from them or drove them away. I now know that their own fear caused them to feel helpless, but I also know that my suffering made me a difficult person to be around. I spoke too often of my own pain and the unfairness of my situation, and my hostility spilled out to those around me. But no one pulled away from my dog Desi when she was sick, because she still gave her love openly even through her suffering.

One of the greatest challenges offered by times of suffering is to remain pleasant while in pain. Indeed, the ultimate test of suffering may be to meet the challenge of loving while hurting. As I learned to ask about others, how they felt about their lives, and to speak less about me and more about the world around me, I sensed people coming back again. Although they were frightened away by my pain, they were drawn back by my teaching about my experiences. I became a doctor, in the literal sense of the word, meaning "to teach."

A *kahuna* summed up this approach by pointing out, "The worse you feel, the more you must try to make others feel good. By doing so, they will be drawn to you by the lessons you have to offer and the joyful *mana* (energy) you give to them. This does not mean that you should not share your pain and say how you feel. It means that you must do so with *aloha*, without being disagreeable, and while still showing concern for your *'ohana* (family). The real test of healing comes with how nice you can be when you really feel mean. Remember reciprocal rebound: what you send out will come back. Send out pleasantness, because that's the medicine you need."

Healing Prompter 4: Your Suffering Is Not Just Yours. You Are Not Important Enough to Be the Most Unlucky Person in the World

Because pain tends to draw us inward, we can become even more selfish and demanding when we are hurting. But exactly the opposite is needed of us in order to heal.

Humbleness through the hurt: Ha'aha'a and suffering "Why me?" It is a question all of us ask—or will ask some day. The common

Western answer is often, "You deserved it. You must have messed up somehow, so get on with it and fight it." The common Eastern answer is the opposite, "Why not you? Life is full of misery. Live with it." The common Oceanic answer is "It's not you. We're all suffering. You're just being more obvious about it right now than the rest of us. You're expressing the suffering for all of us."

Because Polynesians believe we are connected on every level, dealing with pain and suffering requires more intense awareness of the unimportance of the self and the healing power of the whole. Pain's threat is to draw us away from the healing tenderness of our tribe. Pain's challenge is to keep trying to connect even when we hurt so bad we feel like pulling away. Pain's hope is that we will learn that the survival of the physical self is much less important than enjoying the loving, eternal spirit within and among us at each moment.

I have known great pain in my life. I have been totally blinded by the detachment of both retinas, had several kidney stone attacks, had my bones eaten away by cancer, and felt the toxicity of chemotherapy and whole-body radiation. I remember the urge to focus only on myself. The more I did, however, the more I hurt. As my wife and family hugged and held me, the physical pain was not less . . . but it seemed less personalized, pervasive, and permanent.

When I faced moments of death, I learned a profound lesson that I *should* have learned from my own dying patients. There are two stages to leaving this physical world: giving up life, and dying. I have never seen a person at the actual moment of death who felt any pain. There is always a flood of endorphins and other internal painkillers that our body releases for us, flooding the body with all we have that eases pain just when we need it most. It is as if we have a built-in prescription for anesthesia. I have, however, seen terrible struggling and severe pain at the time of giving up life. I have learned we must write our own prescription for lessening the pain of giving up our life.

Polynesians teach that the stage of giving up life has its own spiritual anesthesia, but unlike the natural endorphins that come with physical death, to access our spiritual anesthesia we must realize that loss of the physical self is ultimately irrelevant. A *kahuna* spoke of humble passing and healing *ha'aha'a:* "Once you realize that you are not alone, and the self you have focused on so much is only a convenient illusion, physical passing becomes less fearful. We often are cured by our awareness of the whole, but we can only truly be healed when the self ceases to exist. When you hurt, reach out. When you cry, hold on. When you're afraid, cling hard. When it is time, let go."

Healing Prompter 5: Remember Body over Mind and Relax to Heal. Don't Let the Strain of Pain Be Mainly in Your Brain

The body can do much to help the mind do its healing work. By tuning in to the signals from our body and treating our body as having its own wisdom, we maximize our healing potential.

Tenderness at terrible times: Akahai and suffering Because our brain selfishly protects its body, it usually tenses the body when we hurt emotionally or physically. It gets ready to fight even if an external enemy cannot be identified. One reason a mother comforts, rocks, and sings to her hurt child, saying, "It's okay. . . . You're okay," is to override the brain's battle orientation. All suffering is increased by physical tension, so the best thing you can do when you are emotionally or physically suffering is to take a deep breath, lower your shoulders, and sigh out loud as you exhale. Releasing the body's breath can reduce that part of the pain made worse by our body tension.

The brain's reaction to distress is to fight, but what is needed is to love. One sees many procedures performed in hospitals, and most of them involve some discomfort. What is seen less often in hospitals is true intensive caring and tender loving. Gentle physical contact is almost forbidden or prevented by the nature of hospital life. One of my patients said, "I pay 30 dollars a night for a room at Holiday Inn and I can make love in there all I want. I pay more than 300 dollars a day for my hospital room and my wife and I never get enough privacy to even kiss each other. I haven't been touched sensuously in weeks."

When they hurt emotionally or physically, adults need the same touching, holding, rocking, singing, and tender comfort as children. When we suffer, we need to give as well as receive such tender love. There is much talk in new-age medicine about the healing touch, and research supports its very real power in reducing pain and promoting healing and even curing. Polynesians teach that there is also the need to keep giving physical pleasure and comforting to others, even when we are in distress. To heal, we must not only be the "touchee" but the "toucher." This is the healing power of *akahai,* gentle tenderness.

A *kahuna* summed it up by saying, "When you are dealing with pain, loss, and suffering, you must remember five things. Be patient, for this too shall pass. Stay connected, for relationships must be strong to make the passing possible. Be pleasant through your pain, for that will bring to you the *aloha* you need to heal and give healing to others. Silence your selfish self-pity and avoid self-blame, for you are only doing what we all must do. Most of all, keep giving your *aloha*. Don't use your suffering, share it by opening up to others, teaching them what you are learning from your pain, and holding and comforting them to let them know that they too will be safe when it comes their turn."

Chapter Sixteen

JOY TO THE WORLD: CARING FOR OUR ENCHANTED PLANET

". . . humans are but a brief moment in a continuous flow of life, not its end point. It is in the relationship among species, in present and former communities, that we find the true nature of the world we live in."

— Richard Leakey

Ninety-nine and nine-tenths percent of all species that have ever lived are now extinct.[1] Because of five major extinctions that brought our global biology to the brink of total destruction, almost 30 million of the more than 30 billion species that have existed on earth are gone forever. This last chapter presents the most important of all the practical applications of the five principles of pleasure—the concept of *aloha 'aina*, or the loving care and re-enchantment of the earth. We are a fragile and dependent part of the earth and, ultimately, all healthy pleasure depends on embracing a new ecopsychology for collective and connective balanced planetary joy.

How we love our partner, our families, and our work, and how we survive personal crises, depends as much on how we see and deal with our planet as it does on how we see ourselves. One *kahuna* said, "Instead of just picking flowers for our *leis,* we should see ourselves as flowers that are part of the *lei.* We need the earth much more than the earth needs us. We must be much more loving of our home or we will end up homeless."

A Dire Warning and a Magnificent Hope

I end this book with both a warning and a hope. The warning is that, if we continue to devastate our planet by sucking sustenance from it as if it were separate from us, and if we continue to deplete the planet's bounty to amass personal wealth, there will be no life left to enjoy. Polynesians teach that all health and happiness comes from the *'aina* and from respecting, protecting, and enjoying it in a balanced manner. Unfortunately, in our rush to self-fulfillment, we are destroying the ultimate source of that gratification. Even our most basic needs—food, clothing, and shelter for the earth's population—will no longer be met if we continue to cut down more than two percent of the earth's standing forests every year, dump waste in our oceans, turn the climate toward chaos with human-generated heat, and wreak biological havoc by the invasion and destruction of pristine habitats in the name of "progress." Warned a *kahuna*, "None of us are really tourists any place on earth. We are all of this place and we all live here and need this place to survive. Whether we know it or not, we are home wherever we are." The pleasure prescription calls for us to act that way.

You have read throughout this book that the Third Way to well-being offered by the pleasure prescription promises great hope for a healthy and happy life. Sadly, even as Polynesian *aloha* offers us so many lessons about a wonderful life, it also sends a dire warning: what we call Paradise itself, the islands of the Pacific ocean, are dying.

Primarily due to the influences of the West and East, but also as a result of some uninformed practices by the Polynesians themselves, there is now at least one known extinction per year in the Hawaiian islands.[2] How many other, unknown extinctions occur throughout the islands of Meganesia, I hate to guess. Half of the birds of the Hawaiian islands have become extinct since the first human contact. Radioactive materials left over from the weapons of the East and West pollute the land, air, and water. As I write these words, nuclear testing rocks the islands, throwing fish into the air and killing the plants, animals, and humans who know nothing of continental conflicts over territory.

My home on Maui looks out directly at the island of Kaho'olawe. Its ancient name is *Kanaloa,* for a primordial god of antiquity who was the deity for the ocean and all its animals, fresh water, and all the growth on earth and in the seas.[3] Until a few years ago the military used the island of Kaho'olawe for bombing practice. I could hear the explosions day and night, and they often shook our home. I saw the whales become disoriented and beach themselves. I saw a massive blast of dynamite blow all the spring water from the island. As I sat looking at the suffering island lying just across Honokahua Bay, I could hear it cry. Westerners may find it difficult to believe that one can hear an island cry, but those of us who feel *aloha 'aina* for Hawai'i know we feel its pain and hear it sobbing.

My wife Celest Kalalani has camped out on Kaho'olawe with Protect Kaho'olawe 'Ohana, a group of Hawaiians trying to heal this wounded place. As they camped, Celest and the Kaho'olawe 'Ohana felt the presence of ancestors, who also cried for this place. But they all say they have seldom felt such great potential for healing and happiness as when they go to Kaho'olawe. This lesson—to take part in joyful healing of the Earth—is the true earthly pleasure.

Despite all the talk about self-help, health, and happiness, the Third Way teaches that creating health through helping the planet is the true path to well-being. If we continue to seek selfish, short-term pleasure at the price of causing pain for the *'aina* or Planet Earth, the pleasure potential of the gift of life will be lost forever. And we will have only ourselves to blame.

The Ecopsychology of Healthy Pleasure

There is a relatively new field of psychology, called ecopsychology, that sees health as planetary rather than personal. It stresses the importance of a happy, healthy earth rather than happy, healthy individuals. It suggests that, as dedicated ecologist Richard Leakey also points out, we humans are only the very lucky survivors of more than twenty biotic crises, five of which nearly destroyed all life on earth. He warns that, if we continue to lie down on the therapist's couch to moan about our own personal crises, we will miss the ultimate cause of all suffering: a planet in distress. Unless we start trying to bring more healthy pleasure to our planet, we will all end up like acting-out students who trash their school or arrogant spirits who destroy their paradise.

This perspective of interconnection is not unfamiliar to scientists. Biologist Edward Wilson goes so far as to call humans "environmental abnormalities that cannot persist forever."[4] He writes, "It is possible that intelligence in the wrong kind of species [humans] was foreordained to be a fatal combination for the biosphere. Perhaps a law of evolution is that intelligence usually extinguishes itself."[5] If Wilson is right, and our current focus on *ego-* rather than *eco*-psychology suggests he is, then the next extinction will be the last—the sixth extinction that creates a barren and dead planet.

We must heed the warning of the island people who live in a microcosm of our heavenly planet, floating in the cosmic sea. They feel the dangers we face more immediately than we do because their islands are smaller than our continental islands and the overall planet island. They see the future of the earth in their oceanic home every day.

Eco-Immunity: The Earth's Immune System

A *kahuna* warns that, like humans, the earth also has an immune system. And the earth is now mounting its own defense against the greatest antigen or threat to its survival: us. In the form of planetary autoimmune disease, we ourselves are beginning to be rejected by the planet.

The signs of this immune-defense are everywhere. Antibiotics are no longer as effective as they once were. New deadly viruses emerge from the rain forests and are jetted around the planet in airplanes that become viral bombs. New, stronger, and more adaptive bacteria are killing us in increasing numbers, and old diseases such as malaria and tuberculosis have become invigorated and are killing us once again. New and more lethal flu viruses challenge us every year, and epidemiologists know that it is only a matter of time before a virus that kills a pig in rural China kills millions of people around the world. A book about the pleasurable way to well-being would be irresponsible unless the issue of bringing joy to the world is stressed as a prerequisite for healthy pleasure.

Here is the last test to be offered in this book. It is the most important of all of the quizzes you have taken because it measures the degree to which your very heart and soul are protected and enhanced by you and your family's balanced *aloha*, ecopsychological approach to living. To paraphrase a Western politician of long ago, we will either learn to enjoy our planet paradise together or we will die separately, one by one, as we destroy it.

The Pleasured Planet Test

That's us = 2
That's sometimes us = 1
That's never us = 0

1. Does your family waste very little, leave very little garbage, and use most of what you buy?
2. Does your family recycle?
3. Does your family try to save fossil fuels by lowering the thermostat in winter and using very little air conditioning in the summer?
4. Does your family try to use mass transportation such as buses and trains whenever possible?
5. Does your family avoid wasting energy by turning off lights and adjusting the thermostat when no one is at home?
6. Does your family spend time cleaning up the environment, such as picking up other people's litter, cleaning rivers and streams, and working on community clean-up days?
7. Does your family appreciate nature while avoiding disturbing it?
8. Does your family think of the earth as a living, breathing organism more than something to live on and use?
9. Does your family try to have less "stuff," and to give stuff to others, rather than acquire more stuff?
10. Can your family name at least one thing it has done today as a group that has helped to heal and protect the earth?

Total Pleasured Planet Score: _____

16–20 = Pleasuring the planet
12–15 = Need to pleasure the planet more
11 and below = Urgent need to pleasure the planet

As you complete this last chapter and consider how to apply the pleasure prescription to your life, here are five final pleasure prompters that will help you make the world as joyful as I hope you and your family want to be.

Pleasured Planet Prompter 1: Slow Down. Speed Kills the Planet

Living fast, whether by driving, consuming, or just hurrying though the day at a rapid pace, ultimately robs the planet of energy.

A more patient planet: Ahonui and the planet The accelerated pace of modern living directly or indirectly uses up the earth's natural resources. A tourist said to a Hawaiian tour guide, "I wish I had more time to enjoy this place." Without expecting a response, the Hawaiian asked jokingly, "About how much time do you think it would take?" But the tourist responded, "About two more days. I've rented a jeep, a motorcycle, and a fishing boat. I'd like to go hang-gliding and jet skiing before I leave." This tourist's individual "relaxing" vacation rushed through gallons of fuel, created pounds of pollution, and killed hundreds of sea creatures. The tour guide told me, "One reason everyone who visits Hawai'i wants to come back is that even though they have been here, they haven't really been here. They keep running around looking for paradise even when they are in it."

For humans and for the earth, speed kills. If we slow down, we will give the earth an opportunity to rest and regenerate. A more patient approach to life not only results in more personal joy, it is also good ecological practice. As you have read throughout this book, patience conserves energy and puts less stress on all of the body's systems. Similarly, by putting less pressure on the planet we give it a chance to breathe—to have its own *aloha* which it shares with us. A warning sign about a healthy life and healthy planet might read: "Slow down! Life in progress."

Pleasured Planet Prompter 2: Possessive Pronouns Signal Planet Pain

Don't use "I, me, and mine" so much and start using more "ours."

Sharing the soil: Lokahi and the planet A *kahuna* said, "You will notice that there are very few fences in Polynesia. If there are walls and fences, they were usually put there by *haoles* or because of *haole* law. There are no barriers between the taro fields, no walls on the ocean, and no fence between the earth and sky. We must learn that the earth is not ours to parcel off. Sooner or later, the earth will try to heal the cuts we place upon it. A hurricane will blow the walls down and a tsunami will wash them away."

One of the most important decisions you and your family will make about your health and happiness is whether you will use the earth or be a protective part of it. If your objective is to own, control, build, and develop, you and all of us will eventually suffer severely from the destruction of nature's balance. If you learn to live with a small home instead of a "starter house" in a series of increasingly large homes, one car instead of two, and share the earth joyfully with all of its inhabitants, you and the earth will be rewarded with a happy and healthy life.

Pleasured Planet Prompter 3: Competition and Conflict Kills the Planet

Stop trying to get your piece of the planetary pie and start helping others make a healthier planet.

Healing collaboration: 'Olu'olu and the planet Millions of people have been killed in wars over territory. I have traveled around the world several times and, unlike my home, Hawai'i, most of what I saw has been defiled by wars. Monuments to war heroes are everywhere, as are the scars of killing. The Polynesian view is that all of nature is the ultimate monument, so they do not fight to control or consume land. Because Polynesians are not as territorial as continental people, outsiders who come to Polynesia have been able to put up their walls and fences and claim "ownership." So many hotels dot the coastline of Honolulu and neighbor islands that sewage seeps into the sea, killing the coral and turning soft beach sand to sharp stone. The stench from sewage blows on the trade winds, masking the beautiful odors of the increasingly rare indigenous plants. As one Polynesian put it, "Hawai'i is becoming the place where the affluent meet their own effluent."

Despite claims that competition is natural, it is agreeable collaboration and cooperation that lead to the healthiest and ultimately happiest planet, people, and other earth inhabitants.

Pleasured Planet Prompter 4: Want What You Have Instead of Trying to Get What You Want

Working to have less and to avoid more wealth at others' expense is a key to healthy pleasure.

Giving up goals: Ha'aha'a and the planet Both East and West are driven by goals. The West treasures the attainment of goods, property, and status. The East stresses self-enlightenment and spiritual "liberation." The Oceanic way practices living without goals.

Goal-free living does not mean living without objectives, purpose, or direction. It means leading a graceful life, free of the outward push toward attainment and the inward pull toward making a "better" self. It means living fully in the now, in partnership with nature. It means pausing to see the sunset, walking slowly through the forest, talking gently with the flowers, and helping to create a community that values selfless loving, altruistic working, a broad and caring definition of family, and collective rather than self-healing.

Pleasured Planet Prompter 5: Act as If You Were the Planet's Parent

Treat the earth as if it were a vulnerable, developing child that needs unconditional love every day.

Mothering and fathering the earth: Akahai and the planet

Perhaps more than anything else, healthy pleasure on planet paradise is a gentle, tender, shared loving of the opportunity to be here together. When we forget that we are already in paradise, we become homesick—even though we are already home. I hope this book will give you the chance to begin again to find the joy of daily living with those you love and to extend your *aloha* outward, to be breathed in by every human, plant, and animal. The research I have presented in this book shows that such an ecopsychology of life is the way to health and joy. Ancient Polynesian teachings remind us that everything old can be new again.

Alan Thein Durning, formerly a senior researcher at the Worldwatch Institute and now head of Northwest Watch in Seattle, Washington, warns that whether or not we are able to lead a pleasurable and healthy life depends on whether the richest fifth of the world's people will feel that they have finally met their material needs and are willing to turn their concerns to nonmaterial sources of fulfillment.[6] He asks if we will able to adopt an economy of permanence rather than of consumerism.

As generations of Polynesians have taught over 2000 years, Durning asks if we will be able to find the joy of being home again together. His definition of returning home is similar to the pleasure prescription. A joyful home is a return to " . . . the ancient order of family [*'ohana*], community [*lokahi*], good work [*po'okela*], and a good life [*akahai*], to a reverence for skill, creativity, and creation [*ha'aha'a*], to a daily cadence slow enough to let us watch the sunset and stroll by the water's edge [*ahonui*], to communities worth spending a lifetime in [*'olu'olu*], and to local places pregnant with the memories of generations [*aloha 'aina*]."[7]

Mahalo nui loa (thank you very much) for being willing to consider a new way to wellness. *Aloha kakahiaka kaua!* (Good morning!)

Notes

Introduction

1. These stories are taken from L. Hancock, et al., "Breaking Point," *Newsweek,* 6 March 1995, 56–62.
2. R. J. Bulger, "Narcissus, Pogo, and Lew Thomas' Wager," *Journal of the American Medical Association,* 245, no. 14, 1981, 1450–54. See also L. Dossey, "In Praise of Unhappiness," *Alternative Therapies in Health and Medicine,* 2(1), 1995, 7–10.
3. D. Ling, as quoted in "Sunbeams," *The Sun,* 1995, 235, 40.
4. This wisdom is illustrated in the travels of the Polynesian canoe, Hokulea, which retraced the early Polynesians' travels. See B. Finney, *Voyage of Rediscovery,* Berkeley, CA: University of California Press, 1994.

Chapter 1. Catching Your Breath—and Saving Your Life

1. L. Hancock, et al., "Breaking Point," *Newsweek,* 6 March 1995, 56–61.
2. See J. M. Mossey and E. Shapiro, "Self-rated Health: A Predictor of Mortality Among the Elderly," *American Journal of Public Health,* 72, 1982, 800–807.
3. J. Kabat-Zinn, *Full Catastrophe Living: Using the Wisdom of Your Body and Mind to Face Stress, Pain, and Illness,* New York: Delta, 1990, 17.
4. Because Polynesian culture is unfamiliar to many people, there are stereotypes or misunderstandings about it. For example, most people recognize the hula as a traditional Hawaiian dance, but they don't realize that it is not a dance meant for entertainment; it is a form of prayer, an ancient, sacred tradition. Throughout this book, I hope you will discover and appreciate the true culture of Polynesia in all its richness, depth, and wisdom.
5. The pressures of complying with health warnings and the "sick saint and healthy reprobate" concept is discussed in L. Dossey, *Healing Words,* New York: HarperCollins, 1993.
6. J. McCormick, *Lancet,* August 1994.
7. For a more complete discussion of the work by McCormick and Stone, consult my tape series, *The Pleasure Principle: Discovering a New Way to Health,* Morton Grove, IL: Nightingale-Conant, 1995.
8. For a review of how objective circumstances are unrelated to happiness, see D. G. Myers, *The Pursuit of Happiness,* New York: William Morrow, 1992.

9. As reported in D. Lynch, "Conventional Wisdom on Cancer and Health Is Driving Us to Wrong Conclusions," *The Maui News,* Monday, 25 July 1994, A9.
10. D. Lynch, "Conventional Wisdom on Cancer and Health Is Driving Us to Wrong Conclusions."
11. L. Dossey. *Healing Words,* 7.
12. The "Gaia Hypothesis" suggests that the earth is a living, breathing organism that functions as a whole. This idea was first proposed by J. E. Lovelock, *Gaia: A New Look at Life on Earth,* Oxford, UK: Oxford University Press, 1979.
13. See N. Silver, "Do Optimists Live Longer?" *American Health,* November 1986. For a description of other key factors that predict health and healing and are beyond traditional medical test numbers, see H. Dreher, *The Immune Power Personality,* New York: Dutton Books, 1995.
14. Most elevations in blood pressure are transitory. Even prolonged elevations can be treated by daily doses of pleasure. Medical tests are not as reliable as we may think. For the most balanced description of good medical care and the risk of overreaction to clinical findings, see R. Ornstein and D. Sober, *Healthy Pleasures: Discover the Proven Medical Benefits of Pleasure and Live a Longer, Healthier Life,* Reading, MA: Addison-Wesley, 1989. For data regarding salt and high blood pressure, see L. Dahl, "Salt and Hypertension," *The American Journal of Clinical Nutrition,* 25, no. 231, 1972.
15. If you read the newspapers, it seems that almost everything causes cancer. Researchers often use "relative risk," a descriptive statistic, for their studies. This is a numerical shorthand that describes disease among large groups. A statistical association, however, does not prove causation. Perhaps a better term for cancer would be "cell disease." This term seems less fear-inducing to my patients and can include all cancers, thus reducing the size of one "Big C" to several "little Cs." For a new, successful approach to cancer related to the pleasure prescription, see Linville, "Self-Complexity and Affective Extremity: Don't Put All of Your Eggs in One Cognitive Basket," *Social Cognition,* 3, no. 1, 1985, 94–120.
16. Just as psychology has only recently studied the nature and function of happiness and the other positive emotions, psychoneuroimmunologists are only now focusing on the impact of positive experiences on immunity. See N. Lehrman, "Pleasure Heals: The Role of Social Pleasure—Love in the Broadest Sense—in Medical Practice," *Archives of Internal Medicine,* 153, 26 April 1993, 929–34. Psychologist Aaron Antonovsky has studied "generalized resistance resources" and what he calls "salutogenic" rather than "pathogenic" life factors, and what leads to health rather than what causes illness. See A. Antonovsky, *Unraveling the Mystery of Health,* San Francisco, CA: Jossey-Bass, 1987.
17. For a complete discussion of the issue of stress and its important role in balanced health, see R. M. Sapolsky, *Why Zebras Don't Get Ulcers,* New York: W. H. Freeman, 1994.
18. See A. Montgomery, "Cholesterol Tests: How Accurate Are They?" *Nutrition*

in Action, May 1988, 4–7. See also A. Bonanome and S. M. Grundy, "Effect of Dietary Stearic Acid on Plasma Cholesterol and Lipoprotein Levels," *New England Journal of Medicine,* 313, no. 19, 1988, 1244–48. At the 1981 American College of Cardiology, Dr. James Several of the University of Michigan reported a 20 percent drop in cholesterol after a diet of locust bean gum, an additive commonly used in ice cream. For data on the overreaction to the cholesterol risk, see J. Palumbo, "National Cholesterol Education Program: Does the Emperor Have Any Clothes," *Mayo Clinic Proceedings,* 1988, 63, 88–90. The overreaction to fiber as a health factor is summarized in J. W. Anderson and N. J. Gustafson, "High-Carbohydrate, High-Fiber Diet: Is It Practical and Effective in Treating Hyperlipidemia?" *Postgraduate Medicine,* 82, no. 4, 1987, 400–55.

19. From J. Robbins, *Diet for a New America,* Walpole, NH: Stillpoint Press, 1987.

20. For the evolutionary advantage and importance of symptoms in promoting health and healing, see R. M. Nesse and G. C. Williams, *Why We Get Sick: The New Science of Darwinian Medicine,* New York: Times Books, 1994.

21. M. E. Seligman, "Research in Clinical Psychology: Why Is There So Much Depression Today?" In I. S. Cohen (ed.), *The G. Stanley Hall Lecture Series,* Washington DC: American Psychological Association, 1989, 75–96.

22. For a clear and well-researched discussion of the nature of depression, see M. Seligman, *Learned Optimism,* New York: Random House, 1991.

23. Most data indicates that a pear-shaped body is much less a risk factor than the apple shape. See G. A. Bray, *Obesity in America,* National Institute of Health Publication, no. 79–359, November 1979, 6. Overall, however, body shape alone is not a key health-risk factor. See G. Schwartz, "Disregulation and Systems Theory: A Biobehavioral Framework for Biofeedback and Behavioral Medicine," in N. Biraumer and H. D. Kimmel (eds.), *Biofeedback and Self-Regulation,* Hillsdale, NJ: Erlbaum Publishers, 1984.

24. J. Freedman, *Happy People,* New York: Harcourt Brace Jovanovich, 1978.

25. See M. Seligman, *What You Can Change and What You Can't,* New York: Alfred A. Knopf, 1994. See also D. Hales and R. E. Hales, "How Much Is Enough?" *American Health,* July/August 1983, 37–45. Also R. E. LaPorte, et al., "Cardiovascular Fitness: Is It Really Necessary?" *The Physician and Sports Medicine,* 13, no. 3, 1983, 145–50.

26. See R. Shekelle, J. Billings, and N. Borhanni, "The MRFIT Behavior Pattern Study II. Type A Behavior and Incidence of Coronary Heart Disease," *American Journal of Epidemiology,* 122, no. 599, 1985.

27. S. L. Syme, "Social Support and Risk Reduction," *Mobius,* 4, no. 4, 1984, 44–54.

28. The work of cardiologist Dean Ornish indicates that a joyful connection, along with a low-fat diet and regular exercise, is a key factor in actually helping to clear out clogged arteries without surgery. See D. Ornish, *Dr. Dean Ornish's Program for Reversing Heart Disease,* New York: Random House, 1988.

29. Despite the psychological myths about heart disease and cancer causing personalities, there is no hard evidence that such a relationship exists. See K. R. Pelletier, *Sound Mind, Sound Body: A New Model for Lifelong Health,* New York: Simon and Schuster, 1994.
30. B. Bower, "Blood Pressure Lower for Working Women," *Science News,* 1 July 1995, 148, 6.
31. B. Bower, "Anxiety Before Surgery May Prove Healthful," *Science News,* 20 June 1992, 141, 407.
32. L. A. Sagan, "Family Ties: The Real Reason People Are Living Longer," *The Sciences,* March/April 1988, 21–29.
33. H. C. Mitchell, "The Periodic Health Exam: Genesis of a Myth," *Annals of Internal Medicine,* 95, 1981, 733–35.
34. B. Bower, "Depressing News for Low-Cholesterol Men," *Science News,* 143, 16 January 1993, 137
35. "Exercise: Health Links Need Hard Proof, Say Researchers Studying Mechanisms," *Journal of the American Medical Association,* 265, no. 22, 1991, 298.

Chapter 2. Pleasure—The Seventh Sense

1. M. K. Dudley, *Man, Gods, and Nature,* Honolulu, HI: Na Kane O Ka Malo Press, 1990, 121.
2. A. R. Damasio, *Descartes' Error: Emotion, Reason, and the Human Brain,* New York: Avon Book, 1994.
3. R. Restak, *The Brain Has a Mind of Its Own,* New York: Harmony Books, 1991, 13.
4. For a discussion of the "selfish brain" theory, see A. M. de la Pena, *The Psychobiology of Cancer,* South Hadley, MA: J. F. Bergin Publishers, 1983.
5. For a discussion of *vocatio* and nurturing the soul, see T. Moore, *Care of the Soul,* New York: HarperPerennial, 1992.
6. J. Hillman, *A Blue Fire: Selected Writings by James Hill,* T. Moore, ed., New York: Harper and Row, 1989.
7. C. G. Jung, *Memories, Dreams, Reflections,* R. Winston and C. Winston (trans.), New York: Vintage Books, 1963.

Chapter 3. The Aloha Test

1. For a fascinating description of the way in which the Polynesians have recently proven the validity of claims of their oceanic seamanship, see B. Finney, *Voyage of Rediscovery,* Berkeley, CA: University of California Press, 1994.
2. Western physicians and researchers often use a military metaphor for immunity rather than an *aloha* or loving, sensual metaphor. See S. Sleek, "Rallying the Troops Inside Our Bodies," *The American Psychological Association Monitor,* 26, no. 12, December 1995, 1–25.

3. Most of the lessons from Polynesia in this book are presented in the Hawaiian way. This is the way I know best and the way most readers will be able to apply them to their daily life. Traditionally, knowledge in Polynesia is not in written form. The material from Pilahi Paki is from my attendance at meetings with the *kupuna* (elders) of Hawai'i. The information from Polynesia throughout the book is from my interviews with Polynesian *kupuna, kahuna,* and *kumu.*
4. L. R. Brody and J. A. Hall, "Gender and Emotion," in M. Lewis and J. Haviland (eds.), *Handbook of Emotions,* New York: Guilford Press, 1993.

Chapter 4. Your Invitation to Paradise

1. For a comprehensive review of the research dealing with a healthy orientation to daily living, see G. E. Valliant, *The Wisdom of the Ego,* Cambridge, MA: Harvard University Press, 1993.
2. For one example of research into the "Big Five" healthy personality factors, see R. R. McCrae and P. T. Costa, "Adding Liebe and Arbeit: The Full Five-Factor Model and Well-Being," *Personality and Social Psychology Bulletin,* 17, 1991, 227–32.
3. M. Friedman and R. H. Roseman, *Type A Behavior and Your Heart,* New York: Ballantine, 1974.
4. The complexities of understanding the issue of time pressure and the Type A personality are discussed in R. Shekelle, J. Billings, and N. Borhanni, "The MRFIT Behavior Pattern Study II. Type A Behavior and Incidence of Coronary Heart Disease," *American Journal of Epidemiology,* 122, 1985. See also J. C. Barefoot, et al., "Type A Behavior and Survival. A Follow-up Study of 1,467 Patients with Coronary Artery Disease," *American Journal of Cardiology*, 64, 1989.
5. For a discussion of the physics of time and the concept of eternity as "now," see P. Coveney and R. Highfield, *The Arrow of Time,* New York: Fawcett Columbine, 1991.
6. J. Ogilvy, *Living Without Goals,* New York: Currency/Doubleday, 1995, 17.
7. M. Csikszentmihalyi, *Flow: The Psychology of Optimum Experience,* New York: Harper and Row, 1990.
8. R. R. McCrae and P. T. Costa, "Adding Liebe and Arbeit."
9. The nonprofit group, Live Aloha, promotes this approach to life. For donations, bumper stickers are available with the "Live Aloha" phrase inscribed in 'oli'a lehua flowers. The 'oli'a lehua flower is among the first flowers to push forth from the rocky volcanic landscape. Its simple beauty and enduring strength is symbolic of the resilience, grace, and great pleasure of life in diversity of Hawai'i and Polynesia.
10. T. O'Conner, "Therapy for a Dying Planet," in T. Roszak, M. Gomes, and A. Kanner, *Ecopsychology,* San Francisco, CA: Sierra Club Books, 1995.
11. For example, see D. S. Ones, C. Viswesvaran, and F. L. Schmidt,

"Comprehensive Meta-Analysis of Integrity Test Validities: Findings and Implications for Personnel Selection and Theories of Job Performance," *Journal of Applied Psychology,* 78, 1993, 679–703.
12. R. Williams and V. Williams, *Anger Kills,* New York: HarperPerennial, 1993, 4.
13. R. S. Eliot and D. Breo, *Is It Worth Dying For?* Toronto, Canada: Bantam, 1984, 85.
14. For example, see the work of J. W. Pennebaker, *Opening Up: The Healing Power of Confiding in Others,* New York: Morrow, 1990.
15. B. H. Kaplan, "The Power of Forgiveness: A Comment on *Anger Kills,*" *Advances: The Journal of Mind-Body Health,* 10, no. 2, Spring 1992, 3–14.
16. Williams and Williams, *Anger Kills.*
17. H. S. Friedman (ed.), *Personality and Disease,* New York: John Wiley, 1990. P. T. Costa, et al., "Agreeableness Versus Antagonism: Explication of a Potential Risk Factor for CHD," in A. W. Siegman and T. Dombrowski (eds.), *In Search of Coronary-Prone Behavior,* Hillsdale, NJ: Erlbaum Publishers, 1989, 41–64.
18. As quoted in A. Kohn, *No Contest,* Boston, MA: Houghton Mifflin, 1986, 45.
19. Kohn, *No Contest.*
20. J. H. Hertz (ed.), *Sayings of the Fathers,* New York: Behrman House, 1945.
21. A. Luks, *The Healing Power of Doing Good,* New York: Fawcett Columbine, 1992.
22. For example, see H. S. Friedman (ed.), *Hostility, Coping, and Health,* Washington DC: American Psychological Association, 1992.
23. M. Csikszentmihalyi, *Flow: The Psychology of Optimum Experience,* New York: Harper and Row, 1990, 29–30.
24. Many philosophers and teachers have asked these same questions in different ways. See J. Kornfield and J. Goldstein, *Seeking the Heart of Wisdom,* Boston, MA: Shambhala, 1987.
25. This number is an estimate derived by an informal study I assigned to my "pre-life crisis" students. One-hundred-and-fifty first-year college students did the counting. The average was 163 scene changes in a three-minute period. The highest count was 212, the lowest 68.
26. J. Kornfield, *A Path with Heart,* New York: Bantam, 1993.
27. A. Maslow, *The Farther Reaches of Human Nature,* New York: Penguin, 1971.
28. G. I. Engel, "Sudden and Rapid Death During Psychological Stress: Folk Lore or Folk Wisdom?" *Annals of Internal Medicine,* 74, 1971, 771–82.
29. R. Walsh, "The Psychologies of East and West: Contrasting Views of the Human Condition and Potential," in R. Walsh and D. H. Shapiro (eds.), *Beyond Health and Normality: Explorations in Exceptional Psychological Well-Being,* New York: Van Nostrand Reinhold, 1983, 39–63.
30. L. Dossey, *Healing Words: The Power of Prayer and the Practice of Medicine,* New York: HarperCollins, 1993.
31. D. J. Benor, *Healing Research: Holistic Energy Medicine and Spirituality, Volume I,*

Munich, Germany: Helix Verlag, 1992.
32. J. S. Levin, "How Prayer Heals: A Theoretical Model," *Alternative Therapies,* 2, no. 1, January 1996, 66–73.
33. For a discussion of the "presence of God" orientation to prayer, see B. Lawrence, R. J. Edmundson (trans.), and H. M Helms (ed.), *The Practice of the Presence of God: 1692,* Orleans, MA: Paraclete Press, 1985.
34. S. Hossein Nasr, a prominent Islamic scholar, presented at the Harvard Medical School conference and warned against "using" prayer and the Western way of the relaxation response and meditation. As quoted in R. C. Dujardin, "Faith in Medicine: Experts Explore the Link Between Spirituality and the Healing Arts," *The Detroit Free Press,* Tuesday, 26 December 1995, 6D–7D.
35. R. C. Dujardin, "Faith in Medicine: Experts Explore the Link Between Spirituality and the Healing Arts," 7D.
36. These and many more studies were presented at the Harvard Medical School conference cited in note 34. See also L. Dossey, *Healing Words,* and R. C. Dujardin, "Faith in Medicine: Experts Explore the Link Between Spirituality and the Healing Arts."

Chapter 5. The Re-Enchantment of Everyday Life

1. M. Csikszentlmihalyi, *The Evolving Self,* New York: HarperCollins, 1993.
2. For a complete discussion of our natural evolutionary predilection for negativity, see M. Csikszentmihalyi, *The Evolving Self.*
3. *Ibid.*
4. J. Henry, *Stress, Health, and the Social Environment,* New York: Springer-Verlag, 1977.
5. S. C. Kobasa, "Stressful Life Events, Personality, and Health: An Inquiry Into Hardiness," *Journal of Personality and Social Psychology,* 37, 1979, 1–11. Any research links between cancer and stress have been established from tumors induced in animals by viruses, not from studies of humans. Most of these studies are of rate of growth of tumors, so we know little about how tumors get started in the first place. See M. Fitzmauric, "Physiological Relationships Among Stress, Viruses, and Cancer in Experimental Animals," *International Journal of Neuroscience,* 39, no. 307, 1985.
6. R. M. Sapolsky, *Why Zebras Don't Get Ulcers,* New York: W. H. Freeman, 1994, 15–16.
7. "The Psychologies of East and West: Contrasting Views of the Human Condition and Potential," in R. Walsh and D. H. Shapiro (eds.), *Beyond Health and Normality: Explorations in Exceptional Well-Being,* New York: Van Nostrand Reinhold, 1983, 54–55.
8. B. G. Maslow, *Abraham Maslow: A Memorial Volume,* Monterey, CA: Brooks-Cole, 1972.

9. Physician Larry Dossey speaks about the diminishing barriers between the divine and the self in his article titled "Modern Medicine and the Relationship Between Mind and Matter," in B. Rubick (ed.), *The Interrelationship Between Mind and Matter, Proceedings of a Conference Hosted by the Center for Frontier Sciences,* Philadelphia, PA: The Center for Frontier Sciences, Temple University, 1992, 149–168. See also his books, *Healing Words,* New York: HarperSanFrancisco, 1993, and *Meaning and Medicine: A Doctor's Tales of Breakthrough and Healing,* New York: Bantam Books, 1991. The distinction between Era III and a proposed Era IV is made by J. S. Levin, "How Prayer Heals: A Theoretical Model," *Alternative Therapies,* 2, no. 1, January 1996, 66–73.
10. A. Einstein, "Religion and Science," *Ideas and Opinions,* New York: Crown Publishers, 1954, 36–40.
11. D. Chopra, *Ageless Body, Timeless Mind,* New York: Harmony Books, 1993, 156–57.
12. David Barnhart, editor of Barnhart Dictionary Companion, says that 10,000 to 20,000 new words are created in the English language every year but only about 200 make it into dictionaries. Other recent new words that reflect the delight-deficiency orientation of our society include *anxious class,* referring to middle-class people worried about financial security; *drive-through delivery,* referring to the in-and-out nature of hospital childbirth; *home-meal replacement,* meaning fast food; and *24-7,* referring to working 24 hours a day, seven days a week. Reported in "Explosion of New Words Simply Waymazin," *The Oakland Press,* Saturday, 30 December 1995, A-9.
13. J. Shapiro and D. H. Shapiro, Jr., "Well-Being and Relationship," in R. Walsh and D. H. Shapiro (eds.), *Beyond Health and Normality: Explorations of Exceptional Psychological Well-Being,* New York: Van Nostrand Reinhold, 1983, 207–14.

Chapter 6. Cranial "G-Spots": The Psychoneurology of Pleasure

1. J. Olds and N. Milner, "Positive Reinforcement Produced by Electrical Stimulation of Septal Area and Other Regions of Rat Brain," *Journal of Comparative Physiology and Psychology,* 47, no. 419, 1954.
2. R. G. Heath (ed.), *The Role of Pleasure in Behavior,* New York: Harper and Row, 1964.
3. P. MacLean, "On the Evolution of Three Mentalities," in S. Arieti and G. Chrzanowke (eds.), *New Dimensions in Psychiatry: A World View,* Volume II, New York: John Wiley, 1977.
4. There are many interpretations of ancient Polynesian thought. It can only be understood if you look to your indigenous mind and realize how the Polynesian experience considers the world much differently than the Eastern or Western mind. For a good description of the Polynesian belief system, see M. K. Dudley,

Man, Gods, and Nature, Honolulu, HI: Na Kane O Ka Malo Press, 1990.
5. For a discussion of how emotions ready us to act and how they can determine our patterns of response in social situations, see P. Eckman, "An Argument for Basic Emotions," *Cognition and Emotion,* 6, 1992, 169–200.
6. M. Sarter and H. J. Markowitsch, "Involvement of the Amygdala in Learning and Memory: A Critical Review, with Emphasis on Anatomical Relations," *Behavioral Neuroscience,* 99, 1985, 342–80.
7. E. Thomas, E. Yadin, and C. E. Strickland, "Septal Unit Activity During Classical Conditioning: A Regional Comparison," Brain Research, 103, 1988, 193–210.
8. R. J. Davidson, "Emotion and Affective Style: Hemispheric Substrates," *Psychological Science,* 3, 1992, 39–43.
9. Even what we call "symptoms" of disease may be intended for some degree of pleasure. For example, it is possible to enjoy a good cold once in a while by snuggling up on the couch with a cozy blanket, feeling the healing warmth of a mild fever as it spurs your immune system into action, and reveling in a powerful sneeze that clears your nasal passages. For more on this, see R. M. Nesse and G. C. Williams, *Why We Get Sick: The New Science of Darwinian Medicine,* New York: Times Books, 1994.
10. C. B. Pert., et al., "Opiate Agonists and Antagonists Discriminated by Receptor Binding in the Brain," *Science,* 182, 1973, 1359–61.
11. R. Ornstein and D. Sobel, *Healthy Pleasures,* Reading, MA: Addison-Wesley, 1989, 25–26.
12. There are several sources that document how pleasure equals health. See B. Justice, *Who Gets Sick: Thinking and Health,* Houston, TX: Peak Press, 1987. See also J. D. Matarazzo, et al. (eds.), *Behavioral Health,* New York: John Wiley, 1984. Also Pearsall, *Superimmunity: Master Your Emotions and Improve Your Health,* New York: Fawcett Books, 1987.
13. When we feel sorry because we cry, we behave in accordance with what psychologists call the James-Lange theory of emotion—we come to feel as we behave. See R. W. Levenson, "Autonomic Nervous System Differences Among Emotions," *Psychological Science,* 3, 1992, 23–27.
14. C. Darwin, *The Expression of the Emotions in Man and Animals,* New York: Philosophic Library, 1872.
15. G. B. Duchenne, *The Mechanisms of Human Facial Expression, or Electro-Physiological Analysis of the Expression of the Emotions,* R. A. Cuthberton (trans.), New York: Cambridge University Press, 1990.
16. R. McCraty, et al., "The Effects of Emotions on the Short-Term Power Spectral Analysis of Heart Rate Variability," *American Journal of Cardiology,* 76, 1995, 1089–93.
17. See R. E. Kleiger, et al., "Time Rate Measurements of Heart Rate Variability," *Ambulatory Electrocardiology,* 10, 1992, 487–98.
18. R. McCraty, M. Atkinson, W. A. Tiller, "New Electrophysiological Correlates

Associated with Intentional Heart Focus," Subtle Energies, 4, 1995, 251–68.
19. D. L. Childre, *Freeze Frame: Fast Action Stress Relief,* Boulder Creek, CA: Planetary Publications, 1994.
20. For one of the most readable discussions of the endorphins, see D. Beck and J. Beck, *The Pleasure Connection: How Endorphins Affect Our Health and Happiness,* San Marcos, CA: Synthesis Press, 1987.
21. J. Gorman, *The Man with No Endorphins and Other Reflections on Science,* New York: Penguin Books, 1988, 52–53.
22. See E. Diener and R. S. Cropronzono, "Cognitive Operations Associated with Individual Differences in Affect Intensity," *Journal of Personality and Social Psychology,* 53, no. 4, October 1987, 767–74.
23. R. L. Solomon, "The Opponent Process Theory of Acquired Motivation: The Costs of Pleasure and the Benefits of Pain," *American Psychologist,* 35, 1980, 691–712.
24. J. Hooper, "The Brain's Rivers of Rewards," *American Health,* December 1987, 36–41.
25. H. J. Campbell, *The Pleasure Areas: A New Theory of Behavior,* New York: Delacorte Press, 1973.
26. The pleasure pathway theory is very complex. See N. Milner, "The Discovery of Self-Stimulation and Other Stories," *Neuroscience and Biobehavioral Review,* 13, no. 61, 1989. A complete review of the pleasure pathway and competing pathway theories is in N. Milner, "Brain-Stimulation Reward: A Review," *Canadian Journal of Psychology,* 45, no. 1, 1991.
27. The major findings and breakthroughs in the field of psychoneuroimmunology are in the classic texts: R. Ader (ed.), *Psychoneuroimmunology,* New York: Academic Press, 1981, and R. Ader, D. L. Felten, and N. Cohen (eds.), *Psychoneuroimmunology II,* New York: Academic Press, 1991.
28. As quoted by H. Dreher in *The Immune Power Personality,* New York: Dutton, 1995, 15.
29. The research on neuropeptides and receptors by Dr. Candace Pert is reported in Pert, et al., "Opiate Agonists and Antagonists Discriminated by Receptor Binding in the Brain," *Science,* 182, 1973, 1359–61.
30. For a review of this new field see my book, *Superimmunity,* cited in note 12.
31. R. M. Sapolsky, *Why Zebras Don't Get Ulcers,* New York: W. H. Freeman, 1994, 159.
32. For a fascinating discussion of the universal myth of lost golden ages, see R. Heinberg, *Memories and Visions of Paradise,* Los Angeles, CA: Jeremy Tarcher, 1989.
33. M. Beckwith, *Hawaiian Mythology,* Honolulu, HI: University of Hawaii Press, 1970.
34. K. Ring, *Heading Toward Omega,* New York: Morrow, 1985, 197.
35. As quoted in M. Kinder, *Going Nowhere Fast,* New York: Prentice Hall, 1990, 3.
36. O. Fred Donaldson, "Play to Win and Every Victory Is a Funeral," *Somatics,*

Spring/Summer 1984, 29.
37. R. Heinberg, *Memories and Visions of Paradise,* 249.

Chapter 7. The Pleasure Of Patience—Success Aloha Style

1. How Vincent Foster's and others' deaths relate to intense perfectionism is presented in S. J. Blatt, "The Destructiveness of Perfectionism," *American Psychologist,* 50, 12 November 1995, 1003–20.
2. A detailed discussion of Mr. Foster's high ideals and perfectionism is in D. Von Drehle, "The Crumbing of a Pillar in Washington," *The Washington Post,* 15 August 1993, A20-21.
3. R. J. Samuelson, *The Good Life and Its Discontents,* New York: Times Books, 1996.
4. As reported on *The Evening News,* American Broadcasting Company, Tuesday, 23 January 1996.
5. This quote is an excerpt from R. J. Samuelson, *The Good Life.* Also, "Great Expectations," *Newsweek,* 8 January 1996, 24–33.
6. K. R. Jamison, "Manic-Depressive Illness and Creativity," *Scientific American,* February 1995, 62–67.
7. P. Brickman, "Adaptation Level Determinants of Satisfaction with Equal and Unequal Distributions in Skill and Chance Situations," *Journal of Personality and Social Psychology,* 32, 1975, 191–98.
8. J. Kagan, *Galen's Prophecy: Temperament in Human Nature,* New York: HarperCollins, 1994.
9. J. Kagan, *Galen's Prophecy*, 165.
10. R. S. Weiss, *Staying the Course: The Emotional and Social Lives of Men Who Do Well at Work,* New York: Fawcett-Columbine, 1990. See also S. Covey, *The Seven Habits of Highly Successful People,* New York: Simon and Schuster, 1989.
11. D. C. McClelland, *The Achieving Society,* Princeton, NJ: Van Nostrand, 1971.
12. S. Covey, *The Seven Habits of Highly Effective People,* New York: Simon and Schuster, 1989.
13. F. Herzberg, *Work and the Nature of Man,* Cleveland, OH: World Publishers, 1971.
14. E. L. Deci, J. Nezleck, and L. Sheinman, "Characteristics of the Rewarder and Intrinsic Motivation of the Rewardee," *Journal of Personality and Social Psychology,* 40, 1981, 1–10.
15. K. R. Pelletier, *Healthy People in Unhealthy Places,* New York: Delacorte Press/Seymour Lawrence, 1984.
16. J. M. Rhodes, *When Is Overwork Not Overwork?* Paper delivered at the Annual Meeting of the Academy of Psychosomatic Medicine, 17 November 1978. See also J. I. Walker, "Prescription for the Stressed Physician," *Behavioral Medicine,* September 1980, 12–17.

Chapter 8. The Cycle of Connection—Overcoming the Illusion of Separateness

1. For a brief description of Hawaiian shamanism, see S. K. King, *The Urban Shaman,* New York: Simon and Schuster, 1990.
2. As quoted in J. Borysenko and M. Borysenko, *The Power of the Mind to Heal,* Carson, CA: Hay House, 1994.
3. There is no longer any debate that being connected is one of the best things you can do for your health. For an excellent collection of some of the research in this area, see D. Goleman and J. Gurin (eds.), *Mind/Body Medicine,* Yonkers, NY: Consumer Reports Books, 1993. See also J. Borysenko and M. Borysenko, *The Power of the Mind to Heal.*
4. A. Maslow, *Motivation and Personality,* New York: Harper and Row, 1970.
5. B. L. Goebel and D. R. Brown, "Age Differences in Motivation Related to Maslow's Need Hierarchy," *Developmental Psychology,* 17, 1981, 809–15.
6. Medical author Henry Dreher has written a wonderful book that summarizes in easy-to-read language seven of the modern findings from psychoneuroimmunology that relate to and confirm the ancient Polynesian principles presented throughout this book. The quote from Gary Schwartz is as quoted in H. Dreher, *The Immune Power Personality*, New York: Dutton, 1995, 49.
7. L. Jamner, G. E. Schwartz, and H. Leigh, "The Relationship Between Repressive and Defensive Coping Styles and Monocyte, Eosinophile, and Serum Glucose Levels: Support for the Opioid Peptide Hypothesis of Repression," *Psychosomatic Medicine,* 50, 1988, 567–75.
8. W. Ruberman, et al., "Psychosocial Influences on Mortality After Myocardial Infarction," *New England Journal of Medicine*, 311, no. 9, 1984, 186–204.
9. L. Berkman and S. Syme, "Social Networks, Host Resistance, and Mortality: A Nine-Year Follow-up Study of Alameda Residents," *American Journal of Epidemiology*, 109, 1982, 186–204.
10. J. House, C. Robbins, and H. Metzner, "The Association of Social Relationships and Activities with Mortality: Prospective Evidence from the Tecumseh Study," *American Journal of Epidemiology,* No. 116, 1982, 123–140.
11. For more scientific verification of the health of connection, see J. House, K. R. Landis, and D. Umberson, "Social Relationships and Health," *Science*, 241, 1988, 540–45.
12. Until recently, this support has come from research on baboons in the wild, but recent confirmations have been made for the human "lonely = stress" psychophysiological relationship. See R. M. Sapolsky, "Stress in the Wild," *Scientific American,* January 1990, 116–23.
13. C. D. Jenkins, "Psychological and Social Precursors of Coronary Disease," *New England Journal of Medicine,* 284, 1971, 244–55.
14. The issue of "connective transcendence" as used in this chapter is discussed

in F. Capra and D. Steindl-Rast, *Belonging to the Universe: Explorations from the Frontiers of Science and Spirituality,* New York: HarperSanFrancisco, 1991.
15. Quoted in F. Capra and D. Steindl-Rast, *Belonging to the Universe,* 8–9.
16. F. Capra and D. Steindl-Rast, *Belonging to the Universe,* 98.
17. This quote is found in J. Lee and K. Willis, *People of the Night Rainbow,* Honolulu, HI: Night Rainbow Publishing, 1994.
18. R. Sheldrake, *Seven Experiments That Could Change the World,* New York: Riverhead Books, 1995.
19. R. Sheldrake, *The Presence of the Past: Morphic Resonance and the Habits of Nature,* New York: Times Books, 1988.
20. His new book, *Seven Experiments That Could Change the World,* is reviewed by Larry Dossey, the editor of the journal *Alternative Therapies,* January 1996, 102–104.

Chapter 9. The Power of Pleasantness—No Bliss, No Gain

1. There are many anger assessment inventories. I have chosen a few items in this paragraph from *The Anger Inventory* developed by C. Spielberger in collaboration with G. Jacobs et al. and as modified by M. Seligman in *What You Can Change and What You Can't,* New York: Alfred A. Knopf, 1994, 118–19.
2. Not all the 50 items on the Hostility subtest of the Minnesota Multiphasic Personality Inventory are good predictors of illness and death. Twenty-seven of them are the best predictors. Much more research on this important component of health is needed. See J. C. Barefoot, K. A. Dodge, I. Bercedis, W. G. Dahlstrom, and R. B. Williams, "The Cook-Medley Hostility Scale: Item Content and Ability to Predict Survival," *Psychosomatic Medicine,* 1989, 46–57.
3. R. Williams and V. Williams, *Anger Kills,* New York: HarperPerennial, 1993, 4–14.
4. Expressing anger, not feeling it, raises your blood pressure and decreases the pumping efficiency of your heart by five percent. The research on expressing hostility is summarized in R. Williams and V. Williams, *op. cit.*
5. M. Seligman, *What You Can Change,* 124.
6. J. Hokanson and M. Burgess, "The Effects of Status, Type of Frustration, and Aggression on Vascular Processes," *Journal of Abnormal and Social Psychology,* 655, 1962, 232–37.
7. This research was done at Mayo Clinic in Rochester, Minnesota, and published in the medical journal *Lancet,* February 1996. For a review, see "Heart Patients' Pent-Up Emotions Shorten Life Span," *Body/Mind, The Detroit Free Press,* Thursday, 27 February 1996, 10F.
8. For a description of my own experience with cancer, chemotherapy, radiation, and a bone marrow transplant, see Pearsall, *Making Miracles,* New York: Avon Books, 1991.

9. For a thorough and up-to-date review of the data on TABP (Type A behavior pattern), CHD (coronary heart disease), and the key factor that replaced the Type A cluster—hostility—see M. M. Burg, "Anger, Hostility, and Coronary Heart Disease: A Review," *Mind/Body Medicine,* 1, no. 9, 1995, 159–74.
10. There is debate among anthropologists about whether or not our earliest ancestors resembled the gentle, musical specimens of *Close Encounters of the Third Kind* or the savage predators of *Alien.* Most research indicates, however, that we are descended from a long line of nonpareil killers, and not much about our modern world would convince us otherwise. See R. Ardrey, *The Territorial Imperative,* New York: Atheneum, 1966.
11. See R. M. Sapolsky, *Why Zebras Don't Get Ulcers,* New York: W. H. Freeman, 1994.
12. See D. Kumar and D. Wingate, "Irritable Bowel Syndrome," in D. Kumar and S. Gustavson (eds.), *An Illustrated Guide to Gastrointestinal Motility,* Chichester, MA: John Wiley, 1988.
13. In carefully done studies of monkeys and their anger or urgency response causing plaque formation in the arteries (calciphylactic syndrome), it was found that some primates are "hot" reactors: their sympathetic systems react more quickly and intensely than other primates. See J. Kaplan, "Social Behavior and Gender in Biomedical Investigations Using Monkeys: Studies in Atherogenesis," *Laboratory Animal Science.* In press. Preliminary review in R. Sapolsky, *Why Zebras Don't Get Ulcers,* 45.
14. The Type C theory of cancer personality is in L. Temoshok and H. L. Dreher, *The Type C Connection: The Behavioral Links to Cancer and Your Health,* New York: Random House, 1992.
15. When studying something as complex as cancer, there is a technique called "partial correlation" that can help tell us what the real ingredient is—anger, suppression, lack of a fighting spirit, helplessness, etc.—that may contribute to a higher rate of cancer. This technique is not used in the Type C studies. As a psychoneuroimmunologist, I know that few cancer researchers have had cancer themselves and may not understand many of its dimensions. As a former cancer patient, my guess is that lack of shared pleasure is a key factor in the weakened, imbalanced, or altered immunity that sometimes allows cancer to worsen or spread. The initial cause and process of a tumor's initial formation is not yet known.
16. One study showed more cancer for both exploders and nonexploders. See S. Greer and T. Morris, "Psychological Attributes of Women Who Develop Breast Cancer," *Journal of Psychosomatic Research,* 19, 1975, 147–53. The continued mixed findings regarding "Type C" persons indicate that it is not a very helpful construct for understanding the etiology of cancer.
17. C. Ironson, et al., "Effects of Anger on Left Ventricle Rejection Fraction in Coronary Artery Disease," *American Journal of Cardiology,* 70, 1992, 281–85.

18. M. Weissman and E. Paykel, *The Depressed Woman,* Chicago: University of Chicago Press, 1974, 138–53.
19. S. Nolen-Hoeksma, J. Girgus, and M. Seligman, "Depression in Children of Families in Turmoil," unpublished manuscript. See also H. Friedman, et al., "Psychosocial and Behavioral Predictors of Longevity," *American Psychologist,* 50, no. 2, February 1995, 69–78.
20. J. Wallerstein and S. Blakeley, *Second Chances: Men, Women, and Children a Decade After Divorce,* New York: Ticknor and Fields, 1989.
21. S. Feshbach, "The Catharsis Hypothesis and Some Consequences of Interaction with Aggression and Neutral Play Objects," *Journal of Personality,* 24, 1956, 449–62. See also C. Tavris, *Anger: The Misunderstood Emotion,* New York: Touchstone, 1989.
22. H. Friedman, *op. cit.*
23. M. Seligman, *What You Can Change.*
24. This again is related to the ACE theory of psychologist Gary Schwartz. See N. Birbaumer and H. D. Kimmel (eds.), *Biofeedback and Self-Regulation,* Hillsdale, NJ: Erlbaum Publishers, 1984.
25. D. Goleman, *Emotional Intelligence,* New York: Bantam, 1995, 139.

Chapter 10. The Magic of Modesty—Silencing the Self, Saving the Soul

1. L. Thomas, *The Atlanta Constitution,* 3 May 1980, 1–3, as quoted in R. J. Bulger, "Narcissus, Pogo, and Lew Thomas' Wager," *Journal of the American Medical Association,* 245, no. 14, 1981, 1450–54.
2. S. Covey, *The Seven Habits of Highly Effective People,* New York: Simon and Schuster, 1989.
3. As quoted in J. Lawlor, "Clan of the Seven Habits," *USA Weekend,* 12–14 January 1996, 4–5.
4. J. Lawlor, "Clan of the Seven Habits," 4.
5. M. Csikszentmihalyi, *Flow: The Psychology of Optimum Experience,* New York: Harper and Row, 1990.
6. V. Frankl, *Man's Search for Meaning,* New York: Oxford University Press, 1991.
7. R. D. Putnam, "Bowling Alone: A Harvard Professor Examines America's Dwindling Sense of Community," *The Chronicle of Higher Education,* 1 March 1996, A10–11.
8. J. L. Collier, *The Rise of Selfishness in America,* New York: Oxford University Press, 1991.
9. As quoted by J. Winokur, *The Portable Curmudgeon,* New York: New American Library, 1987.
10. For an excellent review of happiness through a less "consuming and consumed self" see A. T. Durning, "Are We Happy Yet?" in L. R. Brown and J.

Hillman (eds.), *Ecopsychology: Restoring the Earth/Healing the Mind,* San Francisco, CA: Sierra Club Books, 1995.
11. For a review of the data on the psychology of happiness, and for statistics on the degree of happiness in different populations, see D. G. Myers, *The Pursuit of Happiness,* New York: William Morrow, 1992.
12. See A. Campbell, *The Sense of Well-Being in America,* New York: McGraw-Hill, 1981.
13. J. Powell, *Happiness Is an Inside Job,* Valencia, CA: Tabor Press, 1989.
14. As quoted in A. T. Durning, "Are We Happy Yet?" (see note 10).
15. As quoted in A. T. Durning. "Are We Happy Yet?", 71.
16. Henry Dreher describes the myths of the Hydra and Proteus and summarizes research in immunity and health as related to the Western theories that these myths represent, in his book, *The Immune Power Personality,* New York: Dutton, 1995.
17. P. W. Linville, "Self-Complexity as a Cognitive Buffer Against Stress-Related Illness and Depression," *Journal of Personality and Social Psychology,* 1987, 52, no. 4, 663–76.
18. R. Lipton, *The Protean Self: Human Resilience in an Age of Fragmentation,* New York: Basic Books, 1993.

Chapter 11. The Gift from Giving— Try a Little Tenderness

1. L. Dossey, *Meaning and Medicine,* New York: Bantam Books, 1991, 117.
2. D. A. Sadoff, "Values of the Human Body," letter to the Editor, *New England Journal of Medicine,* 308, no. 25, 1983, 1543.
3. G. Murchie, *The Seven Mysteries of Life,* Boston, MA: Houghton Mifflin, 1978, 320.
4. Our body is intrinsically musical, right down to our DNA. Research by Dr. Susumu Ohno, a geneticist at the Beckman Research Institute of the City of Hope in Duarte, California, showed how the four DNA nucleotides, adenine, guanine, cytosine, and thymine, could be matched with the musical notes: *do* (cytosine), *re* and *me* (adenine), *fa* and *so* (guanine), *la* and *ti* (thymine). He and his wife, a musical conductor, were able to play compositions using DNA as the score. See S. Ohno and M. Ohno, "The All-Pervasive Principle of Repetitious Recurrence Governs Not Only Coding Sequence Construction But Also Human Endeavor in Musical Composition," *Immunogenetics,* 24, 1986, 71–78.
5. M. K. Pukui and S. H. Elbert, *Hawaiian Dictionary,* Honolulu, HI: University of Hawaii Press, 1986, 276.
6. For the most complete discussion of the Polynesian concept of a loving, caring family, see M. K. Pukui, E. W. Haertig, and C. A. Lee, *Nana I Ke Kumu* (Look to the Source), Honolulu, HI: Hui Hanai Publishers, 1972. See particularly 166–74.

7. This quote and the concepts behind it are developed in my book, *The Ten Laws of Lasting Love,* New York: Avon Books, 1993.
8. R. Eisler, *Sacred Pleasure,* New York: HarperCollins, 1996.
9. Some of the most carefully designed and thorough research on relationships is done by John Gottman and his colleagues at the University of Washington. I have based many of my recommendations in this chapter on this work. See J. Gottman, *Why Marriages Succeed or Fail,* New York: Simon and Schuster, 1994.
10. For an excellent review of the "complain–criticize–flood–stonewall–criticize" cycle in relationships, see J. Gottman, *What Predicts Divorce: The Relationships Between Marital Processes and Marital Outcomes,* Hillsdale, NJ: Lawrence Erlbaum Associates, 1993.
11. There is a difference between "rate" and "risk." The rate of divorce is the total number of divorces in a given year. Risk refers to the chance that a couple marrying in a given year will end their marriage in divorce.
12. See J. Gottman, *Why Marriages Succeed or Fail.*
13. Research on facial expressions and their emotional and physical impact was conducted by Rubern C. Gur at the University of Pennsylvania Medical School and described by D. Goleman in *Emotional Intelligence,* New York: Bantam, 1995. See also the work of Gottman *op. cits.*
14. P. Ekman and W. Frieson, *Unmasking the Face,* Englewood Cliffs, NJ: Prentice Hall, 1975.
15. J. W. Howard and R. M. Dawes, "Linear Prediction of Marital Happiness," *Personality and Social Psychology Bulletin,* 2, 1976, 478–80.
16. H. B. English, *A Comprehensive Dictionary of Psychological and Psychoanalytic Terms,* New York: David McKay, 1958.
17. The most comprehensive research in the area of confiding is J. W. Pennebaker, *Opening Up: The Healing Power of Confiding in Others,* New York: William Morrow, 1990.
18. J. W. Pennebaker, C. Hughes, and R. C. O'Heeron, "The Psychophysiology of Confession: Linking Inhibitory and Psychosomatic Processes," *Journal of Personality and Social Psychology,* 52, 1987, 781–93.
19. J. W. Pennebaker, "Confession, Inhibition, and Disease," *Advances in Experimental Social Psychology,* 22, 1989, 212–44.
20. J. W. Pennebaker, "The Psychophysiology of Confession: Linking Inhibitory and Psychosomatic Processes." (See note 18.)
21. H. S. Friedman, et al., "Psychosocial and Behavioral Predictors of Longevity," *American Psychologist,* 50, no. 2, February 1995, 69–78.
22. L. M. Terman and M. H. Oden, *Genetic Studies of Genius: The Gifted Children Grow Up, 4,* Stanford, CA: Stanford University Press, 1947.
23. H.S. Friedman, et al., "Psychosocial and Behavioral Predictors of Longevity," 71.
24. C. Tennant, "Parental Loss in Childhood: Its Effects in Adult Life," *Archives of General Psychiatry,* 45, 1988, 1045–50.

25. Data from the National Institute for Healthcare Research, Rockville, Maryland. This study, still in progress, also shows that divorced men in 16 developed countries had higher death rates than other men, teenage children of divorced parents are much more likely to engage in substance abuse, and divorced men are ten times more likely and divorced women five times more likely to experience serious psychiatric and medical problems.
26. R. R. McCrae and P. T. Costa, "Adding Liebe and Arbeit: The Full Five-Factor Model of Well-Being," *Personality and Social Psychology Bulletin,* 17, 1991, 227–32.
27. Friedman, et al., "Psychosocial and Behavioral Predictors of Longevity." (See note 21.)
28. Friedman, et al., "Psychosocial and Behavioral Predictors of Longevity," 76–77.
29. J. Panksepp, N. Najam, and F. Soares, "Morphine Reduces Social Cohesion in Rats," *Pharmacology, Biochemistry, and Behavior,* 11, 1979, 131–34.
30. This and the other recommendations on practicing altruism are based primarily on the research of Allan Luks. Another source is R. Dass and P. Gorman, *How Can I Help?* New York: Alfred A. Knopf, 1986.
31. C. A. Anderson and L. H. Arnault, "An Examination of Perceived Control, Humor, Irrational Beliefs, and Positive Stress as Moderators of the Relation Between Negative Stress and Health," *Basic and Applied Social Psychology,* 10, 1989, 101–17.
32. A. M. Nezu, C. M. Nezu, and S. Blisset, "Sense of Humor as a Moderator of the Relation Between Stressful Events and Psychological Distress: A Prospective Analysis," *Journal of Personality and Social Psychology,* 54, 1988, 520–25.
33. All of these effects of humor and laughter have been discovered in carefully conducted studies. The work on the role of humor in understanding and coping with death and loss was done by J. A. Thorson, "A Funny Thing Happened on the Way to the Morgue: Some Thoughts on Humor and Death, and a Taxonomy of the Humor Associated with Death," *Death Studies,* 9, 1985, 210–16.
34. K. M. Tilton and M. C. Totten, "Psychological Factors, Immunocompetence, and Health of Breast-Feeding Mothers and Their Infants," *Journal of Genetic Psychology,* 2, 1980, 155–62.
35. J. L. Carroll, "The Relationship Between Humor Appreciation and Perceived Physical Health," *Psychology: A Journal of Human Behavior,* 27, 1990, 34–37.

Chapter 12. Making a Pleasurable Partnership

1. J. Gottman, *Why Marriages Succeed or Fail,* New York: Simon and Schuster, 1994.
2. D. Byrne, C. R. Ervin, and J. Lamberth, "Continuity Between Two Experimental Studies of Attraction and Real-Life Couples Dating," *Journal of Personality and Social Psychology,* 16, 1970, 157–65.
3. E. Fromm, *The Art of Loving,* New York: Harper and Row, 1956.

4. Z. Rubin, *Liking and Loving: An Invitation to Social Psychology,* New York: Holt, 1973.
5. R. Driscoll, K. E. Davis, and M. E. Lipetz, "Parental Interference and Romantic Love: True Romeo and Juliet Effect," *Journal of Personality and Social Psychology,* 24, 1972, 1–10.
6. C. Rubenstein, "The Modern Art of Courting Love," *Psychology Today,* July 1983, 40–49.
7. Author Riane Eisler presents a clear and well-documented discussion of the dominator-pain and partnership-pleasure orientation to relationships in *Sacred Pleasure,* New York: HarperCollins, 1996.
8. J. Gottman, *Why Marriages Succeed or Fail,* 28.
9. H. E. Fisher, *Anatomy of Love,* New York: W. W. Norton, 1992.
10. W. M. Sotile, *Heart Illness and Intimacy: How Caring Relationships Aid Recovery,* Baltimore, MD: Johns Hopkins University Press, 1992.
11. For a book that discusses permanence in relationships and the view that two people are a microcosm of the community, see H. Prather and G. Prather, *I Will Never Leave You,* New York: Bantam Books, 1996.
12. P. Pearsall, *A Healing Intimacy,* New York: Crown, 1995.

Chapter 13. Raising Blissful Families in Pressured Times

1. D. Hubel, T. Weisel, and S. Levay, "Plasticity of Ocular Columns in Monkey Striate Cortex," *Philosophical Transaction of the Royal Society of London,* 278, 1977.
2. F. M. Jacobson, et al., "Seasonal Affective Disorder: A Review of the Syndrome and Its Public Health Implications," *American Journal of Public Health,* 77, 1987, 57–60.
3. W. London, "Full-Spectrum Light and Sickness in Pupils," *Lancet,* 21 November 1987, 205–206.
4. T. A. Wehur, D. A. Sack, and N. E. Rosenthal, "Seasonal Affective Disorder with Summer Depression and Winter Hypomania," *American Journal of Psychiatry,* 144, 1987, 1602–1603.
5. B. Kulb, "Brain Development, Plasticity, and Behavior," *American Psychologist,* 44, 1989.
6. R. Davidson, "Symmetric Brain Function, Affective Style, and Psychopathology: The Role of Early Experience and Plasticity," *Development and Psychopathology,* 6, 1994, 741–58.
7. J. Gottman, *What Predicts Divorce: The Relationships Between Marital Processes and Marital Outcomes,* Hillsdale, NJ: Erlbaum Associates, 1993.
8. As described and quoted in D. Goleman, *Emotional Intelligence,* New York: Bantam Books, 1995, 227.
9. For an excellent discussion and presentation of the research in this area, see D. Goleman, *Emotional Intelligence.*

10. K. F. Stone and H. Q. Dillehunt, *Self-Science: The Subject is Me,* Santa Monica, CA: Goodyear Publishing, 1978.
11. M. J. Meaney, et al., "Effect of Neonatal Handling on Age-Related Impairments Associated with the Hippocampus," *Science,* 239, 1988, 755–68.
12. J. Prescott, "Phylogenetic and Ontogenetic Aspects of Human Affectional Development," in R. Gemme and C. Wheeler (eds.), *Selected Proceedings of the 1976 International Congress of Sexology,* New York: Plenum Publishers, 1977.

Chapter 14. Laboring with Love: Health and Balance in the Workplace

1. These first eight quotes of great women and men are found in C. Wade and C. Tavris, *Psychology,* Fourth Edition, New York: HarperCollins College Publishers, 1996, 426–27.
2. S. W. Rabkin, F. A. L. Mathewson, and R. B. Tate, "Chronobiology of Cardiac Sudden Death in Men," *Journal of the American Medical Association,* 244, no. 12, 1980, 1357–58.
3. MIT Press, *Work in America: Report of a Special Task Force to the Secretary of Health, Education, and Welfare,* Cambridge, MA: MIT Press, 1973.

Chapter 15. Loving and Learning Through the Hard Times

1. This premise is the starting point for one of the most popular books of all time, *The Road Less Traveled,* by M. Scott Peck, New York: Simon and Schuster, 1978.
2. For an excellent discussion of suffering from a crisis and suffering in daily living, see M. A. Budd, "Human Suffering: Road to Illness or Gateway to Learning?" *Advances,* 9, no. 3, 1993, 28–35.
3. H. R. Markus and S. Kitayama, "Culture and the Self: Implications for Cognition, Emotion, and Motivation," *Psychological Review,* 98, 1991, 224–53.
4. F. M. Rothbaum, et al., "Changing the World and Changing the Self: A Two-Process Model of Achieving Control," *Journal of Personality and Social Psychology,* 42, 1982, 5–37.
5. W. Berland, "Unexpected Cancer Recovery: Why Patients Believe They Survive," *Advances,* 11, no. 4, Fall 1995, 5–19.
6. Berland, "Unexpected Cancer Recovery," 13.
7. H. Azuma, "Secondary Control as a Heterogeneous Category," *American Psychologist,* 39, 1984, 970–71.
8. As quoted in Berland, "Unexpected Cancer Recovery," 13.
9. S. E. Taylor, R. R. Lictman, and J. V. Wood, "Attributions, Beliefs About Control, and Adjustment to Breast Cancer," *Journal of Personality and Social Psychology,* 46, 1984, 489–502.

Chapter 16. Joy to the World: Caring for Our Enchanted Planet

1. The statistics used in this chapter are from a careful, well-documented, and thoughtful discussion of the threat to our planet's survival by R. Leakey with R. Lewin, *The Sixth Extinction: Patterns of Life and the Future of Humankind,* New York: Doubleday, 1995.
2. S. Pimm, from a manuscript as quoted in Leakey, *The Sixth Extinction.*
3. For a sensitive and accurate description of this island and the life that surrounds it, see C. K. Maxwell, Sr., "The Kohola in Hawai'i," *Na Poe Hawai'i* (The Hawaiian Magazine), Winter 1996, 6–7.
4. E. O. Wilson, "Is Humanity Suicidal?" *New York Times Magazine,* 30 May 1993, 26.
5. E. O. Wilson, "Is Humanity Suicidal?" 26. See also E. O. Wilson, *The Diversity of Life,* New York: W. W. Norton, 1992, 192.
6. A. T. Durning, "Are We Happy Yet?" in L. R. Brown and J. Hillman (eds.), *Ecopsychology: Restoring the Earth and Healing the Mind,* San Francisco, CA: Sierra Club Books, 1995, 68–76.
7. A. T. Durning, "Are We Happy Yet?" 76.

Polynesian Glossary

The following are some of the Hawaiian and Polynesian words used throughout the text. Many other Polynesian islands have their own words and phrases. For simplicity and brevity this book uses primarily Hawaiian words and myths as an example of the powerful and beautiful languages of Polynesia.The definitions are based on *The Hawaiian Dictionary* by M. K. Pukui and S. H. Elbert (Honolulu: University of Hawai'i Press, 1986) and given enhanced meaning from my interviews with *kupuna* (elders), *kahuna* (healers), and *kumu* (teachers) in Hawai'i.

The Hawaiian language has the shortest alphabet in the world—12 letters. In oversimplified form, here is a simple guide to pronouncing Hawaiian words:

vowels	**consonants and diacritical marks**
a, like a in above	*p, k,* about the same as in English but with less aspiration
e, like e in bet	*h, l, m, n,* about as in English
i, like y in city	*w,* after *i* and *e* usually like *v,* after *u* and *o* usually like *w,* initially and after *a* like *v* or *w*
o, like o in sole	', a glottal stop *('okina),* similar to the sound between oh's in the English "oh-oh"
u, like oo in moon	-, a macron *(kahako)* over a vowel; prolongs the sound of the vowel

Ahonui: Patience; enduring and tolerant

A'i: Neck

'Aka 'aka: To laugh

Akahai: Gentle, loving, tender

Aloha: Compassion, love, caring, sympathy, kindness, and many other meanings related to a shared joy in living

Aloha 'aina: Love of the land, meaning to live with great respect for and sharing and protection of all things

Aumakua: Family or personal gods, deified ancestors who might assume the shape of sharks or other fish or animals

Ha'ina: Confession

Ha'aha'a: Humble, unpretentious, modest, unassuming

Ha'awina: Lesson, assignment, task, gift

Hanai: To raise, nurture, love, and care for a child given by his or her natural parents to another person or family to raise

Hava'iki: Sacred land of the ancestors

Hei mai: Come here!

Ho'i mai: Come back

Holo'oko'a: Whole

Ho'okipa: Generosity; giving, caring, sharing

Ho'oponopono: A sacred system of re-establishing balance and health in a distressed family system

Hula: Polynesian dance to express connection with the *'aina,* ancestors, and *'ohana*

Kalo: The taro plant, the substance of life in Polynesia

Kahiko: Ancient traditional form of hula

Kahuna: Priest, healer, sorcerer; a "keeper of the secret" of a healthy, happy life

Ke Akua: God, the Supreme Being

Keiki: Child, offspring, descendant

Kohola: Whale

Kokua: To help

Kumu: Teacher

Kupuna: Respected elder, grandparent, relative

Lamalama ka'ili: To glow with health

Lokahi: Unity, accord, harmony

Lolo: Brains, bone-marrow

Makua: Parent

Malama: To take care of, tend, protect, maintain

Malamalama: Light of knowledge, enlightenment, clarity of thinking

Mana: Supernatural or divine power or energy, often miraculous in nature

Mana'o: Thought, idea, belief, opinion

Na'auao: Learned, enlightened, intelligent, wise

'Ohana: Family, relative, kin group in the broadest sense, often including ancestors

'Oli'a lehua: One of the first flowers to push forth from the silent volcanic landscape, said to be favored by *Hi'iaka i ka poli Pele* (the sister of volcano goddess Pele)

'Olu'olu: Pleasant, agreeable, nice

Pa'anai: To bask gleefully in the wonders of the everyday world

Pahaku: Rock or stone

Paio: To quarrel or fight

Pana'i: Reciprocity, reward, revenge

Pu'uwai aloha: Giving from the heart

Pele: Volcano goddess

Pili: To join, adjoin, to become close

Poi: The Hawaiian staff of life, made from cooked taro corns; seen as symbolic of life, family, and ancestors

Pololei: Correctly or rightly connected or joined

Pono: Balance, righteousness, correctness; the "way" life and living should be

Po'okela: Excellent, foremost; achieved by a life of values and not objectives

Pule: A prayer or blessing expressing connection with the *'aina,* ancestors, and the Creator

Uhane: Soul, spirit, but more similar in meaning to the Western concept of "ego"

Unihipili: Spirit of a dead person represented in their bones and hair and cared for lovingly, but more similar in meaning to the Western concept of "id"

Waiwai: Great wealth; from the word for water, meaning much wealth from respectful treatment and appreciation of the gifts of nature

Bibliography

Ader, R. (ed.). *Psychoneuroimmunology.* New York: Academic Press, 1981.

Ader, R., D. L. Felten, and N. Cohen (eds.). *Psychoneuroimmunology II.* New York: Academic Press, 1991.

Anderson, C. A. and L. H. Arnault. "An Examination of Perceived Control, Humor, Irrational Beliefs, and Positive Stress as Moderators of the Relation Between Negative Stress and Health." *Basic and Applied Social Psychology* 10 (1989) 101–17.

Anderson, J. W. and N. J. Gustafson. "High-Carbohydrate, High-Fiber Diet: Is It Practical and Effective in Treating Hyperlipidemia." *Postgraduate Medicine* 82:4 (1987) 400–55.

Antonovsky, A. *Unraveling the Mystery of Health.* San Francisco, CA: Jossey-Bass, 1987.

Ardrey, R. *The Territorial Imperative.* New York: Atheneum, 1966.

Aristotle. *Nicomachean Ethics: Book I and Book IX.*

Azuma, H. "Secondary Control as a Heterogeneous Category." *American Psychologist* 39 (1984) 970–71.

Barefoot, J. C., et al. "The Cook-Medley Hostility Scale: Item Content and the Ability to Predict Survival." *Psychosomatic Medicine* (1989) 46–57.

_________, et al. "Type A Behavior and Survival: A Follow-up Study of 1,467 Patients with Coronary Artery Disease." *American Journal of Cardiology* 64 (1989).

Barnhart, D. "Explosion of New Words Simply Waymazin." *The Oakland Press* Saturday, 30 December 1995, A-9.

Beck, J. and D. Beck. *The Pleasure Connection: How Endorphins Affect Our Health and Happiness.* San Marcos, CA: Synthesis Press, 1987.

Beckwith, M. *Hawaiian Mythology.* Honolulu, HI: University of Hawaii Press, 1970.

Benor, D. J. *Healing Research: Holistic Energy Medicine and Spirituality, I.* Munich, Germany: Helix Verlag, 1992.

Berkman, L. and S. Syme. "Social Networks, Host Resistance, and Mortality: A Nine-Year Follow-up Study of Alameda Residents." *American Journal of Epidemiology* 109 (1982) 186–204.

Berland, W. "Unexpected Cancer Recovery: Why Patients Believe They Survive." *Advances* 11:4 (1995) 5–19.

Birbaumer, N. and H. D. Kimmel (eds.). *Biofeedback and Self-Regulation.* Hillsdale, NJ: Erlbaum Publishers, 1984.

Blatt, S. J. "The Destructiveness of Perfectionism." *American Psychologist* 50 (November 1995) 1003–20.

Bonanome, A. and S. M. Grundy. "Effect of Dietary Stearic Acid on Plasma Cholesterol and Lipoprotein Levels." *New England Journal of Medicine* 313:19 (1988) 1244–48.

Borysenko, J. and M. Borysenko. *The Power of the Mind to Heal.* Carson, CA: Hay House, 1994.

Bower, B. "Anxiety Before Surgery May Prove Healthful." *Science News* 20 June 1992, 141, 407.

________. "Blood Pressure Lower for Working Women." *Science News* 1 July 1995, 148, 6.

________. "Depressing News for Low-Cholesterol Men." *Science News* 16 January 1993, 137, 143.

Bray, G. A. *Obesity in America.* Washington DC: National Institute of Health Publication No. 79–359, November 1979.

Brickman, P. "Adaptation Level Determinants of Satisfaction with Equal and Unequal Distributions in Skill and Chance Situations." *Journal of Personality and Social Psychology* 32 (1975) 191–98.

Brody, L. R. and J. A. Hall. "Gender and Emotion." In M. Lewis and J. Haviland (eds.) *Handbook of Emotions.* New York: Guilford Press, 1993.

Bruhn, J., et al. "Psychological Predictors of Sudden Death in Myocardial Infarction." *Journal of Psychosomatic Research* 18 (1974).

Budd, M. A. "Human Suffering: Road to Illness or Gateway to Learning?" *Advances* 9:3 (1993) 28–35.

Bulger, R. J. "Narcissus, Pogo, and Lew Thomas' Wager." *Journal of the American Medical Association* 245:14 (1981) 1450–54.

Burg, M. M. "Anger, Hostility, and Coronary Heart Disease: A Review." *Mind/Body Medicine* 1:9 (1995) 159–74.

Byrne, D., C. R. Ervin, and J. Lamberth. "Continuity Between Two Experimental Studies of Attraction and Real-Life Couples Dating." *Journal of Personality and Social Psychology* 16 (1970) 157–65.

Campbell, A. *The Sense of Well-Being in America.* New York: McGraw-Hill, 1981.

Campbell, H. J. *The Pleasure Areas: A New Theory of Behavior.* New York: Delacorte Press, 1973.

Campbell, J., and B. Meyers. *The Power of Myth.* New York: Anchor, 1988.

Capra, F. and D. Steindl-Rast. *Belonging to the Universe: Explorations from the Frontiers of Science and Spirituality.* New York: HarperSanFrancisco, 1991.

Carroll, J. L. "The Relationship Between Humor Appreciation and Perceived Physical Health." *Psychology: A Journal of Human Behavior* 27 (1990) 34–37.

Chopra, D. *Ageless Body, Timeless Mind.* New York: Harmony Books, 1993.

Childre, D. L. *Freeze-Frame: Fast Action Stress Relief.* Boulder Creek, CA: Planetary Publications, 1994.

Collier, J. L. *The Rise of Selfishness in America.* New York: Oxford University Press, 1991.

Costa, T., R. R. McCrae, and T. Dembroski. "Agreeableness Versus Antagonism: Explication of a Potential Risk Factor for CHD." In A. W. Siegman and T. M. Dombroski (eds.) *In Search of Coronary-Prone Behavior.* Hillsdale, NJ: Erlbaum Publishers, 1989, 41–64.

Coveney, P. and R. Highfield. *The Arrow of Time.* New York: Fawcett Columbine, 1991.

Covey, S. *The Seven Habits of Highly Effective People.* New York: Simon and Schuster, 1989.

Csikszentmihalyi, M. *The Evolving Self.* New York: HarperCollins, 1993.

__________. *Flow: The Psychology of Optimum Experience.* New York: Harper and Row, 1990.

Dahl, L. "Salt and Hypertension." *The American Journal of Clinical Nutrition* 25:231 (1972).

Damasio, A. R. *Descartes' Error: Emotion, Reason, and the Human Brain*. New York: Avon Book, 1994.

Darwin, C. *The Expression of the Emotions in Man and Animals.* New York: Philosophic Library, 1872.

Dass, R. and P. Gorman, *How Can I Help?* New York: Alfred A. Knopf, 1986.

Davidson, R. "Symmetric Brain Function, Affective Style, and Psychopathology: The Role of Early Experience and Plasticity." *Development and Psychopathology* 6 (1994) 741–58.

Davidson, R. J. "Emotion and Affective Style: Hemispheric Substrates." *Psychological Science* 3 (1992) 39–43.

Deci, E. L., J. Nezleck, and L. Sheinman. "Characteristics of the Rewarder and Intrinsic Motivation of the Rewardee." *Journal of Personality and Social Psychology* 40 (1981) 1–10.

de la Pena, A. M. *The Psychobiology of Cancer.* South Hadley, MA: J. F. Bergin, 1983.

Diener, E. and R. S. Cropronzono. "Cognitive Operations Associated with Individual Differences in Affect Intensity." *Journal of Personality and Social Psychology* 53:4 (1987) 767–74.

Donaldson, O. Fred. "Play to Win and Every Victory is a Funeral." *Somatics* (Spring/Summer 1984).

Dossey, L. *Healing Words.* New York: HarperCollins, 1993.

_________. "In Praise of Unhappiness." *Alternative Therapies in Health and Medicine* 2 (1995) 7–10.

_________. *Meaning and Medicine: A Doctor's Tales of Breakthroughs and Healing.* New York: Bantam Books, 1991.

_________. "Modern Medicine and the Relationship Between Mind and Matter." In B. Rubick (ed.). *The Interrelationship Between Mind and Matter, Proceedings of a Conference Hosted by the Center for Frontier Sciences.* Philadelphia, PA: The Center for Frontier Sciences, Temple University, (1992) 149–68.

________. Review of R. Sheldrake's *Seven Experiments That Could Change the World.* In *Alternative Therapies* (January 1996) 102–04.

Dreher, H. *The Immune Power Personality.* New York: Dutton Books, 1995.

Driscoll, R., K. E. Davis, and M. E. Lipetz. "Parental Interference and Romantic Love: True Romeo and Juliet Effect." *Journal of Personality and Social Psychology* 24 (1972) 1–10.

Duchenne, G. B. *The Mechanisms of Human Facial Expression, or Electro-Physiological Analysis of the Expression of the Emotions.* R. A. Cuthberton (trans.) New York: Cambridge University Press, 1990.

Dudley, M. K. *Man, Gods, and Nature.* Honolulu, HI: Na Kane O Ka Malo Press, 1990.

Dujardin, R. C. "Faith in Medicine: Experts Explore the Link Between Spirituality and the Healing Arts." *The Detroit Free Press* 26 December 1995, 6D–7D.

Durning, A. T. "Are We Happy Yet?" In L. R. Brown and J. Hillman (eds.). *Ecopsychology: Restoring the Earth/Healing the Mind.* San Francisco, CA: Sierra Club Books, 1995.

Eckman, P. "An Argument for Basic Emotions." *Cognition and Emotion* 6 (1992) 169–200.

Einstein, A. "Religion and Science." In *Ideas and Opinions.* New York: Crown Publishers, 1954, 36–40.

Eisler, R. *Sacred Pleasure.* New York: HarperCollins, 1996.

Ekman, P. and W. Frieson. *Unmasking the Face.* Englewood Cliffs, NJ: Prentice Hall, 1975.

Eliot, R. S. and D. Breo. *Is It Worth Dying For?* Toronto, Canada: Bantam Books, 1984.

Engel, G. I. "Sudden and Rapid Death During Psychological Stress: Folk Lore or Folk Wisdom?" *Annals of Internal Medicine* 74 (1971) 771–82.

English, H. B. and A. C. English. *A Comprehensive Dictionary of Psychological and Psychoanalytical Terms: A Guide to Usage.* New York: David McKay, 1958.

Erikson, E. *Identity.* London: Faber and Faber, 1958.

Feshbach, S. "The Catharsis Hypothesis and Some Consequences of Interaction with Aggression and Neutral Play Objects." *Journal of Personality* 24 (1956) 449–62.

Finney, B. *Voyage of Rediscovery.* Berkeley, CA: University of California Press, 1994.

Fisher, H. E. *Anatomy of Love.* New York: W. W. Norton, 1992.

Fitzmauric, M. "Physiological Relationships Among Stress, Viruses, and Cancer in Experimental Animals." *International Journal of Neuroscience* 39:307 (1985) 22–34.

Frankl, V. *Man's Search for Meaning.* New York: Oxford University Press, 1991.

Freedman, J. *Happy People.* New York: Harcourt Brace Jovanovich, 1978.

Friedman, H. S. (ed.). *Hostility, Coping, and Health.* Washington DC: American Psychological Association, 1992.

________. (ed.). *Personality and Disease.* New York: John Wiley, 1990.

________, et al. "Psychosocial and Behavioral Predictors of Longevity." *American Psychologist* 50:2 (February 1995) 69–78.

________. "The Disease-Prone Personality: A Meta-Analysis of the Construct." *American Psychologist* 42 (1987) 539–55.

Friedman, M. and R. H. Roseman. *Type A Behavior and Your Heart.* New York: Ballantine Books, 1974.

Fromm, E. *The Art of Loving.* New York: Harper and Row, 1956.

Goebel, B. L. and D. R. Brown. "Age Differences in Motivation Related to Maslow's Need Hierarchy." *Developmental Psychology*, 17 (1981) 809–15.

Goleman, D. *Emotional Intelligence.* New York: Bantam, 1995.

________, and Gurin, J. (eds.). *Mind/Body Medicine.* Yonkers, NY: Consumer Reports Books, 1993.

Gorman, J. *The Man with No Endorphins and Other Reflections on Science.* New York: Penguin Books, 1988.

Gottman, J. *Why Marriages Succeed or Fail.* New York: Simon and Schuster, 1994.

________. *What Predicts Divorce: The Relationship Between Marital Processes and Marital Outcomes.* Hillsdale, NJ: Erlbaum Associates, 1993.

Greer, S. and T. Morris. "Psychological Attributes of Women Who Develop Breast Cancer." *Journal of Psychosomatic Research* 19 (1975) 147–53.

Hales, D. and R. E. Hales. "How Much Is Enough?" *American Health* (July/August 1983) 37–45.

Hancock, L., et al. "Breaking Point." *Newsweek* 6 March 1995, 56–62.

"Heart Patients' Pent-Up Emotions Shorten Life Span." *Body/Mind, Detroit Free Press* Thursday, 27 February 1996, 10F.

Heath, R. G. (ed.). *The Role of Pleasure in Behavior.* New York: Harper and Row, 1964.

Henry, J. *Stress, Health, and the Social Environment.* New York: Springer-Verlag, 1977.

Hertz, J. H. (ed.). *Sayings of the Fathers.* New York: Behrman House, 1945.

Herzberg, F. *Work and the Nature of Man.* Cleveland, OH: World Publishers, 1971.

Hillman, J. *A Blue Fire: Selected Writings by James Hill.* T. Moore (ed.). New York: Harper and Row, 1989.

Heinberg, R. *Memories and Visions of Paradise.* Los Angeles, CA: Jeremy Tarcher, 1989.

Hokanson, J. and M. Burgess. "The Effects of Status, Type of Frustration and Aggression on Vascular Processes." *Journal of Abnormal and Social Psychology* 655 (1962) 232–37.

Hooper, J. "The Brain's Rivers of Rewards." *American Health* (December 1987) 36–41.

House, J., K. R. Landis, and D. Umberson. "Social Relationships and Health." *Science* 241 (1988) 540–45.

House, J., C. Robbins, and H. Metzner. "The Association of Social Relationships and Activities with Mortality: Prospective Evidence from the Tecumseh Study." *American Journal of Epidemiology* 116 (1982) 123–40.

Howard, J. W. and R. M. Dawes. "Linear Prediction of Martial Happiness." *Personality and Social Psychology Bulletin* 2 (1976) 478–80.

Hubel, D., T. Weisel, and S. Levay. "Plasticity of Ocular Columns in Monkey Striate Cortex." *Philosophical Transactions of the Royal Society of London* 278 (1977).

Ironson, C., et al. "Effects of Anger on Left Ventricle Rejection Fraction in Coronary Artery Disease." *American Journal of Cardiology* 70 (1992) 281–85.

Jacobson, F. M., et al. "Seasonal Affective Disorder: A Review of the Syndrome and Its Public Health Implications." *American Journal of Public Health* 77 (1987) 57–60.

Jamison, K. R. "Manic-Depressive Illness and Creativity." *Scientific American* (February 1995) 62–67.

Jamner, L., G. E. Schwartz, and H. Leigh. "The Relationship Between Repressive and Defensive Coping Styles and Monocyte, Eosinophile, and Serum Glucose Levels: Support for the Opioid Peptide Hypothesis of Repression." *Psychosomatic Medicine* 50 (1988) 567–75.

Jenkins, C. D. "Psychological and Social Precursors of Coronary Disease." *New England Journal of Medicine* 284 (1971) 244–55.

Jung, C. G. *Memories, Dreams, Reflections.* R. Winston and C. Winston (trans.) New York: Vintage Books, 1963.

Justice, B. *Who Gets Sick: Thinking and Health.* Houston, TX: Peak Press, 1987.

Kabat-Zinn, J. *Full Catastrophe Living: Using the Wisdom of Your Body and Mind to Face Stress, Pain, and Illness.* New York: Delta Press, 1990.

Kagan, J. *Galen's Prophecy: Temperament in Human Nature.* New York: HarperCollins, 1994.

Kaplan, B. H. "Social Health and the Forgiving Heart." *Journal of Behavioral Medicine* 15 (1992) 3–14.

_________. "The Power of Forgiveness: A Comment on *Anger Kills.*" In *Advances: The Journal of Body-Mind Health* 10:2 (Spring 1994) 61–63.

Kaplan, J. "Social Behavior and Gender in Biomedical Investigations Using Monkeys: Studies in Artherogenesis." *Laboratory Animal Science.* In press.

Kinder, M. *Going Nowhere Fast.* New York: Prentice Hall, 1990.

King, S. K. *The Urban Shaman.* New York: Simon and Schuster, 1990.

Kirchoff, B. K. "A Holistic Aesthetic for Science." *Journal for Scientific Exploration* 9 (1995) 565–78.

Kleiger, R. E. et al. "Time Rate Measurements of Heart Rate Variability." *Ambulatory Electrocardiology* 10 (1992) 487–98.

Kobasa, S. C. "Stressful Life Events, Personality, and Health: An Inquiry Into Hardiness." *Journal of Personality and Social Psychology* 37 (1979) 1–11.

Kohn, A. *No Contest.* Boston, MA: Houghton Mifflin, 1986.

Kornfield, J. *A Path with Heart.* New York: Bantam, 1993.

Kornfield, J., and J. Goldstein. *Seeking the Heart of Wisdom.* Boston, MA: Shambhala, 1987.

Kulb, B. "Brain Development, Plasticity, and Behavior." *American Psychologist* 44 (1989) 12–56.

Kumar, D. and D. Wingate. "Irritable Bowel Syndrome." *An Illustrated Guide to Gastrointestinal Motility*. Chichester, MA: John Wiley, 1988.

Kumar, J. "Social Behavior and Gender in Biomedical Investigations Using Monkeys: Studies in Atherogenesis." *Laboratory Animal Science.* In press.

LaPorte, R.E., S. Dearwater, and J. A. Cauley. "Cardiovascular Fitness: Is It Really Necessary?" *The Physician and Sports Medicine* 13:3 (1983) 145–50.

Lawlor, J. "Clan of the Seven Habits." *USA Weekend* (12–14 January 1996) 4–5.

Lawrence, B. and R. J. Edmundson (trans.) and H. M. Helms (ed.). *The Practice of the Presence of God: 1692.* Orleans, MA: Paraclete Press, 1985.

Leakey, R. with R. Lewin. *The Sixth Extinction: Patterns of Life and the Future of Humankind.* New York: Doubleday, 1995.

Lee, J. and K. Willis. *People of the Night Rainbow.* Honolulu, HI: Night Rainbow Publishing Company, 1994.

Lehrman, N. "Pleasure Heals: The Role of Social Pleasure—Love in the Broadest Sense—in Medical Practice." *Archives of Internal Medicine* 153, (26 April 1993) 929–34.

Levenson, R. W. "Autonomic Nervous System Differences Among Emotions." *Psychological Sciences* 3 (1992) 23–27.

Levin, J. S. "How Prayer Heals: A Theoretical Model." *Alternative Therapies* 2:1 (1996) 66–73.

Lipton, R. *The Protean Self: Human Resilience in an Age of Fragmentation.* New York: Basic Books, 1993.

Liliuokalani (Hawaii's Queen). *Hawaii's Story.* Honolulu: Mutual Publishing Company, 1990.

Ling, D. "Sunbeams." *The Sun* 235 (1995).

Linville, P. W. "Self-Complexity and Affective Extremity: Don't Put All Of Your Eggs in One Cognitive Basket." *Social Cognition* 3:1 (1985) 94–120.

_________. "Self-Complexity as a Cognitive Buffer Against Stress-Related Illness and Depression." *Journal of Personality and Social Psychology* 52 (1987) 663–76.

London, W,. "Full-Spectrum Light and Sickness in Pupils." *Lancet* (21 November 1987) 205–06.

Lovelock, J. E. *Gaia: A New Look at Life on Earth.* Oxford, U.K.: Oxford University Press, 1979.

Luks, A. *The Healing Power of Doing Good.* New York: Fawcett Columbine, 1992.

Lynch, D. "Conventional Wisdom on Cancer and Health Is Driving Us to Wrong Conclusions." *The Maui News* Monday, 25 July 1994, A9.

MacLean, P. "On the Evolution of Three Mentalities." In S. Arieti and G. Chrzanowke (eds.). *New Dimensions in Psychiatry: A World View. II.* New York: John Wiley, 1977.

Maier, S. "Figures Show Decline in Divorce." *The Oakland Michigan Press*, 29 December 1995, A14.

Markus, H. R. and S. Kitayama. "Culture and the Self: Implications for Cognition, Emotion, and Motivation." *Psychological Review* 98 (1991) 224–53.

Maslow, A. *Motivation and Personality.* New York: Harper and Row, 1970.

________. *The Farther Reaches of Human Nature.* New York: Penguin, 1971.

Maslow, B. G. *Abraham Maslow: A Memorial Volume*. Monterey, CA: Brooks-Cole, 1972.

Matarazzo, J. D., et al. (eds.). *Behavioral Health.* New York: John Wiley, 1984.

Maxell, C. K., Sr. "The Kohola in Hawai'i." *Na Poe Hawai'i* (The Hawaiian Magazine) (Winter 1996) 6–7.

McClelland, D. C. *The Achieving Society.* Princeton, NJ: Van Nostrand, 1971.

McCormick, J. *Lancet.* (August 1994).

McCrae, R. R. and P. T. Costa. "Adding Liebe and Arbeit: The Full Five-Factor Model of Well-Being." *Personality and Social Psychology Bulletin* 17 (1991) 227–32.

McCraty, R., M. Atkinson, and W. A. Tiller. "New Electrophysiological Correlates Associated with Intentional Heart Focus." *Subtle Energies* 4 (1995) 251–68.

_______, et al. "The Effects of Short-Term Heart Rate Variability Using Power Spectrum Analysis." *American Journal of Cardiology* 76 (1995) 1089–93.

Meaney, M. J., et al. "Effect of Neonatal Handling on Age-Related Impairments Associated with the Hippocampus." *Science* 239 (1988) 755–68.

Meyers, D. G. *The Pursuit of Happiness.* New York: William Morrow, 1992.

Milner, N. "Brain Stimulation Reward: A Review." *Canadian Journal of Psychology* 45:1 (1991).

________. "The Discovery of Self-Stimulation and Other Stories." *Neuroscience and Biobehavioral Review* 13:61 (1989).

Mitchell, D. Kilolani. *Resource Units in Hawaiian Culture.* Honolulu, HI: Kamehameha Schools Press, 1992.

Mitchell, H. C. "The Periodic Health Exam: Genesis of a Myth." *Annals of Internal Medicine* 95 (1981) 733-35.

Montgomery, A. "Cholesterol Tests: How Accurate Are They?" *Nutrition in Action* (May 1988) 4–7.

Moore, T. *Care of the Soul.* New York: HarperPerennial, 1992.

Mossey, J. M. and Shapiro, E. "Self-Rated Health: A Predictor of Mortality Among the Elderly." *American Journal Of Public Health* 72 (1982) 800–07.

Murchie, G. *The Seven Mysteries of Life.* Boston, MA: Houghton Mifflin, 1978.

Nesse, R. M. and G. C. Williams. *Why We Get Sick: The New Science of Darwinian Medicine.* New York: Vintage, 1994.

Nezu, A. M., C. M. Nezu, and S. Blissett. "Sense of Humor as a Moderator of the Relation Between Stressful Events and Psychological Distress: A Prospective Analysis." *Journal of Personality and Social Psychology* 54 (1988) 520–25.

Nolen-Hoeksma, S., J. Girgus, and M. Seligman. "Depression in Children of Families in Turmoil." Unpublished manuscript.

O'Connor, T. "Therapy for a Dying Planet." In T. Roszak, M. Gomes, and A. Kanner (eds.). *Ecopsychology.* San Francisco, CA: Sierra Club Books, 1995.

Ogilvy, J. *Living Without Goals.* New York: Currency/Doubleday, 1995.

Ohno, S. and M. Ohno "The All-Pervasive Principle of Repetitious Recurrence Governs Not Only Coding Sequence Construction But Also Human Endeavor in Musical Composition." *Immunogenetics* 24 (1986) 71–78.

Olds, J. and N. Milner. "Positive Reinforcement Produced by Electrical Stimulation of Septal Area and Other Regions of Rat Brain." *Journal of Comparative Physiology and Psychology* 47:419 (1954).

Ones, D. S., C. Viswesvaran, and F. L. Schmidt. "Comprehensive Meta-Analysis of Integrity Test Validities: Findings and Implications for Personnel Selection and Theories of Job Performance." *Journal of Applied Psychology* 78 (1993) 679–703.

Ornish, D. *Dr. Dean Ornish's Program for Reversing Heart Disease.* New York: Random House, 1988.

Ornstein, R. and D. Sobel. *Healthy Pleasures: Discover the Proven Medical Benefits of Pleasure and Live a Longer, Healthier Life.* Reading, MA: Addison-Wesley, 1989.

Palumbo, J. "National Cholesterol Education Program: Does the Emperor Have Any Clothes." *Mayo Clinic Proceedings* 63 (1988) 88–90.

Panksepp, J., N. Najam and F. Soares. "Morphine Reduces Social Cohesion in Rats." *Pharmacology, Biochemistry, and Behavior* 11 (1979) 131–34.

Pearsall, P. *A Healing Intimacy: The Power of Loving Connections.* New York: Crown, 1994.

_________. *Making Miracles.* New York: Avon Books, 1991.

_________. *The Pleasure Principle: Discovering a New Way to Health.* Audiotape Series. Morton Grove, IL: Nightingale-Conant Corporation, 1995.

_________. *Superimmunity: Master Your Emotions and Improve Your Health.* New York: McGraw-Hill, 1987.

_________. *The Ten Laws of Lasting Love.* New York: Avon Books, 1993.

Peck, M. S. *The Road Less Traveled.* New York: Simon and Schuster, 1978.

Pelletier, K. R. *Healthy People in Unhealthy Places.* New York: Delacorte Press/Seymore Lawrence, 1984.

_________. *Sound Mind, Sound Body: A New Model for Lifelong Health.* New York: Simon and Schuster, 1994.

Pennebaker, J. W., C. Hughes and R. C. O'Heeron. "The Psychophysiology of Confession: Linking Inhibitory and Psychosomatic Processes." *Journal of Personality and Social Psychology* 52 (1987) 781–93.

_________. *Opening Up: the Healing Power of Confiding in Others.* New York: William Morrow, 1990.

Pert, C. B., G. Pasternak, and S. H. Snyder. "Opiate Agonists and Antagonists Discriminated by Receptor Binding in the Brain." *Science* 182:4119 (1973) 1359–61.

Pimm, S. Manuscript as quoted in R. Leakey. *The Sixth Extinction.* New York: Doubleday, 1995.

Powell, J. *Happiness Is an Inside Job.* Valencia, CA: Tabor Press, 1989.

Prather, H. and G. Prather. *I Will Never Leave You.* New York: Bantam, 1996.

Prescott, J. "Phylogenetic and Ontogenetic Aspects of Human Affectional Development." In R. Gemme and C. Wheeler (eds.). *Selected Proceedings of the 1976 International Congress of Sexology.* New York: Plenum, 1977.

Pukui, M. K. and Elbert, S. H. *Hawaiian Dictionary.* Honolulu, HI: University of Hawaii Press, 1986.

Pukui, M. K., E. W. Haertig, and C. A. Lee. *Nana I Ke Kumu* (Look to the Source). Honolulu, HI: Hui Hanai Publishers, 1972.

Putnam, R. D. "Bowling Alone: A Harvard Professor Examines America's Dwindling Sense of Community." *The Chronicle of Higher Education.* 1 March 1996, A10–11.

Rabkin, S. W., F. A. L. Mathewson, and R. B. Tate. "Chronobiology of Cardiac Sudden Death in Men." *Journal of the American Medical Association* 244:12 (1980) 1357–58.

Restak, R. *The Brain Has a Mind of Its Own.* New York: Harmony Books, 1991.

Rhodes, J. M. *When Is Overwork Not Overwork?* Paper delivered at the Annual Meeting of the Academy of Psychosomatic Medicine, 17 November 1978.

Ring, K. *Heading Toward Omega.* New York: Morrow, 1985.

Robbins, J. *Diet for a New America.* Walpole, NH: Stillpoint Press, 1987.

Rothbaum, F. M., et al. "Changing the World and Changing the Self: A Two-Process Model of Achieving Control." *Journal of Personality and Social Psychology* 42 (1982) 5–37.

Rubenstein, C. "The Modern Art of Courting Love." *Psychology Today* (July 1983) 40–49.

Ruberman, W., et al. "Psychosocial Influences on Mortality After Myocardial Infarction." *New England Journal of Medicine* 311:9 (1984) 186–204.

Rubin, Z. *Liking and Loving: An Invitation to Social Psychology.* New York: Holt, 1973.

Sadoff, D. A. "Values of the Human Body." Letter to the Editor. *New England Journal of Medicine* 308:25 (1983) 1543.

Sagan, L. A. "Family Ties: The Real Reason People Are Living Longer." *The Sciences* (March/April 1988) 21–29.

Samuelson, R. J. "Great Expectations." *Newsweek* 8 January 1996, 24–33.

_________. *The Good Life and Its Discontents.* New York: Times Books, 1996.

Sapolsky, R. M. "Stress in the Wild." *Scientific American* (January 1990) 116–123.

_________. *Why Zebras Don't Get Ulcers.* New York: W. H. Freeman, 1994.

Sarter, M. and H. J. Markowitsch, "Involvement of the Amygdala in Learning and Memory. A Critical Review, with Emphasis on Anatomical Relations." *Behavioral Neuroscience* 99 (1985) 342–80.

Schwartz, G. "Disregulation and Systems Theory: A Biobehavioral Framework for Biofeedback and Behavioral Medicine." In N. Biraumer and H. D. Kimmel (eds.). *Biofeedback and Self-Regulation.* Hillsdale, NJ: Erlbaum Publishers, 1984.

Seligman, M. *Learned Optimism.* New York: Random House, 1991.

________. "Research in Clinical Psychology: Why Is There So Much Depression Today?" In I. S. Cohen (ed.). *The G. Stanley Hall Lecture Series.* Washington DC: American Psychological Association, 1989, 75–96.

________. *What You Can Change and What You Can't.* New York: Alfred A. Knopf, 1994.

Shapiro, J. and D. H. Shapiro, Jr. "Well-Being and Relationship." In R. Walsh and D. Shapiro (eds.). *Beyond Health and Normality: Explorations of Exceptional Psychological Well-Being.* New York: Van Nostrand Reinhold, 1983.

Shekelle, R., J. Billings, and N. Borhanni. "The MRFIT Behavior Pattern Study II: Type A Behavior and Incidence of Coronary Heart Disease." *American Journal of Epidemiology* 122:599 (1985).

Sheldrake, R. *Seven Experiments That Could Change the World.* New York: Riverhead Books, 1995.

________. *The Presence of the Past: Morphic Resonance and the Habits of Nature.* New York: Times Books, 1988.

Silver, N. "Do Optimists Live Longer?" *American Health* (November 1986).

Sleek, S. "Rallying the Troops Inside Our Body." *The American Psychological Association Monitor* 26:12 (December 1995) 1–25.

Solomon, R. L. "The Opponent Process Theory of Acquired Motivation: The Costs of Pleasure and the Benefits of Pain." *American Psychologist* 35 (1980) 691–712.

Sotile, W. M. *Heart Illness and Intimacy: How Caring Relationships Aid Recovery.* Baltimore, MD: Johns Hopkins University Press, 1992.

Stone, K. F. and H. Q. Dillehunt. *Self-Science: The Subject Is Me.* Santa Monica, CA: Goodyear Publishing, 1978.

Stor, A. *Churchill's Black Dog, Kafka's Mice.* New York: Ballantine Books, 1988.

Syme, S. L. "Social Support and Risk Reduction." *Mobius* 4:4 (1984) 44–54.

Tavris, C. *Anger: The Misunderstood Emotion.* New York: Touchstone, 1989.

Taylor, S. E., R. R. Lictman, and J. V. Wood. "Attributions, Beliefs About Control, and Adjustment to Breast Cancer." *Journal of Personality and Social Psychology* 46 (1984) 489–502.

Temoshok, L. and H. L. Dreher. *The Type C Connection: The Behavioral Links to Cancer and Your Health.* New York: Random House, 1992.

Tennant, C. "Parental Loss in Childhood: Its Effects in Adult Life." *Archives of General Psychiatry* 45 (1988) 1045–50.

Terman, L. M. and M. H. Oden. *Genetic Studies of Genius: The Gifted Children Grow Up,* 4. Stanford, CA: Stanford University Press, 1947.

Thomas, E., E. Yadin, and C. E. Strickland. "Septal Unit Activity During Classical Conditioning: A Regional Comparison." *Brain Research* 103 (1988) 193–210.

Thomas, L. *The Atlanta Constitution* (May 1980) 1–3.

Thorson, J. A. "A Funny Thing Happened on the Way to the Morgue: Some Thoughts On Humor and Death, and a Taxonomy of the Humor Associated with Death." *Death Studies* 9 (1985) 210–16.

Tiller, W. A., et al. "Cardiac Coherence: A New, Noninvasive Measure of Autonomic Nervous System Order." *Alternative Therapies* 2 (January 1996) 52–65.

Tilton, K. M. and M. C. Totten. "Psychological Factors, Immunocompetence, and Health of Breast-Feeding Mothers and Their Infants." *Journal of Genetic Psychology* 2 (1980) 155–62.

Valliant, G. E. *The Wisdom of the Ego.* Cambridge, MA: Harvard University Press, 1993.

Von Drehle, D. "The Crumbling of a Pillar in Washington." *The Washington Post* 15 August 1993, A20–21.

Wade, C. and C. Tavris. *Psychology.* Fourth Edition. New York: HarperCollins College Publishers, 1996.

Walker, J. I. "Prescription for the Stressed Physician." *Behavioral Medicine* (September 1980) 12–17.

Wallerstein, J. and S. Blakeley. *Second Chances: Men, Women, and Children a Decade After Divorce.* New York: Ticknor and Fields, 1989.

Walsh, R. and D. H. Shapiro. *Beyond Health and Normality: Explorations in Exceptional Well-Being.* New York: Van Nostrand Reinhold, 1983.

Wehur, T. A., D. A. Sack, and N. E. Rosenthal. "Seasonal Affective Disorder with Summer Depression and Winter Hypomania." *American Journal of Psychiatry* 144 (1987) 1602–03.

Weiss, R. S. *Staying the Course: The Emotional and Social Lives of Men Who Do Well at Work.* New York: Fawcett-Columbine, 1990.

Weissman, M. and E. Paykel. *The Depressed Woman.* Chicago, IL: University of Chicago Press, 1974.

Williams, R. and V. Williams. *Anger Kills.* New York: HarperPerennial, 1993.

Wilson, E. O. "Is Humanity Suicidal?" *New York Times Magazine* (May 1993) 26.

_________. *The Diversity of Life.* New York: W. W. Norton, 1992.

Winokur, J. *The Portable Curmudgeon.* New York: New American Library, 1987.

Work in America: Report of a Special Task Force to the Secretary of Health, Education, and Welfare. Cambridge, MA: MIT Press, 1973.

Index

A

B

C

D

E

F

G

H

I

J

K

L

M

N

S

T

U

V

W

TO CONTACT THE AUTHOR

Dr. Paul Ka'ikena Pearsall presents lectures and lecture concerts and consults all over the world to medical, educational, business, and lay audiences. To contact him to schedule appearances or to order his other books or tapes, please write to his mainland office:

Dr. Paul Ka'ikena Pearsall, Founder and President
Ho'ala Hou (To Reawaken), Inc.
P.O. Box 1632
Dearborn MI 48121-1632

Hunter House
BOOKS ON SEXUALITY

SEXUAL PLEASURE: Reaching New Heights of Sexual Arousal and Intimacy
by Barbara Keesling, Ph.D.

This book is for everyone interested in enhancing his or her sex life and experiencing lovemaking as a deeply pleasurable physical and emotional exchange. It shows how to develop sensual awareness and learn to replace anxiety with enjoyment. A series of graduated sensual exercises reveal the three secrets of sexual pleasure: enjoying touching; enjoying being touched; and merging touching and feeling as an ecstatic experience

The exercises take readers from basic body-awareness techniques to ecstatic levels of arousal and release. Tasteful pictures by leading erotic photographers are included throughout the book.

224 pages … 14 illus. … Paperback $12.95 … Hard cover $21.95

SEXUAL HEALING: A Self-help Program to Enhance Your Sensuality and Overcome Common Sexual Problems
by Barbara Keesling, Ph.D.

In this insightful book, Barbara Keesling explores the profound, complex, and soulful nature of sexuality and its power to heal. Using her sixteen years of experience as both a surrogate partner and a sex therapist, Dr. Keesling explains that touch heals, intimacy heals, and the intimate sexual bond between committed partners is most healing of all.

Keesling offers advice on how to recognize a healing partner, and how to introduce sexual healing into a relationship at any stage. She describes the many health benefits of good sex, including a stronger immune system, improved circulation, and healthier hair, skin, and eyes. The warm tone of the book is complemented in sensual photographs that make this book a perfect gift.

256 pages … 14 illus. … Paperback … $12.95

WOMEN, SEX & DESIRE: Exploring Your Sexuality at Every Stage of Life
by Elizabeth Davis; Foreword by Germaine Greer

A woman's sexuality is a synthesis of her emotion, intuition, energy, and spirituality, and it affects all aspects of her life and self. *Women, Sex & Desire* is not about sexual technique or performance but rather is an exploration of the natural cycles of a woman's sexuality over the days, weeks, months, and years of her life. Elizabeth Davis, a longtime midwife, tells why desire comes and goes and reveals what women can do to keep a sensual balance. The influences of hormone changes on sexuality are discussed along with the impact of pregnancy, child rearing, stress, joy, grief, and aging. This is a comprehensive classic in-the-making, rewarding the reader with "courage at every turn."

256 pages … 15 illus. … Paperback $12.95 … Hard cover $22.95

Prices subject to change without notice—
see last page for ordering or call 1-800-266-5592